Shaw on Theatre

George Bernard SHAW

Shaw on Theatre

Edited by E. J. WEST

MACGIBBON & KEE

Manufactured in the United States of America
by The Colonial Press Inc.

NOTE ON SHAW'S USAGES

Many of the pieces reprinted in this volume were copy-edited to conform to the house usages of the publications (some of them cisatlantic) that first printed them; and the printed versions are therefore no guide to how Shaw wanted various words spelled and various locutions punctuated. To avoid the clash of codes, some of them at odds with his known preferences, we have harmonized the spellings throughout (except in quoted matter) with the usages that prevail in the Messrs. Constable and Company's Standard Edition of the Works of Bernard Shaw. These usages include Elizabethan forms (*shew*), quasi-American reforms (*honor, labor,* etc., and also *glamor,* which Shaw treated as if it were of the *honor-labor* class), Oxford or American *z* for British *s* in such words as *recognize* and *organization,* and *Shakespear.* Italics or quotation marks are omitted from titles of published works and of periodicals, periods from such abbreviations as *Mr., Dr.,* and *St.* (for *Saint*), and apostrophes from *don't, isn't,* etc. In details about which the Standard Edition is inconsistent—as it is in various hyphenations and the retention of the final comma in series of the form *a, b, and c*—we have used the patterns that seem to have a clear preponderance.

The application of this system introduces the fallacy of an assumption that Shaw did not change his mind about any of these details between 1891 and 1950; but it seems better to accept that small fallacy than slavishly to follow printed versions containing a motley of usages many of which were always anathema to the author of *Back to Methuselah.*

THE PUBLISHERS

ACKNOWLEDGMENTS

To Arthur W. Wang and Eric Bentley the editor expresses sincere gratitude for inspiration, aid, encouragement, and patient and tolerant understanding in the preparation of the present volume.

E. J. West (1903–58) of the University of Colorado was a notable teacher, critic, and stage director. His edition of Bernard Shaw's *Advice to a Young Critic* appeared in 1955, *Shaw on Theatre* a few months before his death.

Owing to Mr. West's untimely death, corrections for the second impression had to be made by another hand. The publishers wish to express their gratitude to Mr. Dan Laurence for a generous and expert contribution.

Contents

Introduction

Bernard Shaw was one of the greatest and also one of the most prolific of dramatic critics. The Standard Edition of his works includes three volumes of play reviews, four of music criticism, *Major Critical Essays* ("The Quintessence of Ibsenism," "The Perfect Wagnerite," and "The Sanity of Art"), and *Pen Portraits and Reviews*—nine volumes, with over a third of their contents devoted to the theatre arts in general. Obiter dicta on the stage and the script, on dramaturgy and dramatic production, are to be found throughout his prefaces to his own and others' works and his essays on sociological, political, and miscellaneous subjects. There are also uncounted items of value on library shelves, some of them buried in the bound volumes of newspapers and periodicals including long discontinued and forgotten ones, and some in other writers' volumes long out of print.

From an admittedly incomplete bibliography compiled during a quarter century I assembled a short check list of uncollected Shaviana on theatre and drama that appeared serially in *The Shavian* of the Shaw Society of London, September 1955 to December 1957. It was meant partly as propaganda for the publication of at least some of this material; for much of it was communicative not only to the dedicated Shavian but also to the general reader interested in the protean personality of "the Man of the Century," as Archibald Henderson called Shaw. It was material packed with comments on his own and others' plays, on the theatre of his time and earlier, on the craft and art of playwright, director, actor, and the other artists of the theatre. From my check list I excluded many pieces of merit—for examples, those collected by Mander and Mitchenson in their *Theatrical Companion to Shaw;* Shaw's testimony before the censorship committee, published by the Shaw Society (London) as

a Shavian Tract; and the "Author's Apology" from
Mrs Warren's Profession, published in England with
the Stage Society edition of the play and in the United
States by itself (by Brentano's, with introduction by
John Corbin). And from the present collection I have
excluded much that was in my check list. (See ap-
pended bibliography.) The pages that follow are, then,
a selection from a selection; and if they are but a
tantalizing fraction of the quantity that could be gathered, they incorporate the quality that comes of a
repeated winnowing.

Our volume well represents, then, the whole range
and richness of the eligible material. And it includes
some items that may provide surprises for those whose
reading has been cursory. For example, various pieces
on the cutting and editing of Shakespeare for the modern stage exhibit Shaw in the unexpected role of a
scholar—a scholar even in the narrower textual sense.
There is Shaw's last piece of official dramatic criticism,
"The Dying Tongue of Great Elizabeth." And I have
rescued the important dramatist's credo of 1894, "A
Dramatic Realist to His Critics." The Malvern Festival
Books of 1931–39 are sampled as copiously as space
permits. A shortage of room and, in a few instances,
problems of copyright have compelled me to leave out
some matter that it would have been a pleasure to include—more program notes containing Shaw's dicta
on his own plays; letters to Ellen Terry, Mrs. Pat
Campbell, Lillah McCarthy, Florence Farr, Robert
Loraine, Harcourt Williams, and B. Iden Payne not
less interesting than those that I have included to Janet
Achurch, Louis Calvert, and others. But the omissions,
all told, do not prevent these pages from supplying a
conspectus of the many-sided mind behind them. Furthermore it strikingly illustrates the unity that under-
lies the many-sidedness. For there is a remarkable con-
tinuity in Shaw's critical precepts and in his application of them. Our selections, more of them concerned
with dramaturgy than not, cover the span from 1891 to
1950, and in them the man of ninety-four, as vividly

alive as he ever was, is still affirming the principles laid down by the man of thirty-five.

To the innate gifts of the good critic—awareness, conscience, justice, courage—Shaw added an intensive and very practical self-education in public speaking, literary criticism, art criticism, music criticism, play-writing, and stage managing. The total result was the kind of executive virtuosity defined early in Shaw's career by the articulate pugilist of *Cashel Byron's Profession:* "What is it that you need to know then, in order to act up to your fine ideas? Why, you want to know how to hit him, when to hit him, and where to hit him; and then you want the nerve to go in and do it." Cashel continued with the warning: "Now, nothing can be what you might call artistically done if it's done with an effort. If a thing can't be done light and easy, steady and certain, let it not be done at all." How light and easy, steady and certain was Bernard Shaw's performance of the critic's task for the fifty-nine years from 1891, the pages that follow will cogently attest. The selections are arranged in chronological order.

E. J. West

Boulder, Colorado
March 1958

Appendix to *The Quintessence of Ibsenism*

(Appeared only in the first edition, 1891.)

I have a word or two to add as to the difficulties which Ibsen's philosophy places in the way of those who are called on to impersonate his characters on the stage in England. His idealist figures, at once higher and more mischievous than ordinary Philistines, puzzle by their dual aspect the conventional actor, who persists in assuming that if he is to be selfish on the stage he must be villainous; that if he is to be self-sacrificing and scrupulous he must be a hero; and that if he is to satirize himself unconsciously he must be comic. He is constantly striving to get back to familiar ground by reducing his part to one of the stage types with which he is familiar, and which he has learnt to present by rule of thumb. The more experienced he is, the more certain is he to de-Ibsenize the play into a melodrama or a farcical comedy of the common sort. Give him Helmer to play, and he begins by declaring that the part is a mass of "inconsistencies," and ends by suddenly grasping the idea that it is only Joseph Surface over again. Give him Gregers Werle, the devotee of Truth, and he will first play him in the vein of George Washington, and then, when he finds that the audience laughs at him instead of taking him respectfully, rush to the conclusion that Gregers is only his old friend the truthful milkman in A Phenomenon in a Smock Frock, and begin to play for the laughs and relish them. That is, if there are only laughs enough to make the part completely comic. Otherwise he will want to omit the passages which provoke them. To be laughed at when playing a serious part is hard upon an actor, and still more upon an actress: it is derision, than which nothing is more terrible to those whose livelihood depends on public approbation, and whose calling produces an abnormal

development of self-consciousness. Now Ibsen undoubtedly does freely require from his artists that they
shall not only possess great skill and power on every
plane of their art, but that they shall also be ready to
make themselves acutely ridiculous sometimes at the
very climax of their most deeply felt passages. It is
not to be wondered at that they prefer to pick and
choose among the lines of their parts, retaining the
great professional opportunities afforded by the tragic
scenes, and leaving out the touches which complete
the portrait at the expense of the model's vanity. If
an actress of established reputation were asked to play
Hedda Gabler, her first impulse would probably be
to not only turn Hedda into a Brinvilliers,* or a
Borgia,† or a "Forget-me-not," § but to suppress all
the meaner callosities and odiousnesses which detract
from Hedda's dignity as dignity is estimated on the
stage. The result would be about as satisfactory to a
skilled critic as that of the retouching which has made
shop window photography the most worthless of the
arts. The whole point of an Ibsen play lies in the exposure of the very conventions upon which are based
those by which the actor is ridden. Charles Surface or
Tom Jones may be very effectively played by artists
who fully accept the morality professed by Joseph
Surface and Blifil. Neither Fielding nor Sheridan forces
upon either actor or audience the dilemma that since
Charles and Tom are lovable, there must be something
hopelessly inadequate in the commercial and sexual
morality which condemns them as a pair of blackguards. The ordinary actor will tell you that the
authors "do not defend their heroes' conduct," not seeing that making them lovable is the most complete
defence of their conduct that could possibly be made.

* In *La Marquise de Brinvilliers,* a musical pastiche with libretto by Scribe and Castil-Blaze and music by Auber, Cheru-
bini, and others; first performed in 1831. It treated a grim
subject with levity.
† Lucrezia Borgia was one of Adelaide Ristori's more lurid roles.
§ Geneviève Ward's most popular role, in a play written for
her by Merivale and Grove.

How far Fielding and Sheridan saw it—how far
Molière or Mozart was convinced that the statue had
right on his side when he threw Don Juan into the
bottomless pit—how far Milton went in his sympathy
with Lucifer: all these are speculative points which
no actor has hitherto been called upon to solve. But
they are the very subjects of Ibsen's plays: those whose
interest and curiosity are not excited by them find him
the most puzzling and tedious of dramatists. He has
not only made "lost" women lovable; but he has
recognized and avowed that this is a vital justification
for them, and has accordingly explicitly argued on
their side and awarded them the sympathy which
poetic justice grants only to the righteous. He has
made the terms "lost" and "ruined" in this sense
ridiculous by making women apply them to men with
the most ludicrous effect. Hence Ibsen cannot be
played from the conventional point of view: to make
that practicable the plays would have to be rewritten.
In the rewriting, the fascination of the parts would
vanish, and with it their attraction for the performers.
A Doll's House was adapted in this fashion, though not
at the instigation of an actress; but the adaptation
fortunately failed. Otherwise we might have to endure
in Ibsen's case what we have already endured in that
of Shakespear, many of whose plays were supplanted
for centuries by incredibly debased versions, of which
Cibber's Richard III and Garrick's Katharine and
Petruchio have lasted to our own time.

Taking Talma's estimate of eighteen years as the
apprenticeship of a completely accomplished stage
artist, there is little encouragement to offer Ibsen parts
to our finished actors and actresses. They do not
understand them, and would not play them in their
integrity if they could be induced to attempt them. In
England only two women in the full maturity of their
talent have hitherto meddled with Ibsen. One of these,
Miss Geneviève Ward, who "created" the part of Lona
Hessel in the English version of Pillars of Society, had
the advantage of exceptional enterprise and intelli-

gence, and of a more varied culture and experience of life and art than are common in her profession. The other, Mrs Theodore Wright, the first English Mrs Alving, was hardly known to the dramatic critics, though her personality and her artistic talent as an amateur reciter and actress had been familiar to the members of most of the advanced social and political bodies in London since the days of the International. It was precisely because her record lay outside the beaten track of newspaper criticism that she was qualified to surprise its writers as she did. In every other instance, the women who first ventured upon playing Ibsen heroines were young actresses whose ability had not before been fully tested and whose technical apprenticeships were far from complete. Miss Janet Achurch, though she settled the then disputed question of the feasibility of Ibsen's plays on the English stage by her impersonation of Nora in 1889, which still remains the most complete artistic achievement in the new genre, had not been long enough on the stage to secure a unanimous admission of her genius, though it was of the most irresistible and irrepressible kind. Miss Florence Farr, who may claim the palm for artistic courage and intellectual conviction in selecting for her experiment Rosmersholm, incomparably the most difficult and dangerous, as it is also the greatest, of Ibsen's later plays, had almost relinquished her profession from lack of interest in its routine, after spending a few years in acting farcical comedies. Miss Elizabeth Robins and Miss Marion Lea, to whose unaided enterprise we owe our early acquaintance with Hedda Gabler on the stage, were, like Miss Achurch and Miss Farr, juniors in their profession. All four were products of the modern movement for the higher education of women, literate, in touch with advanced thought, and coming by natural predilection on the stage from outside the theatrical class, in contradistinction to the senior generation of inveterately sentimental actresses, schooled in the old fashion if at all, born into their profession, quite out of the political and social movement around them—in short, intellectually naïve to the last degree. The new school says to the old, You cannot play Ibsen because you are ignoramuses. To which the old school retorts, You cannot play anything because you are amateurs. But taking amateur in its sense of un-practised executant, both schools are amateur as far as Ibsen's plays are concerned. The old technique breaks down in the new theatre; for though in theory it is a technique of general application, making the artist so plastic that he can mould himself to any shape designed by the dramatist, in practice it is but a stock of tones and attitudes out of which, by appropriate selection and combination, a certain limited number of conventional stage figures can be made up. It is no more possible to get an Ibsen character out of it than to contrive a Greek costume out of an English wardrobe; and some of the attempts already made have been so grotesque, that at present, when one of the more specifically Ibsenian parts has to be filled, it is actually safer to entrust it to a novice than to a competent and experienced actor.

A steady improvement may be expected in the performances of Ibsen's plays as the young players whom they interest gain the experience needed to make mature artists of them. They will gain this experience not only in plays by Ibsen himself, but in the works of dramatists who will have been largely influenced by Ibsen. Playwrights who formerly only compounded plays according to the received prescriptions for producing tears or laughter, are already taking their profession seriously to the full extent of their capacity, and venturing more and more to substitute the incidents and catastrophes of spiritual history for the swoons, surprises, discoveries, murders, duels, assassinations, and intrigues which are the common-places of the theatre at present. Others, who have no such impulse, find themselves forced to raise the quality of their work by the fact that even those who witness Ibsen's plays with undisguised weariness and aversion, find, when they return to their accustomed theatrical fare, that they have suddenly become conscious of absurdities and artificialities in it which never troubled them before. In just the same way the painters of the Naturalist school reformed their opponents much more extensively than the number of their own direct admirers indicates: for example, it is still common to hear the most contemptuous abuse and ridicule of Monet and Whistler from persons who have nevertheless had their former tolerance of the unrealities of the worst type of conventional studio picture wholly destroyed by these painters. Until quite lately, too, musicians were to be heard extolling Donizetti in the same breath with which they vehemently decried Wagner. They would make wry faces at every chord in Tristan and Isolde, and never suspected that their old faith was shaken until they went back to La Favorita, and found that it had become as obsolete as the rhymed tragedies of Lee and Otway. In the drama then, we may depend on it that though we shall not have another Ibsen, yet nobody will write for the stage after him as most playwrights wrote before him. This will involve a corresponding change in the technical stock-in-trade of the actor, whose ordinary training will then cease to be a positive disadvantage to him when he is entrusted with an Ibsen part.

No one need fear on this account that Ibsen will gradually destroy melodrama. It might as well be assumed that Shakespear will destroy music-hall entertainments, or the prose romances of William Morris supersede the Illustrated Police News. All forms of art rise with the culture and capacity of the human race; but the forms rise together: the higher forms do not return and submerge the lower. The wretch who finds his happiness in setting a leash of greyhounds on a hare or in watching a terrier killing rats in a pit, may evolve into the mere blockhead who would rather go to a "free-and-easy" and chuckle over a dull, silly, obscene song; but such a step will not raise him to the level of the frequenter of music halls of the better class, where, though the entertainment is administered in small separate doses or "turns," yet the turns have some artistic pretension. Above him again is the patron of that elementary form of sensational drama in which there is hardly any more connection between the incidents than the fact that the same people take part in them and call forth some very simple sort of moral judgment by being consistently villainous or virtuous throughout. As such a drama would be almost as enjoyable if the acts were played in the reverse of their appointed order, no inconvenience except that of a back seat is suffered by the playgoer who comes in for half price at nine o'clock. On a higher plane we have dramas with a rational sequence of incidents, the interest of any one of which depends on those which have preceded it; and as we go up from plane to plane we find this sequence becoming more and more organic until at last we come to a class of play in which nobody can understand the last act who has not seen the first also. Accordingly, the institution of half price at nine o'clock does not exist at theatres devoted to plays of this class. The highest type of play is completely homogeneous, often consisting of a single very complex incident; and not even the most exhaustive information as to the story enables a spectator to receive the full force of the impression aimed at in any given passage if he enters the theatre for that passage alone. The success of such plays depends upon the exercise by the audience of powers of memory, imagination, insight, reasoning, and sympathy, which only a small minority of the playgoing public at present possesses. To the rest the higher drama is as disagreeably perplexing as the game of chess is to a man who has barely enough capacity to understand skittles. Consequently, just as we have the chess club and the skittle alley prospering side by side, we shall have the theatre of Shakespear, Molière, Goethe, and Ibsen prospering alongside that of Henry Arthur Jones and Gilbert; of Sardou, Grundy, and Pinero; of Buchanan and Ohnet, as naturally as these already prosper alongside that of Pettit and Sims, which again does no more harm to the music halls than the music halls do to the waxworks or even the ratpit, although this last is dropping into the limbo of discarded brutalities by the same progressive movement that has led the intellectual playgoer to discard Sardou and take to Ibsen. It has often been said that political parties progress serpent-wise, the tail being today where the head was formerly, yet never overtaking the head. The same figure may be applied to grades of playgoers, with the reminder that this sort of serpent grows at the head and drops off joints of his tail as he glides along. Therefore it is not only inevitable that new theatres should be built for the new first class of playgoers, but that the best of the existing theatres should be gradually converted to their use, even at the cost of ousting, in spite of much angry protest, the old patrons who are being left behind by the movement.

The resistance of the old playgoers to the new plays will be supported by the elder managers, the elder actors, and the elder critics. One manager pities Ibsen for his ignorance of effective playwriting, and declares that he can see exactly what ought to have been done to make a real play of Hedda Gabler. His case is parallel to that of Mr Henry Irving, who saw exactly what ought to have been done to make a real play of Goethe's Faust, and got Mr Wills to do it. A third manager, repelled and disgusted by Ibsen, condemns Hedda as totally deficient in elevating moral sentiment. One of the plays which he prefers is Sardou's La Tosca! Clearly these three representative gentlemen, all eminent both as actors and managers, will hold by the conventional drama until the commercial success of Ibsen forces them to recognize that in the course of nature they are falling behind the taste of the day. Mr Thorne, at the Vaudeville Theatre, was the first leading manager who ventured to put a play of Ibsen's into his evening bill; and he did not do so until Miss Elizabeth Robins and Miss Marion Lea had given ten experimental performances at his theatre at their own risk. Mr Charrington and Miss Janet Achurch, who, long before that, staked their capital and reputation on A Doll's House, had to take a theatre and go into management themselves for the purpose. The production of Rosmersholm was not a managerial enterprise in the ordinary sense at all: it was an experiment made by Miss Farr, who played Rebecca—an experiment, too, which was considerably hampered by the refusal of the London managers to allow members of their companies to take part in the performance. In short, the senior division would have nothing to say for themselves in the matter of the one really progressive theatrical movement of their time, but for the fact that Mr W. H. Vernon's effort to obtain a hearing for Pillars of Society in 1880 was the occasion of the first appearance of the name of Ibsen on an English playbill.

But it had long been obvious that the want of a playhouse at which the aims of the management should be unconditionally artistic was not likely to be supplied either at our purely commercial theatres or at those governed by actor-managers reigning absolutely over all the other actors, a power which a young man abuses to provide opportunities for himself, and which an older man uses in an old-fashioned way. Mr. William Archer, in an article in The Fortnightly Review, invited private munificence to endow a National Theatre; and some time later a young Dutchman, Mr J. T. Grein, an enthusiast in theatrical art, came forward with a somewhat similar scheme. Private munificence remained irresponsive—fortunately, one must think, since it was a feature of both plans that the management of the endowed theatre should be handed over to committees of managers and actors of established reputation—in other words, to the very people whose deficiencies have created the whole difficulty. Mr Grein, however, being prepared to take any practicable scheme in hand himself, soon saw the realities of the situation well enough to understand that to wait for the floating of a fashionable

Utopian enterprise, with the Prince of Wales as President and a capital of at least £20,000, would be to wait for ever. He accordingly hired a cheap public hall in Tottenham Court Road, and, though his resources fell far short of those with which an ambitious young professional man ventures upon giving a dance, made a bold start by announcing a performance of Ghosts to inaugurate "The Independent Theatre" on the lines of the Théâtre Libre of Paris. The result was that he received sufficient support both in money and gratuitous professional aid to enable him to give the performance at the Royalty Theatre; and throughout the following week he shared with Ibsen the distinction of being abusively discussed to an extent that must have amply convinced him that his efforts had not passed unheeded. Possibly he may have counted on being handled generously for the sake of his previous services in obtaining some consideration for the contemporary English drama on the continent, even to the extent of bringing about the translation and production in foreign theatres of some of the most popular of our recent plays; but if he had any such hope it was not fulfilled; for he received no quarter whatever. And at present it is clear that unless those who appreciate the service he has rendered to theatrical art in England support him as energetically as his opponents attack him, it will be impossible for him to maintain the performances of the Independent Theatre at the pitch of efficiency and frequency which will be needed if it is to have any wide effect on the taste and seriousness of the playgoing public. One of the most formidable and exasperating obstacles in his way is the detestable censorship exercised by the official licenser of plays, a public nuisance of which it seems impossible to rid ourselves under existing Parliamentary conditions. The licenser has the London theatres at his mercy through his power to revoke their licenses; and he is empowered to exact a fee for reading each play submitted to him, so that his income depends on his allowing no play to be produced without going through that ordeal. As these powers are granted to him in order that he may forbid the performance of plays which would have an injurious effect on public morals, the unfortunate gentleman is bound in honor to try to do his best to keep the stage in the right path—which he of course can set about in no other way than by making it a reflection of his individual views, which are necessarily dictated by his temperament and by the political and pecuniary interests of his class. This he does not dare to do: self-mistrust and the fear of public opinion paralyze him whenever either the strong hand or the open mind claims its golden opportunity; and the net result is that indeceny and vulgarity are rampant on the London stage, from which flows the dramatic stream that irrigates the whole country; whilst Shelley's Cenci tragedy and Ibsen's Ghosts are forbidden, and have in fact only been performed once "in private": that is, before audiences of invited non-paying guests. It is now so well understood that only plays of the commonest idealist type can be sure of a license in London, that the novel and not the drama is the form adopted as a matter of course by thoughtful masters of fiction. The merits of the case ought to be too obvious to need restating: It is plain that every argument that supports a censorship of the stage supports with tenfold force a censorship of the press, which is admittedly an abomination. What is wanted is the entire abolition of the censorship and the establishment of Free Art in the sense in which we speak of Free Trade. There is not the slightest ground for protecting theatres against the competition of music halls, or for denying to Mr Grein as a theatrical entrepreneur the freedom he would enjoy as a member of a publishing firm. In the absence of a censorship a manager can be prosecuted for an offence against public morals, just as a publisher can. At present, though managers may not touch Shelley or Ghosts, they find no difficulty in obtaining official sanction, practically amounting to indemnity, for indecencies from which our uncensored

novels are perfectly free. The truth is that the real
support of the censorship comes from those Puritans
who regard Art as a department of original sin. To
them the theatre is an unmixed evil, and every re-
striction on it a gain to the cause of righteousness.
Against them stand those who regard Art in all its
forms as a department of religion. The Holy War between the two sides has played a considerable part in
the history of England, and is just now being prosecuted with renewed vigor by the Puritans. If their
opponents do not display equal energy, it is quite
possible that we shall presently have a reformed censorship ten times more odious than the existing one, the
very absurdity of which causes it to be exercised with
a halfheartedness that prevents the licenser from doing his worst as well as his best. The wise policy for
the friends of Art just now is to use the Puritan agitation in order to bring the matter to an issue, and then
to make a vigorous effort to secure that the upshot shall
be the total abolition of the censorship.

As it is with the actors and managers, so it is with
the critics: the supporters of Ibsen are the younger
men. In the main, however, the Press follows the managers instead of leading them. The average newspaper
dramatic critic is not a Lessing, a Lamb, or a Lewes:
there was a time when he was not necessarily even an
accustomed playgoer, but simply a member of the
reporting or literary staff told off for theatre duty without any question as to his acquaintance with dramatic
literature. At present, though the special nature of his
function is so far beginning to be recognized that ap-
pointments of the kind usually fall now into the hands
of inveterate frequenters of the theatre, yet he is still
little more than the man who supplies accounts of
what takes place in the playhouses just as his colleague
supplies accounts of what takes place at the police
court—an important difference, however, being that
the editor, who generally cares little about Art and
knows less, will himself occasionally criticize, or ask
one of his best writers to criticize, a remarkable police

case, whereas he never dreams of theatrical art as a subject upon which there could be any editorial policy. Sir Edwin Arnold's editorial attack on Ibsen was due to the accidental circumstance that he, like Richelieu, writes verses between whiles. In fact, the "dramatic critic" of a newspaper, in ordinary circumstances, is at his best a good descriptive reporter, and at his worst a mere theatrical newsman. As such he is a person of importance among actors and managers, and of no importance whatever elsewhere. Naturally he frequents the circles in which alone he is made much of; and by the time he has seen so many performances that he has formed some critical standards in spite of himself, he has also enrolled among his personal acquaintances every actor and manager of a few years' standing, and become engaged in all the private likes and dislikes, the quarrels and friendships, in a word, in all the partialities which personal relations involve, at which point the value of his verdicts may be imagined. Add to this that if he has the misfortune to be attached to a paper to which theatrical advertisements are an object, or of which the editor and proprietors (or their wives) do not hesitate to incur obligations to managers by asking for complimentary admissions, he may often have to choose between making himself agreeable and forfeiting his post. So that he is not always to be relied on even as a newsman where the plain truth would give offence to any individual.

Behind all the suppressive forces with which the critic has to contend comes the law of libel. Every adverse criticism of a public performer is a libel; and any agreement among the critics to boycott artists who appeal to the law is a conspiracy. Of course the boycott does take place to a certain extent; for if an artist, manager, or agent shows any disposition to retort to what is called a "slating" by a lawyer's letter, the critic, who cannot for his own sake expose his employers to the expenses of an action or the anxiety attending the threat of one, will be tempted to shun the danger by simply never again referring to the liti-

giously disposed person. But although this at first sight
seems to sufficiently guarantee the freedom of criticism
(for most public persons would suffer more from being
ignored by the papers than from being attacked in
them, however abusively) its operation is really re-
stricted on the one side to the comparatively few and
powerful critics who are attached to important papers
at a fixed salary, and on the other to those entrepreneurs and artists about whom the public is not
imperatively curious. Most critics get paid for their
notices at so much per column or per line, so that their
incomes depend on the quantity they write. Under
these conditions they fine themselves every time they
ignore a performance. Again, a dramatist or a manager may attain such a position that his enterprises
form an indispensable part of the news of the day. He
can then safely intimidate a hostile critic by a threat
of legal proceedings, knowing that the paper can afford
neither to brave nor ignore him. The late Charles
Reade, for example, was a most dangerous man to
criticize adversely; but the very writers against whom
he took actions found it impossible to boycott him;
and what Reade did out of a natural overflow of indignant pugnacity, some of our more powerful artistic
entrepreneurs occasionally threaten to do now after
a deliberate calculation of the advantages of their
position. If legal proceedings are actually taken, and
the case is not, as usual, compromised behind the
scenes, the uncertainty of the law receives its most
extravagant illustration from a couple of lawyers ar-
guing a question of fine art before a jury of men of
business. Even if the critic were a capable speaker
and pleader, which he is not in the least likely to be,
he would be debarred from conducting his own case
by the fact that his comparatively wealthy employer
and not himself would be the defendant in the case. In
short, the law is against straightforward criticism at
the very points where it is most needed; and though
it is true that an ingenious and witty writer can make
any artist or performance acutely ridiculous in the

eyes of ingenious and witty people without laying himself open to an action, and indeed with every appearance of good-humored indulgence, such applications of wit and ingenuity do criticism no good; whilst in any case they offer no remedy to the plain critic writing for plain readers.

All this does not mean that the entire Press is hopelessly corrupt in its criticism of Art. But it certainly does mean that the odds against the independence of the Press critic are so heavy that no man can maintain it completely without a force of character and a personal authority which are rare in any profession, and which in most of them can command higher pecuniary terms and prospects than any which journalism can offer. The final degrees of thoroughness have no market value on the Press; for, other things being equal, a journal with a critic who is good-humored and compliant will have no fewer readers than one with a critic who is inflexible where the interest of Art and the public are concerned. I do not exaggerate or go beyond the warrant of my own experience when I say that unless a critic is prepared not only to do much more work than the public will pay him for, but to risk his livelihood every time he strikes a serious blow at the powerful interests vested in artistic abuses of all kinds (conditions which in the long run tire out the strongest man), he must submit to compromises which detract very considerably from the trustworthiness of his criticism. Even the critic who is himself in a position to brave these risks must find a sympathetic and courageous editor-proprietor who will stand by him without reference to the commercial advantage—or disadvantage—of his incessant warfare. As all the economic conditions of our society tend to throw our journals more and more into the hands of successful moneymakers, the exceeding scarcity of this lucky combination of resolute, capable, and incorruptible critic, sympathetic editor, and disinterested and courageous proprietor, can hardly be appreciated by those who only know the world of journalism through its black and white veil.

On the whole, though excellent criticisms are written every week by men who, either as writers distinguished in other branches of literature and journalism, or as civil servants, are practically independent of this or that particular appointment as dramatic critic (not to mention the few whom strong vocation and force of character have rendered incorruptible) there remains a great mass of newspaper reports of theatrical events which is only called dramatic criticism by courtesy. Among the critics properly so called opinions are divided about Ibsen in the inevitable way into Philistine, idealist, and realist (more or less). Just at present the cross firing between them is rather confusing. Without being necessarily an Ibsenist, a critic may see at a glance that abuse of the sort quoted * is worthless; and he may for the credit of his cloth attack it on that ground. Thus we have Mr A. B. Walkley, of The Speaker, one of the most able and independent of our critics, provoking Mr Clement Scott beyond measure by alluding to the writers who had just been calling the admirers of Ibsen "muck-ferreting dogs," as "these gentry," with a good-humored but very perceptible contempt for their literary attainments. Thereupon Mr Scott publishes a vindication of the literateness of that school, of which Mr Walkley makes unmerciful fun. But Mr Walkley is by no means committed to Ibsenism by his appreciation of Ibsen's status as an artist, much less by his depreciation of the literary status of Ibsen's foes. On the other hand there is Mr Frederick Wedmore, a professed admirer of Balzac, conceiving such a violent antipathy to Ibsen that he almost echoes Sir Edwin Arnold, whose denunciations are at least as applicable to the author of Vautrin as to the author of Ghosts. Mr George Moore, accustomed to fight on behalf of Zola against the

* By William Archer in "Ghosts and Gibberings," *The Pall Mall Gazette*, April 8, 1891.

men who are now attacking Ibsen, takes the field promptly against his old enemies in defence, not of Ibsenism, but of Free Art. Even Mr William Archer expressly guards himself against being taken as an Ibsenist doctrinaire. In the face of all this, it is little to the point that some of the critics who have attacked Ibsen have undoubtedly done so because—to put it bluntly —they are too illiterate and incompetent in the sphere of dramatic poetry to conceive or relish anything more substantial than the theatrical fare to which they are accustomed; or that others, intimidated by the outcry raised by Sir Edwin Arnold and the section of the public typified by Pastor Manders (not to mention Mr Pecksniff), against their own conviction join the chorus of disparagement from modesty, caution, compliance—in short, from want of the courage of their profession. There is no reason to suppose that if the whole body of critics had been endowed with a liberal education and an independent income, the number of Ibsenists among them would be much greater than at present, however the tone of their adverse criticism might have been improved. Ibsen, as a pioneer in stage progress no less than in morals, is bound to have the majority of his contemporaries against him, whether as actors, managers, or critics.

Finally, it is necessary to say, by way of warning, that many of the minor combatants on both sides have either not studied the plays at all, or else have been so puzzled that they have allowed themselves to be misled by the attacks of the idealists into reading extravagant immoralities between the lines, as, for instance, that Oswald in Ghosts is really the son of Pastor Manders, or that Lövborg is the father of Hedda Tesman's child. It has even been asserted that horrible exhibitions of death and disease occur in almost every scene of Ibsen's plays, which, for tragedies, are exceptionally free from visible physical horrors. It is not too much to say that very few of the critics have yet got so far as to be able to narrate accurately the stories of the plays they have witnessed.

No wonder, then, that they have not yet made up
their minds on the more difficult point of Ibsen's
philosophic drift—though I do not myself see how
performances of his plays can be quite adequately
judged without reference to it. One consequence of
this is that those who are interested, fascinated, and
refreshed by Ibsen's art misrepresent his meaning
benevolently quite as often as those who are perplexed and disgusted misrepresent it maliciously; and it
already looks as if Ibsen might attain undisputed supremacy as a modern playwright without necessarily
converting a single critic to Ibsenism. Indeed it is not
possible that his meaning should be fully recognized,
much less assented to, until Society as we now know
it loses its self-complacency through the growth of
the conviction foretold by Richard Wagner when he
declared that "Man will never be that which he can
and should be until, by a conscious following of that
inner natural necessity which is the only true necessity, he makes his life a mirror of nature, and frees
himself from his thraldom to outer artificial counter-
feits. Then will he first become a living man, who
now is a mere wheel in the mechanism of this or that
Religion, Nationality, or State."

A Dramatic Realist to His Critics

(*The New Review* XI, July 1894)

I think very few people know how troublesome
dramatic critics are. It is not that they are morally
worse than other people; but they know nothing. Or,
rather, it is a good deal worse than that: they know
everything wrong. Put a thing on the stage for them
as it is in real life, and instead of receiving it with the
blank wonder of plain ignorance, they reject it with
scorn as an imposture, on the ground that the real
thing is known to the whole world to be quite dif-

ferent. Offer them Mr Crummles's real pump and tubs, and they will denounce both as spurious on the ground that the tubs have no handles, and the pump no bung-hole.

I am, among other things, a dramatist; but I am not an original one, and so have to take all my dramatic material either from real life at first hand, or from authentic documents. The more usual course is to take it out of other dramas, in which case, on tracing it back from one drama to another, you finally come to its origin in the inventive imagination of some original dramatist. Now a fact as invented by a drama-tist differs widely from the fact of the same name as it exists or occurs objectively in real life. Not only stage pumps and tubs, but (much more) stage morality and stage human nature differ from the realities of these things. Consequently to a man who derives all his knowledge of life from witnessing plays, nothing appears more unreal than objective life. A dramatic critic is generally such a man; and the more exactly I reproduce objective life for him on the stage, the more certain he is to call my play an extravaganza.

It may be asked here whether it is possible for one who every day contemplates the real world for four-teen of his waking hours, and the stage for only two, to know more of the stage world than the real world. As well might it be argued that a farmer's wife, churning for only two hours a week, and contem-plating nature almost constantly, must know more about geology, forestry, and botany than about butter. A man knows what he works at, not what he idly stares at. A dramatic critic works at the stage, writes about the stage, thinks about the stage, and under-stands nothing of the real life he idly stares at until he has translated it into stage terms. For the rest, see-ing men daily building houses, driving engines, march-ing to the band, making political speeches, and what not, he is stimulated by these spectacles to *imagine* what it is to be a builder, an engine-driver, a soldier, or a statesman. Of course, he imagines a stage builder, engine-driver, soldier, and so on, not a real one. Simple as this is, few dramatic critics are intelligent enough to discover it for themselves. No class is more idiotically confident of the reality of its own unreal knowledge than the literary class in general and dramatic critics in particular.

We have, then, two sorts of life to deal with: one subjective or stagey, the other objective or real. What are the comparative advantages of the two for the purposes of the dramatist? Stage life is artificially simple and well understood by the masses; but it is very stale; its feeling is conventional; it is totally unsuggestive of thought because all its conclusions are foregone; and it is constantly in conflict with the real knowledge which the separate members of the audience derive from their own daily occupations. For instance, a naval or military melodrama only goes down with civilians. Real life, on the other hand, is so ill understood, even by its clearest observers, that no sort of consistency is discoverable in it; there is no "natural justice" corresponding to that simple and pleasant concept, "poetic justice"; and, as a whole, it is unthinkable. But, on the other hand, it is credible, stimulating, suggestive, various, free from creeds and systems—in short, it is real.

This rough contrast will suffice to show that the two sorts of life, each presenting dramatic potentialities to the author, will, when reproduced on the stage, affect different men differently. The stage world is for the people who cannot bear to look facts in the face, because they dare not be pessimists, and yet cannot see real life otherwise than as the pessimist sees it. It might be supposed that those who conceive all the operations of our bodies as repulsive, and of our minds as sinful, would take refuge in the sects which abstain from playgoing on principle. But this is by no means what happens. If such a man has an artistic or romantic turn, he takes refuge, not in the conventicle, but in the theatre, where, in the contemplation of the idealized, or stage life, he finds some relief from his haunting conviction of omnipresent foulness and baseness. Confront him with anything like reality, and his chronic pain is aggravated instead of relieved; he raises a terrible outcry against the spectacle of cowardice, selfishness, faithlessness, sensuality—in short, everything that he went to the theatre to escape from. This is not the effect on those pessimists who dare face facts and profess their own faith. They are great admirers of the realist playwright, whom they embarrass greatly by their applause. Their cry is "Quite right: strip off the whitewash from the sepulchre; expose human nature in all its tragi-comic baseness; tear the mask of respectability from the smug bourgeois, and show the liar, the thief, the coward, the libertine beneath."

Now to me, as a realist playwright, the applause of the conscious, hardy pessimist is more exasperating than the abuse of the unconscious, fearful one. I am not a pessimist at all. It does not concern me that, according to certain ethical systems, all human beings fall into classes labelled liar, coward, thief, and so on. I am myself, according to these systems, a liar, a coward, a thief, and a sensualist; and it is my deliberate, cheerful, and entirely self-respecting intention to continue to the end of my life deceiving people, avoiding danger, making my bargains with publishers and managers on principles of supply and demand instead of abstract justice, and indulging all my appetites, whenever circumstances commend such actions to my judgment. If any creed or system deduces from this that I am a rascal incapable on occasion of telling the truth, facing a risk, foregoing a commercial advantage, or resisting an intemperate impulse of any sort, then so much the worse for the creed or system, since I have done all these things, and will probably do them again. The saying "All have sinned," is, in the sense in which it was written, certainly true of all the people I have ever known. But the sinfulness of my friends is not unmixed with saintliness: some of their

actions are sinful, others saintly. And here, again, if
the ethical system to which the classifications of saint
and sinner belong, involves the conclusion that a line
of cleavage drawn between my friends' sinful actions
and their saintly ones will coincide exactly with one
drawn between their mistakes and their successes (I
include the highest and widest sense of the two
terms), then so much the worse for the system; for
the facts contradict it. Persons obsessed by systems
may retort; "No; so much the worse for your friends"
—implying that I must move in a circle of rare
blackguards; but I am quite prepared not only to
publish a list of friends of mine whose names would
put such a retort to open shame, but to take any
human being, alive or dead, of whose actions a
genuinely miscellaneous unselected dozen can be
brought to light, to show that none of the ethical systems habitually applied by dramatic critics (not to
mention other people) can verify their inferences. As
a realist dramatist, therefore, it is my business to get
outside these systems. For instance, in the play of
mine which is most in evidence in London just now,
the heroine has been classified by critics as a minx, a
liar, and a *poseuse*. I have nothing to do with that: the
only moral question for me is, does she do good or
harm? If you admit that she does good, that she
generously saves a man's life and wisely extricates herself from a false position with another man, then you
may classify her as you please—brave, generous, and
affectionate; or artful, dangerous, faithless—it is all
one to me: you can no more prejudice me for or
against her by such artificial categorizing than you
could have made Molière dislike Monsieur Jourdain
by a lecture on the vanity and pretentiousness of that
amiable "bourgeois gentilhomme." The fact is, though
I am willing and anxious to see the human race
improved, if possible, still I find that, with reasonably
sound specimens, the more intimately I know people
the better I like them; and when a man concludes
from this that I am a cynic, and that he, who prefers

stage monsters—walking catalogues of the systematized virtues—to his own species, is a person of wholesome philanthropic tastes, why, how can I feel towards him except as an Englishwoman feels towards the Arab who, faithful to *his* system, denounces her indecency in appearing in public with her mouth uncovered?

The production of Arms and the Man at the Avenue Theatre, about nine weeks ago, brought the misunderstanding between my real world and the stage world of the critics to a climax, because the misunderstanding was itself, in a sense, the subject of the play. I need not describe the action of the piece in any detail: suffice it to say that the scene is laid in Bulgaria in 1885–6, at a moment when the need for repelling the onslaught of the Servians made the Bulgarians for six months a nation of heroes. But as they had only just been redeemed from centuries of miserable bondage to the Turks, and were, therefore, but beginning to work out their own redemption from barbarism—or, if you prefer it, beginning to contract the disease of civilization—they were very ignorant heroes, with boundless courage and patriotic enthusiasm, but with so little military skill that they had to place themselves under the command of Russian officers. And their attempts at Western civilization were much the same as their attempts at war—instructive, romantic, ignorant. They were a nation of plucky beginners in every department. Into their country comes, in the play, a professional officer from the high democratic civilization of Switzerland—a man completely acquainted by long, practical experience with the realities of war. The comedy arises, of course, from the collision of the knowledge of the Swiss with the illusions of the Bulgarians. In this dramatic scheme Bulgaria may be taken as symbolic of the stalls on the first night of a play. The Bulgarians are dramatic critics; the Swiss is the realist playwright invading their realm; and the comedy is the comedy of the collision of the realities represented by the realist playwright

with the preconceptions of stageland. Let us follow this
comedy a little into particulars.

War, as we all know, appeals very strongly to the
romantic imagination. We owe the greatest realistic
novel in the world, Don Quixote, to the awakening
lesson which a romantically imaginative man received
from some practical experience of real soldiering.
Nobody is now foolish enough to call Cervantes a
cynic because he laughed at Amadis de Gaul, or Don
Quixote a worthless creature because he charged wind-
mills and flocks of sheep. But I have been plentifully
denounced as a cynic, my Swiss soldier as a coward,
and my Bulgarian Don Quixote as a humbug, because
I have acted on the same impulse and pursued the
same method as Cervantes. Not being myself a
soldier like Cervantes, I had to take my facts at
second hand; but the difficulties were not very great,
as such wars as the Franco-Prussian and Russo-Turk-
ish have left a considerable number of experienced
soldiers who may occasionally be met and consulted
even in England; whilst the publication of such long-
delayed works as Marbot's Memoirs, and the success
with which magazine editors have drawn some of our
generals, both here and in America, on the enthralling
subject of military courage, has placed a mass of
documentary evidence at the disposal of the realist.
Even realistic fiction has become valuable in this way:
for instance, it is clear that Zola, in his Débâcle, has
gone into the evidence carefully enough to give high
authority to his description of what a battle is really
like.

The extent to which the method brought me into
conflict with the martial imaginings of the critics is
hardly to be conveyed by language. The notion that
there could be any limit to a soldier's courage, or any
preference on his part for life and a whole skin over
a glorious death in the service of his country, was
inexpressibly revolting to them. Their view was simple,
manly, and straightforward, like most impracticable
views. A man is either a coward or he is not. If a

brave man, then he is afraid of nothing. If a coward, then he is no true soldier; and to represent him as such is to libel a noble profession.

The tone of men who know what they are talking about is remarkably different. Compare, for instance, this significant little passage from no less an authority than Lord Wolseley, who, far from being a cynic, writes about war with an almost schoolboyish enthusiasm, considering that he has seen so much of it:

One of the most trying things for the captain or subaltern is to make their men who have found some temporary haven of refuge from the enemy's fire, leave it and spring forward in a body to advance over the open upon a position to be attacked. It is even difficult to make a line of men who have lain down, perhaps to take breath after a long advance at a running pace, rise up again. (*Fortnightly Review*, August, 1888.)

This, you will observe, is your British soldier, who is quite as brave as any soldier in the world. It may be objected, however, by believers in the gameness of blue blood, that it is the British officer who wins our battles, on the playing fields of Eton and elsewhere. Let me, therefore, quote another passage from our veteran commander:

I have seen a whole division literally crazy with terror when suddenly aroused in the dark by some senseless alarm. I have known even officers to tackle and wound their own comrades upon such occasions. Reasoning men are for the time reduced to the condition of unreasoning animals who, stricken with terror, will charge walls or houses, unconscious of what they do. [Here Lord Wolseley describes a scare which took place on a certain occasion.] In that night's panic several lost their lives; and many still bear the marks of wounds then received. (*Ibid.*, pp. 284–5.)

Now let us hear General Horace Porter, a veteran of the American War, which had the advantage of being a civil war, the most respectable sort of war, since there is generally a valuable idea of some kind at

stake in it. General Porter, a cooler writer than our
General, having evidently been trained in the world,
and not in the army, delivers himself as follows:

The question most frequently asked of soldiers is "How
does a man feel in battle?" There is a belief, among some
who have never indulged in the pastime of setting themselves up as targets to be shot at, that there is a delicious
sort of exhilaration experienced in battle, which arouses
a romantic enthusiasm; surfeits the mind with delightful
sensations; makes one yearn for a lifetime of fighting, and
feel that peace is a pusillanimous sort of thing at best.
Others suppose, on the contrary, that one's knees rattle
like a Spanish ballerina's castanets, and that one's mind
dwells on little else than the most approved means of
running away.
A happy mean between these two extremes would doubtless define the condition of the average man when he finds
that, as a soldier, he is compelled to devote himself to
stopping bullets as well as directing them. He stands his
ground and faces the dangers into which his profession
leads him, under a sense of duty and a regard for his self-
respect, but often feels that the sooner the firing ceases,
the better it would accord with his notion of the general
fitness of things, and that if the enemy is going to fall
back, the present moment would be as good a time as any
at which to begin such a highly judicious and commendable
movement. Braving danger, of course, has its compensa-
tions. "The blood more stirs to rouse a lion than to start
a hare." In the excitement of a charge, or in the enthusiasm of approaching victory, there is a sense of pleasure
which no one should attempt to underrate. It is the
gratification which is always born of success, and, coming
to one at the supreme moment of a favorable crisis in
battle, rewards the soldier for many severe trials and
perilous tasks. (Article in *The Century*, June 1888, p. 251.)

Probably nothing could convey a more sickening
sense of abandoned pusillanimity to the dramatic
critic than the ignoble spectacle of a soldier dodg-
ing a bullet. Bunn's* sublime conception of Don

* Alfred Bunn (1798–1860) was stage manager, translator of
Scribe, facile versifier, and opera librettist (*The Bohemian Girl*).

Caesar de Bazan, with his breast "expanding to the ball," has fixed for ever the stage ideal of the soldier under fire. General Porter falls far beneath Bunn in this passage:

> I can recall only two persons who, throughout a rattling musketry fire, always sat in their saddles without moving a muscle or even winking an eye. One was a bugler in the regular cavalry; and the other was General Grant.

It may be urged against me here that in my play I have represented a soldier as shying like a nervous horse, not at bullets, but at such trifles as a young lady snatching a box of sweets from him and throwing it away. But my soldier explains that he has been three days under fire; and though that would, of course, make no difference to the ideal soldier, it makes a considerable difference to the real one, according to General Porter.

> Courage, like everything else, wears out. Troops used to go into action during our late war, displaying a coolness and steadiness the first day that made them seem as if the screeching of shot and shell was the music on which they had been brought up. After fighting a couple of days their nerves gradually lost their tension; their buoyancy of spirits gave way; and dangers they would have laughed at the first day, often sent them panic-stricken to the rear on the third. It was always a curious sight in camp after a three days' fight to watch the effect of the sensitiveness of the nerves: men would start at the slightest sound, and dodge the flight of a bird or a pebble tossed at them. One of the chief amusements on such occasions used to be to throw stones and chips past one another's heads to see the active dodging that would follow.

A simple dramatic paraphrase of that matter-of-fact statement in the first act of Arms and the Man has received as a wild topsy-turvyist invention; and when Captain Bluntschli said to the young lady, "If I were in camp now they'd play all sorts of tricks on me," he was supposed to be confessing himself the champion coward of the Servian army. But the truth

is that he was rather showing off, in the style characteristic of the old military hand. When an officer
gets over the youthful vanity of cutting a figure as a
hero, and comes to understand that courage is a
quality for use and not for display, and that the
soldier who wins with the least risk is the best soldier,
his vanity takes another turn; and, if he is a bit of a
humorist, he begins to appreciate the comedy latent
in the incongruity between himself and the stage
soldier which civilians suppose him. General Porter
puts this characteristic of the veteran before us with
perfect clearness:

> At the beginning of the war officers felt that, as untested
> men, they ought to do many things for the sake of ap-
> pearance that were wholly unnecessary. This at times led to
> a great deal of posing for effect and useless exposure of
> life. Officers used to accompany assaulting columns over
> causeways on horseback, and occupy the most exposed
> positions that could be found. They were not playing the
> Bravo: they were confirming their own belief in their
> courage, and acting under the impression that bravery
> ought not only to be undoubted, but conspicuous. They
> were simply putting their courage beyond suspicion.
>
> At a later period of the war, *when men began to plume
> themselves as veterans,* they could afford to be more con-
> servative: they had won their spurs; their reputations were
> established; they were beyond reproach. Officers then dis-
> mounted to lead close assaults, dodged shots to their hearts'
> content, did not hesitate to avail themselves of the cover
> of earthworks when it was wise to seek such shelter, and
> resorted to many acts which conserved human life and in
> no wise detracted from their efficiency as soldiers. There
> was no longer anything done for buncombe: they had
> settled down to practical business. (*Ibid.,* p. 249.)

In Arms and the Man, this very simple and intelligible picture is dramatized by the contrast between
the experienced Swiss officer, with a high record for
distinguished services, and the Bulgarian hero who
wins the battle by an insanely courageous charge for
which the Swiss thinks he ought to be court-martialled.
Result: the dramatic critics pronounce the Swiss "a

poltroon." I again appeal to General Porter for a precedent both for the Swiss's opinion of the heroic Bulgarian, and the possibility of a novice, in "sheer ignorance of the art of war" (as the Swiss puts it), achieving just such a success as I have attributed to Sergius Saranoff:

Recruits sometimes rush into dangers from which veterans would shrink. When Thomas was holding on to his position at Chickamauga on the afternoon of the second day, and resisting charge after charge of an enemy flushed with success, General Granger came up with a division of troops, many of whom had never before been under fire. As soon as they were deployed in front of the enemy, they set up a yell, sprang over the earthworks, charged into the ranks, and created such consternation that the Confederate veterans were paralyzed by the very audacity of such conduct. Granger said, as he watched their movements, "Just look at them: they don't know any better; they think that's the way it ought to be done. I'll bet they'll never do it again."

According to the critics, Granger was a cynic and a worldling, incapable of appreciating true courage.

I shall perhaps here be reminded by some of my critics that the charge in Arms and the Man was a cavalry charge; and that I am suppressing the damning sneer at military courage implied in Captain Bluntschli's reply to Raïna Petkoff's demand to have a cavalry charge described to her:

Bluntschli—You never saw a cavalry charge, did you?

Raïna—No: how could I?

Bluntschli—Of course not. Well, it's a funny sight. It's like slinging a handful of peas against a window pane—first one comes, then two or three close behind them, and then all the rest in a lump.

Raïna (*thinking of her lover, who has just covered himself with glory in a cavalry charge*)—Yes; first one, the bravest of the brave!

Bluntschli—Hm! you should see the poor devil pulling at his horse.

Raïna—Why should he pull at his horse?

Bluntschli—It's running away with him, of course: do

you suppose the fellow wants to get there before the others
and be killed?

Imagine the feelings of the critics—countrymen of
the heroes of Balaclava, and trained in warfare by
repeated contemplation of the reproduction of Miss
Elizabeth Thompson's pictures in the Regent Street
shop windows, not to mention the recitations of Ten-
nyson's Charge of the Light Brigade, which they have
criticized—on hearing this speech from a mere Swiss!
I ask them now to put aside these authorities for a
moment and tell me whether they have ever seen a
horse bolt in Piccadilly or the Row. If so, I would then
ask them to consider whether it is not rather likely
that in a battlefield, which is, on the whole, rather a
startling place, it is not conceivable and even likely
that at least one horse out of a squadron may bolt in
a charge. Having gently led them to this point, I
further ask them how they think they would feel if
they happened to be on the back of that horse, with
the danger that has so often ended in death in Rotten
Row complicated with the glory of charging a regiment practically single-handed. If we are to believe
their criticisms, they would be delighted at the distinction. The Swiss captain in my play takes it for
granted that they would pull the horse's head off.
Leaving the difference of opinion unsettled, there can
be no doubt as to what their duty would be if they
were soldiers. A cavalry charge attains its maximum
effect only when it strikes the enemy solid. This fact
ought to be particularly well known to Balaclava
amateurs; for Kinglake, the popular authority on the
subject, gives us specimens of the orders that were
heard during the frightful advance down "the valley
of death." The dramatic-critical formula on that occasion would undoubtedly have been, "Charge, Ches-
ter, charge! on, Stanley, on!" Here is the reality:

The crash of dragoons overthrown by round shot, by
grape and by rifle-ball, was alternate with dry technical
precepts: "Back, right flank!" "Keep back, private This,"

"Keep back, private That!" "Close in to your centre!" "Do look to your dressing!" "Right squadron, right squadron, keep back!"

There is cynicism for you! Nothing but "keep back!" Then consider the conduct of Lord Cardigan, who rode at the head of the Light Brigade. Though he, too, said "Keep back," when Captain White tried to force the pace, he charged the centre gun of the battery just like a dramatic critic, and was the first man to sweep through the Russian gunners. In fact, he got clean out at the other side of the battery, happening to hit on a narrow opening by chance. The result was that he found himself presently riding down, quite alone, upon a mass of Russian cavalry. Here was a chance to cut them all down single-handed and plant the British flag on a mountain of Muscovite corpses. By refusing it, he flinched from the first-nighter's ideal. Realizing the situation when he was twenty yards from the foe, he pulled up and converted that twenty yards into 200 as quickly as was consistent with his dignity as an officer. The stage hero finds in death the supreme consolation of being able to get up and go home when the curtain falls; but the real soldier, even when he leads Balaclava charges under conditions of appalling and prolonged danger, does not commit suicide for nothing. The fact is, Captain Bluntschli's description of the cavalry charge is taken almost verbatim from an account given privately to a friend of mine by an officer who served in the Franco-Prussian war. I am well aware that if I choose to be guided by men grossly ignorant of dramatic criticism, whose sole qualification is that they have seen cavalry charges on stricken fields, I must take the consequences. Happily, as between myself and the public, the consequences have not been unpleasant; and I recommend the experiment to my fellow dramatists with every confidence.

But great as has been the offence taken at my treating a soldier as a man with no stomach for unnecessary danger, I have given still greater by treating him

as a man with a stomach for necessary food. Nature
provides the defenders of our country with regular
and efficient appetites. The taxpayer provides, at
considerable cost to himself, rations for the soldier
which are insufficient in time of peace and necessarily
irregular in time of war. The result is that our young,
growing soldiers sometimes go for months without
once experiencing the sensation of having had enough
to eat, and will often, under stress of famine, condescend to borrow florins and other trifles in silver from
the young ladies who walk out with them, in order to
eke out "the living wage." Let me quote from
Cobbett's description of his soldiering days in his
"Advice to Young Men," which nobody who has read
the book ever forgets:

I remember, and well I may! that, upon occasion, I,
after all absolutely necessary expenses, had, on Friday,
made shift to have a halfpenny in reserve, which I had
destined for the purchase of a *red herring* in the morning;
but, when I pulled off my clothes at night, so hungry then
as to be hardly able to endure life, I found that I had *lost
my halfpenny*. I buried my head under the miserable sheet
and rug and cried like a child.

I am by no means convinced that the hidden tears
still shed by young soldiers (who would rather die
than confess to them) on similar provocation would
not fill a larger cask than those shed over lost comrades
or wounds to the national honor of England. In the
field the matter is more serious. It is a mistake to
suppose that in a battle the waiters come round
regularly with soup, fish, an entrée, a snack of game,
a cut from the joint, ice pudding, coffee and cigarettes,
with drinks at discretion. When battles last for several days, as modern battles often do, the service of
food and ammunition may get disorganized or cut off
at any point; and the soldier may suffer exceedingly
from hunger in consequence. To guard against this
the veteran would add a picnic hamper to his equipment if it were portable enough and he could afford
it, or if Fortnum and Mason would open a shop on

the field. As it is, he falls back on the cheapest, most portable, and most easily purchased sort of stomach-stayer, which, as every cyclist knows, is chocolate. This chocolate, which so shocks Raïna in the play —for she, poor innocent, classes it as "sweets"—and which seems to so many of my critics to be the climax of my audacious extravagances, is a commonplace of modern warfare. I know of a man who lived on it for two days in the Shipka Pass.

By the way, I have been laughed at in this connection for making my officer carry an empty pistol, preferring chocolate to cartridges. But I might have gone further and represented him as going without any pistol at all. Lord Wolseley mentions two officers who seldom carried any weapons. One of them had to defend himself by shying stones when the Russians broke into his battery at Sebastopol. The other was Gordon.

The report that my military realism is a huge joke has once or twice led audiences at the Avenue Theatre to laugh at certain grim touches which form no part of the comedy of disillusionment elsewhere so constant between the young lady and the Swiss. Readers of General Marbot's Memoirs will remember his description of how, at the battle of Wagram, the standing corn was set on fire by the shells and many of the wounded were roasted alive. "This often happens," says Marbot, coolly, "in battles fought in summer." The Servo-Bulgarian war was fought in winter; but Marbot will be readily recognized as the source of the incident of Bluntschli's friend Stolz, who is shot in the hip in a wood-yard and burnt in the conflagration of the timber caused by the Servian shells. There is, no doubt, a certain barbarous humor in the situation—enough to explain why the Bulgarian, on hearing Raïna exclaim, "How horrible!" adds bitterly, "And how ridiculous!" but I can assure those who are anxious to fully appreciate the fun of the travesty of war discovered in my work by the critics, and whose rule is, "When in doubt, laugh," that I should not laugh at

that passage myself were I looking at my own play.
Marbot's picture of the fire-eaters fire-eaten is one
which I recommend to our music-hall tableauists when
they are in need of a change. Who that has read that
Wagram chapter does not remember Marbot forcing
his wretched horse to gallop through the red-hot straw
embers on his way to Massena; finding that general
with no aide-de-camp left to send on a probably fatal
errand except his only son; being sent in the son's
place as soon as he had changed his roasted horse for
a fresh one; being followed into the danger by the
indignant son; and, finally—Nature seldom fails with
her touch of farce—discovering that the son could not
handle his sabre, and having to defend him against
the pursuing cavalry of the enemy, who, as Bluntschli
would have prophesied, no sooner found that they had
to choose between two men who stood to fight and
hundreds who were running away and allowing themselves to be slaughtered like sheep, than they devoted
themselves entirely to the sheep, and left Marbot to
come out of the battle of Wagram with a whole skin?

I might considerably multiply my citations of documents; but the above will, I hope, suffice to show that
what struck my critics as topsy-turvy extravaganza,
having no more relation to real soldiering than Mr Gilbert's Pinafore has to real sailoring, is the plainest
matter-of-fact. There is no burlesque: I have stuck to
the routine of war, as described by real warriors, and
avoided such farcical incidents as Sir William Gordon
defending his battery by throwing stones, or General
Porter's story of the two generals who, though brave
and capable men, always got sick under fire, to their
own great mortification. I claim that the dramatic
effect produced by the shock which these realities give
to the notions of romantic young ladies and fierce civilians is not burlesque, but legitimate comedy, none the
less pungent because, on the first night at least, the
romantic young lady was on the stage and the fierce
civilians in the stalls. And since my authorities, who
record many acts almost too brave to make pleasant

reading, are beyond suspicion of that cynical disbelief in courage which has been freely attributed to me, I would ask whether it is not plain that the difference between my authenticated conception of real warfare and the stage conception lies in the fact that in real warfare there is real personal danger, the sense of which is constantly present to the mind of the soldier, whereas in stage warfare there is nothing but glory? Hence Captain Bluntschli, who thinks of a battlefield as a very busy and very dangerous place, is incredible to the critic who thinks of it only as a theatre in which to enjoy the luxurious excitements of patriotism, victory, and bloodshed without risk or retribution.

There are one or two general points in the play on which I may as well say a word whilst I have the opportunity. It is a common practice in England to speak of the courage of the common soldier as "bulldog pluck." I grant that it is an insulting practice—who would dream of comparing the spirit in which an ancient Greek went to battle with the ferocity of an animal?—though it is not so intended, as it generally comes from people who are thoughtless enough to suppose that they are paying the army a compliment. A passage in the play which drove home the true significance of the comparison greatly startled these same thoughtless ones. Can we reasonably apply such a word as valor to the quality exhibited in the field by, for instance, the armies of Frederick the Great, consisting of kidnapped men, drilled, caned, and flogged to the verge of suicide, and sometimes over it? Flogging, sickeningly common in English barracks all through the most "glorious" periods of our military history, was not abolished here by any revolt of the English soldier against it: our warriors would be flogging one another today as abjectly as ever but for the interference of humanitarians who hated the whole conception of military glory. We still hear of soldiers severely punished for posting up in the barrack stables a newspaper paragraph on the subject of an army grievance. Such absurd tyranny would, in a dockyard

or a factory full of matchgirls, produce a strike; but
it cows a whole regiment of soldiers. The fact is, armies
as we know them are made possible, not by valor in
the rank and file, but by the lack of it; not by physical
courage (we test the eyes and lungs of our recruits,
never their courage), but by civic impotence and
moral cowardice. I am afraid of a soldier, not because
he is a brave man, but because he is so utterly un-
manned by discipline that he will kill me if he is told,
even when he knows that the order is given because
I am trying to overthrow the oppression which he
fears and hates. I respect a regiment for a mutiny more
than for a hundred victories; and I confess to the
heartiest contempt for the warlike civilian who pays
poor men a pittance to induce them to submit to be
used as pawns on a battlefield in time of war, he himself, meanwhile, sitting at home talking impudent nonsense about patriotism, heroism, devotion to duty, the
inspiring sound of a British cheer, and so on. "Bulldog
pluck" is much more sensible and candid. And so the
idealist in my play continues to admit nightly that his
bull terrier, which will fight as fiercely as a soldier,
will let himself be thrashed as helplessly by the man
in authority over him. One critic seems to think that
it requires so much courage to say such things that he
describes me as "protecting" myself by "ostensibly
throwing the burden of my attack upon a couple of
small and unimportant nationalities," since "there
would have been a certain danger in bringing my
malevolent mockery too near home." I can assure the
gentleman that I meant no mockery at all. The observation is made in the play in a manner dramatically
appropriate to the character of an idealist who is made
a pessimist by the shattering of his illusions. His conclusion is that "life is a farce." My conclusion is that a
soldier ought to be made a citizen and treated like any
other citizen. And I am not conscious of running any
risk in making that proposal, except the risk of being
foolishly criticized.

I have been much lectured for my vulgarity in introducing certain references to soap and water in Bui-

garia. I did so as the shortest and most effective way of bringing home to the audience the stage of civilization in which the Bulgarians were in 1885, when, having clean air and clean clothes, which made them much cleaner than any frequency of ablution can make us in the dirty air of London, they were adopting the washing habits of big western cities as pure ceremonies of culture and civilization, and not on hygienic grounds. I had not the slightest intention of suggesting that my Bulgarian major, who submits to a good wash for the sake of his social position, or his father, who never had a bath in his life, are uncleanly people, though a cockney, who by simple exposure to the atmosphere becomes more unpresentable in three hours than a Balkan mountaineer in three years, may feel bound to pretend to be shocked at them, and to shrink with disgust from even a single omission of the daily bath which, as he knows very well, the majority of English, Irish, and Scotch people do not take, and which the majority of the inhabitants of the world do not even tell lies about.

Major Petkoff is quite right in his intuitive perception that soap, instead of being the radical remedy for dirt, is really one of its worst consequences. And his remark that the cultus of soap comes from the English because their climate makes them exceptionally dirty, is one of the most grimly and literally accurate passages in the play, as we who dwell in smoky towns know to our cost. However, I am sorry that my piece of realism should have been construed as an insult to the Bulgarian nation; and perhaps I should have hesitated to introduce it had I known that a passionate belief in the scrupulous cleanliness of the inhabitants of the Balkan peninsula is a vital part of Liberal views on foreign policy. But what is done is done. I close the incident by quoting from the daily papers of the 5th May last the following item of Parliamentary intelligence, which gives a basis for a rough calculation of the value of English cleanliness as measured by the pecuniary sacrifices we are willing to make for it:

ARMY BEDDING

The SECRETARY for WAR, replying to Mr. Hanbury's
question as to the provision made in the Army for the
washing of soldiers' bedding, stated that soldiers are now
allowed to have their sheets washed once a month, and
their blankets once a year; and the right hon. gentleman
stated that the cost of allowing clean sheets fortnightly
instead of monthly would amount to something like £10,-
000 a year, money which might be spent more advanta-
geously in other directions, he thought. (Hear, hear.)

I am afraid most of my critics will receive the above
explanations with an indulgent sense of personal in-
gratitude on my part. The burden of their mostly very
kind notices has been that I am a monstrously clever
fellow, who has snatched a brilliant success by amusingly whimsical perversions of patent facts and pi-
quantly cynical ridicule of human nature. I hardly
have the heart to turn upon such friendly help with
a cold-blooded confession that all my audacious origi-
nalities are simple liftings from stores of evidence
which is ready to everybody's hand. Even that triumph
of eccentric invention which nightly brings down the
house, Captain Bluntschli's proposal for the hand of
Raïna, is a paraphrase of an actual proposal made by
an Austrian hotel proprietor for the hand of a member
of my own family. To that gentleman, and to him alone,
is due the merit of the irresistible joke of the four
thousand tablecloths and the seventy equipages of
which twenty-four will hold twelve inside. I have
plundered him as I have plundered Lord Wolseley and
General Porter and everyone else who had anything
that was good to steal. I created nothing; I invented
nothing; I imagined nothing; I perverted nothing; I
simply discovered drama in real life.

I now plead strongly for a theatre to supply the
want of this sort of drama. I declare that I am tired to
utter disgust of imaginary life, imaginary law, imaginary ethics, science, peace, war, love, virtue, villainy, and imaginary everything else, both on the stage
and off it. I demand respect, interest, affection for

human nature as it is and life as we must still live it even when we have bettered it and ourselves to the utmost. If the critics really believe all their futile sermonizing about "poor humanity" and the "seamy side of life" and meanness, cowardice, selfishness, and all the other names they give to qualities which are as much and as obviously a necessary part of themselves as their arms and legs, why do they not shoot themselves like men instead of coming whimpering to the dramatist to pretend that they are something else? I, being a man like to themselves, know what they are perfectly well; and as I do not find that I dislike them for what they persist in calling their vanity, and sensuality, and mendacity, and dishonesty, and hypocrisy, and venality, and so forth; as, furthermore, they would not interest me in the least if they were otherwise, I shall continue to put them on the stage as they are to the best of my ability, in the hope that some day it may strike them that if they were to try a little self-respect, and stop calling themselves offensive names, they would discover that the affection of their friends, wives, and sweethearts for them is not a reasoned tribute to their virtues, but a human impulse towards their very selves. When Raïna says in the play, "Now that you have found me out, I suppose you despise me," she discovers that that result does not follow in the least, Captain Bluntschli not being quite dramatic critic enough to feel bound to repudiate the woman who has saved his life as "a false and lying minx," because, at twenty-three, she has some generous illusions which lead her into a good deal of pretty nonsense.

I demand, moreover, that when I deal with facts into which the critic has never inquired, and of which he has had no personal experience, he shall not make his vain imaginations the criterion of my accuracy. I really cannot undertake, every time I write a play, to follow it up by a textbook on mortgages, or soldiering, or whatever else it may be about, for the instruction of gentlemen who will neither accept the result of my study of the subject (lest it should destroy their

cherished ideals), nor undertake any study on their
own account. When I have written a play the whole
novelty of which lies in the fact that it is void of
malice to my fellow creatures, and laboriously exact
as to all essential facts, I object to be complimented
on my "brilliancy" as a fabricator of cynical extrava-
ganzas. Nor do I consider it decent for critics to call
their own ignorance "the British public," as they almost invariably do.

It must not be supposed that the whole Press has
gone wrong over Arms and the Man to the same extent
and in the same direction. Several of the London cor-
respondents of the provincial papers accustomed to
deal with the objective world outside the theatre, came
off with greater credit than the hopelessly specialized
critics. Some of the latter saved themselves by a strong
liking for the play, highly agreeable to me; but most
of them hopelessly misunderstood me. I should have
lain open to the retort that I had failed to make myself
comprehensible had it not been for the masterly critical exploit achieved by Mr A. B. Walkley, whose
article in The Speaker was a completely successful
analysis of my position. Mr Walkley here saved the
critics from the reproach of having failed where the
actors had succeeded. Nobody who has seen Mr Yorke
Stephens's impersonation of the Swiss captain will suspect him for a moment of mistaking his man, as most
of the critics did, for "a poltroon who prefers chocolate
to fighting." It was Mr Walkley who recognized that
Bluntschli, "dogged, hopelessly unromantic, incurably
frank, always *terre à terre*, yet a man every inch of him,
is one of the most artistic things Mr Yorke Stephens
has done."

Here we have the actor making Bluntschli appear
to a fine critic, as he undoubtedly did to the gallery,
a brave, sincere, unaffected soldier; and yet some of
the other critics, unable to rise to the actor's level,
moralized in a positively dastardly way about a "cow-
ardly and cynical mercenary." Imagine English dramatic critics, who, like myself, criticize for the paper

that pays them best, without regard to its politics, and whose country's regular army is exclusively a paid professional one, waxing virtuous over a "mercenary" soldier! After that, one hardly noticed their paying tribute to the ideal woman (a sort of female George Washington) by calling Raïna a minx, and feebly remonstrating with Miss Alma Murray for charming them in such a character; whilst as to the heroic Sergius, obsessed with their own ideals, and desperately resolved to live up to them in spite of his real nature, which he is foolish enough to despise, I half expected them to stone him; and I leave Mr Bernard Gould and Mr Walkley to divide the credit, as actor and critic, the one of having realized the man, and the other of having analyzed him—the nicety of the second operation proving the success of the first.

Here I must break off, lest I should appear to talk too much about my own play. I should have broken off sooner but for the temptation of asserting the right of the authors to decide who is the best critic, since the critics take it upon themselves to decide who is the best writer.

Preface to *The Theatrical "World" of 1894,* by William Archer

(London, Walter Scott, Ltd., 1895)

My qualification for introducing this annual record is, as I have vainly urged upon my friend the author, the worst qualification possible. For years past those readers of The World whose interest in art gave them an appetite for criticism, turned every Tuesday from a page on the drama by W. A. to a page on music by G. B. S. Last year the death of Edmund Yates closed a chapter in the history of the paper; and G. B. S., having exhausted his message on the subject of contemporary music, took the occasion to write Finis at the end

of his musical articles. But the old association was so
characteristic, and is still so recent, that we have
resolved to try whether the reader will not, just this
once more, turn over the page and pass from G. B. S.
to W. A., by mere force of habit, without noticing the
glaring fact that the musical duties of G. B. S., by
cutting him off almost entirely from the theatre, have
left him, as aforesaid, quite the most unsuitable person
to meddle in a book about the theatre and nothing
else.

However, one can learn something about the theatre
even at the opera: for instance, that there are certain
permanent conditions which deeply affect every artistic
performance in London. No journalist, without intolerable injustice to artists and managers whose livelihood is at stake, can pass judgment without taking
these conditions into account; and yet he may not
mention them, because their restatement in every
notice would be unbearable. The journalist is therefore forced to give his reader credit for knowing the
difficulties under which plays are produced in this
country, just as the writer of the leading article is
forced to assume that his reader is acquainted with
the British constitution and the practical exigencies of
our system of party government. And it is because the
reader hardly ever does know these things that newspapers so often do more harm than good.

Obviously Mr Archer, in reprinting his weekly articles exactly as they appeared, and thereby preserving
all their vividness and actuality, preserves also this
dependence of the journalist on the public for a con-
siderate and well-informed reading of his verdicts.
I need hardly add that he will not get it, because his
readers, though interested in the art of the theatre,
neither know nor care anything about the business of
the theatre; and yet the art of the theatre is as dependent on its business as a poet's genius is on his
bread and butter. Theatrical management in this
country is one of the most desperate commercial forms
of gambling. No one can foresee the fate of a play:

the most experienced managers carefully select failure after failure for production; and the most feather-headed beginners blunder on successes. At the London West End theatres, where all modern English dramas are born, the minimum expense of running a play is about £400 a week, the maximum anything you please to spend on it. And all but the merest fraction of it may be, and very frequently is, entirely lost. On the other hand, success may mean a fortune of fifty thousand pounds accumulated within a single year. Very few forms of gambling are as hazardous as this. At roulette you can back red or black instead of yellow. On the turf you can take the low odds against the favorite instead of the high odds against the outsider. At both games you can stake as much or as little as you choose. But in the theatre you must play a desperate game for high stakes, or not play at all. And the risk falls altogether on the management. Everybody, from the author to the charwoman, must be paid before the management appropriates a farthing.

The scientific student of gambling will see at once that these are not the conditions which permanently attract the gambler. They are too extreme, too inelastic; besides, the game requires far too much knowledge. Consequently, the gambler pure and simple never meddles with the theatre: he has ready to his hand dozens of games that suit him better. And what is too risky for the gambler is out of the question for the man of business. Thus, from the purely economic point of view, the theatre is impossible. Neither as investment nor speculation, enterprise nor game, earnest nor jest, can it attract a single sovereign of capital. You must disturb a man's reason before he will even listen to a proposal to run a playhouse.

It will now be asked why, under these circumstances, have we a couple of dozen West End theatres open in London. Are they being run by people whose reason is disturbed? The answer is, emphatically, Yes. They are the result of the sweeping away of all reasonable economic prudence by the immense force of an artistic

instinct which drives the actor to make opportunities
at all hazards for the exercise of his art, and which
makes the theatre irresistibly fascinating to many rich
people who can afford to keep theatres just as they
can afford to keep racehorses, yachts, or newspapers.
The actor who is successful enough to obtain tolerably
continuous employment as "leading man" in London
at a salary of from twenty to forty pounds a week,
can in a few years save enough to try the experiment
of taking a theatre for a few months and producing a
play on his own account. The same qualities which
have enabled him to interest the public as an actor
will help him, as actor-manager, to interest the rich
theatre fanciers, and to persuade them to act as his
"backers." If the enterprise thus started be watered
now and then by the huge profits of a successful play,
it will take a great deal to kill it. With the help of
these profits and occasional subsidies, runs of ill luck
are weathered with every appearance of brilliant pros-
perity, and are suspected only by experienced acting-
managers, and by shrewd observers who have noticed
the extreme scepticism of these gentlemen as to the
reality of any apparently large success.

The system of actor-manager and backer is practically supreme in London. The drama is in the hands
of Mr Irving, Mr Alexander, Mr Beerbohm Tree, Mr
Lewis Waller, Mrs John Wood, Mr Hare, Mr Terry,
Mr Wyndham, Mr Penley, and Mr Toole. Nearly all
the theatres other than theirs are either devoted, like
the Adelphi and Drury Lane, to the routine of those
comparatively childish forms of melodrama which
have no more part in the development of the theatre as
one of the higher forms of art than Madame Tussaud's
or the Christy Minstrels, or else they are opera-houses.

We all know by this time that the effect of the
actor-manager system is to impose on every dramatic
author who wishes to have his work produced in first-
rate style, the condition that there shall be a good part
for the actor-manager in it. This is not in the least due
to the vanity and jealousy of the actor-manager: it is

due to his popularity. The strongest fascination at a
theatre is the fascination of the actor or actress, not of
the author. More people go to the Lyceum Theatre to
see Mr Irving and Miss Ellen Terry than to see Shakespear's plays; at all events, it is certain that if Mr
Irving were to present himself in as mutilated a condition as he presented King Lear, a shriek of horror
would go up from all London. If Mr Irving were to
produce a tragedy, or Mr Wyndham a comedy, in
which they were cast for subordinate parts, the public
would stay away; and the author would have reason
to curse the self-denial of the actor-manager. Mr
Hare's personally modest managerial policy is anything but encouraging to authors and critics who wish
that all actor-managers were even as he. The absence
of a strong personal interest on his part in the plays
submitted to him takes all the edge off his judgment
as to their merits; and except when he is falling back
on old favorites like Caste and Diplomacy, or holding
on to A Pair of Spectacles, which is as much a one-
part actor-manager's play as Hamlet is, he is too often
selecting all the failures of the modern drama, and
leaving the successes to the actor-managers whose
selective instincts are sharpened by good parts in
them. We thus see that matters are made worse instead of mended by the elimination of personal motives
from actor-management; whilst the economic conditions are so extremely unfavorable to anyone but an
actor venturing upon the management of any but a
purely routine theatre, that in order to bring up the
list of real exceptions to the London rule of actor-
management to three, we have to count Mr Daly and
Mr Grein of the Independent Theatre along with Mr
Comyns Carr. Mr Grein, though his forlorn hopes
have done good to the drama out of all apparent
proportion to the show they have been able to make,
tells us that he has lost more by his efforts than anybody but a fanatic would sacrifice; whilst Mr Daly, as
the manager and proprietor of a London theatre (New
York is his centre of operations), has had little success

except in the Shakespearean revivals which have enabled him to exploit Miss Ada Rehan's unrivalled charm of poetic speech.

Taking actor-management, then, as inevitable for the moment, and dismissing as untenable the notion that the actor-manager can afford to be magnanimous any more than he can afford to be lazy, why is it that, on the whole, the effect of the system is to keep the theatre lagging far behind the drama? The answer is, that the theatre depends on a very large public, and the drama on a very small one. A great dramatic poet will produce plays for a bare livelihood, if he can get nothing more. Even if a London theatre would perform them on the same terms, the sum that will keep a poet for a year—or five years at a pinch—will not keep the theatre open for more than a week. Ibsen, the greatest living dramatic poet, produces a play in two years. If he could sell twenty thousand copies of it at five shillings apiece within the following two years, he would no doubt consider himself, for a poet, a most fortunate man in his commercial relations. But unless a London manager sees some probability of from 50,000 to 75,000 people paying him an average five shillings apiece within three months, he will hardly be persuaded to venture. In this book the reader will find an account of the production for the first time in England of Ibsen's Wild Duck, a masterpiece of modern tragi-comedy, famous throughout Europe. It was by no means lacking in personal appeal to the actor-manager; for it contains two parts, one of which, old Ekdal, might have been written for Mr Hare, whilst the other, Hjalmar Ekdal, would have suited Mr Beerbohm Tree to perfection. What actually happened, however, was that no London manager could afford to touch it; and it was not until a few private persons scraped together a handful of subscriptions that two modest little representations were given by Mr Grein under great difficulties. Mr Tree had already, by the experiment of a few matinées of An Enemy of the People, ascertained that such first-rate work as Ibsen's is still far above the very low level represented by the average taste of the huge crowd of playgoers requisite to make a remunerative run for a play. The Wild Duck, therefore, had to give place to commoner work. This is how the theatre lags behind its own published literature. And the evil tends to perpetuate itself in two ways: first, by helping to prevent the formation of a habit of playgoing among the cultivated section of the London community; and second, by diverting the best of our literary talent from the theatre to ordinary fiction and journalism, in which it becomes technically useless for stage purposes.

The matter is further complicated by the conditions on which the public are invited to visit the theatre. These conditions, in my opinion, are sufficient by themselves to make most reasonable people regard a visit to the theatre rather as a troublesome and costly luxury to be indulged in three or four times a year under family pressure, than as the ordinary way of passing an unoccupied evening. The theatrical managers will not recognize that they have to compete with the British fireside, the slippers, the easy chair, the circulating library, and the illustrated press. They persist in expecting a man and his wife to leave their home after dinner, and, after worrying their way to the theatre by relays of train and cab or omnibus, pay seven-and-sixpence or half a guinea apiece for comfortable seats. In the United States, where prices are higher in other things, the accommodation can be had for five and six shillings. The cheaper parts of the London theatres are below the standard of comfort now expected by third-class travellers on our northern railway lines. The result is, not that people refuse to go to the theatre at all, but that they go very seldom, and then only to some house of great repute, like Mr Irving's, or to see some play which has created the sort of mania indicated by the term "catching on." No doubt, when this mania sets in, the profits are, as we have seen, enormous. But when it does not—and this is the more frequent case—the acting-manager

is at his wit's end to find people who will sit in his
half-guinea stalls and seven-and-sixpenny balcony seats
for nothing, in order to persuade the provincial playgoer, when his turn comes to see the piece "on tour"
from an excellent seat costing only a few shillings, that
he is witnessing a "great London success." In the long
run this system will succumb to the action of competition, and to the growing discrepancy between the
distribution of prices in the theatre; but the reader
who wishes to intelligently understand the failures and
successes recorded in this book, must take account of
the fact that, with the exception of the shilling gallery,
every seat in a West End London theatre is at present
charged for at a rate which makes it impossible for
theatrical enterprise to settle down from a feverish speculation into a steady industry.

Among other effects of this state of things is an
extreme precariousness of employment for actors, who
are compelled to demand unreasonably high salaries in
order that they may earn in the course of the year dis-
couragingly small incomes. As we have seen, the few
who have sufficient adaptable ability and popularity
to be constantly employed, save rapidly enough to
become actor-managers and even to build theatres for
themselves. The result is that it becomes more and
more difficult to obtain a fine cast for a play. The "star
system," which is supposed to have disappeared in
London, is really rampant there as far as acting is
concerned. Compare, for example, the Opera, where
the actor-manager is unknown, with the Lyceum
Theatre. Sir Augustus Harris can present an opera
with a whole constellation of stars in it. One of the
greatest operas in the world, sung by half-a-dozen of
the greatest dramatic singers in the world, is a phenomenon which, as a musical critic, I have seen, and
found fault with, at Covent Garden. Now try to imagine Mr Irving attempting to do for a masterpiece
of Shakespear's what Sir Augustus Harris does for
Lohengrin. All the other stars are like Mr Irving: they
have theatres of their own, and are competing with

him as men of business, instead of co-operating with
him as artists. The old receipt for an opera company,
"Catalani and a few dolls," is, leaving scenery and
mounting out of the question, as applicable to a Shakespearean performance at the Lyceum today as it was
to the provincial starring exploits of the late Barry
Sullivan. One expects every month to hear that Mr
Waring, Mr Fred Terry, Mr Yorke Stephens, Mr
Forbes-Robertson, Mr Brandon Thomas, and Mr Haw-
trey are about to follow Mr Alexander and Mr Waller
into actor-management. We should then have sixteen
actor-managers competing with one another in sixteen
different theatres, in a metropolis hardly containing
good actors enough to cast three good plays simultaneously, even with the sixteen actor-managers counted
in. No doubt such an increased demand for actors and
plays as six additional managers would set up might
produce an increased and improved supply if the demand of the public for theatrical amusements kept
pace with the ambition of actors to become actor-
managers; but is there, under existing conditions as
to growth of population and distribution of income,
the slightest likelihood of such an upward bound of
public demand without a marked reduction of prices?

There is yet another momentous prospect to be taken
into consideration. We have at present nine actor-managers and only one actress-manageress—Mrs John
Wood. So far, our chief actresses have been content
to depend on the position of "leading lady" to some
actor-manager. This was sufficient for all ordinary am-
bitions ten years ago; but since then the progress of
a revolution in public opinion on what is called the
Woman Question has begun to agitate the stage. In
the highest class of drama the century has produced,
the works of Richard Wagner, we find the Elsa of
Lohengrin, the most highly developed of the operatic
"prima donnas" whose main function it is to be hon-
ored with the love of the hero, supplanted by a race
of true heroines like Brynhild and Isolde, women in
no sense secondary to the men whose fate is bound

up with their own, and indeed immeasurably superior
in wisdom, courage, and every great quality of heart
and mind, to the stage heroes of the middle Victorian
period of Romance. The impulse felt in heroic music
drama has now reached domestic prose comedy; and
Esther Eccles and Diplomacy Dora are succeeded by
Nora Helmer, Rebecca West, Hedda Gabler, and Hilda
Wangel. The change is so patent, that one of the plays
criticized by Mr Archer in the pages which follow is
called The New Woman. Now it is not possible to put
the new woman seriously on the stage in her relation
to modern society, without stirring up, both on the
stage and in the auditorium, the struggle to keep her
in her old place. The play with which Ibsen conquered the world, A Doll's House, allots to the "leading man" the part of a most respectable bank manager,
exactly the sort of person on whose quiet but irresistible
moral superiority to women Tom Taylor insisted with
the fullest public applause in his Still Waters Run
Deep. Yet the play ends with the most humiliating exposure of the vanity, folly, and amorous beglamorment
of this complacent person in his attitude towards his
wife, the exposure being made by the wife herself.
His is not the sort of part that an actor-manager likes
to play. Mr Wyndham has revived Still Waters Run
Deep; he will not touch A Doll's House. The one part
that no actor as yet plays willingly is the part of a hero
whose heroism is neither admirable nor laughable. A
villain if you like, a hunchback, a murderer, a kicked,
cuffed, duped pantaloon by all means; but a hero
manqué, never. Man clings to the old pose, the old
cheap heroism; and the actor in particular, whose life
aspiration it has been to embody that pose, feels, with
inexpressible misgiving, the earth crumbling beneath
his feet as the enthusiasm his heroism once excited
turns to pity and ridicule. But this misgiving is the
very material on which the modern dramatist of the
Ibsen school seizes for his tragi-comedy. It is the
material upon which I myself have seized in a play of
my own criticized in this book, to which I only allude

here to gratify my friend the author, who has begged me to say something about Arms and the Man. I comply by confessing that the result was a misunderstanding so complete, that but for the pleasure given by the acting, and for the happy circumstance that there was sufficient fun in the purely comic aspect of the piece to enable it to filch a certain vogue as a novel sort of extravaganza, its failure would have been as evident to the public as it was to me when I bowed my acknowledgments before the curtain to a salvo of entirely mistaken congratulations on my imaginary success as a conventionally cynical and paradoxical castigator of "the seamy side of human nature." The whole difficulty was created by the fact that my Bulgarian hero, quite as much as Helmer in A Doll's House, was a hero shown from the modern woman's point of view. I complicated the psychology by making him catch glimpse after glimpse of his own aspect and conduct from this point of view himself, as all men are beginning to do more or less now, the result, of course, being the most horrible dubiety on his part as to whether he was really a brave and chivalrous gentleman, or a humbug and a moral coward. His actions, equally of course, were hopelessly irreconcilable with either theory. Need I add that if the straightforward Helmer, a very honest and ordinary middle-class man misled by false ideals of womanhood, bewildered the public, and was finally set down as a selfish cad by all the Helmers in the audience, *a fortiori* my introspective Bulgarian hero never had a chance, and was dismissed, with but moderately spontaneous laughter, as a swaggering impostor of the species for which contemporary slang has invented the term "bounder"?

But what bearing have the peculiarities of Helmer and my misunderstood Bulgarian on the question of the actress-manageress? Very clearly this, that it is just such peculiarities that make characteristically modern plays as repugnant to the actor as they are attractive to the actress, and that, consequently, the actress who is content to remain attached to an actor-manager as "leading lady," forfeits all chance of creating any of the fascinating women's parts which come at intervals of two years from the Ibsen mint. Among the newest parts open to the leading lady, Paula Tanqueray counts as "advanced," although she would be perfectly in her place in a novel by Thackeray or Trollope, to either of whom Nora Helmer would have been an inconceivable person. A glance at our theatres will show that the higher artistic career is practically closed to the leading lady. Miss Ellen Terry's position at the Lyceum Theatre may appear an enviable one; but when I recall the parts to which she has been condemned by her task of "supporting" Mr Irving, I have to admit that Miss Janet Achurch, for instance, who made for herself the opportunity of "creating" Nora Helmer in England by placing herself in the position virtually of actress-manageress, is far more to be envied. Again, if we compare Miss Elizabeth Robins, the creator of Hedda Gabler and Hilda Wangel, with Miss Kate Rorke at the Garrick Theatre, or the records of Miss Florence Farr and Miss Marion Lea with that of Miss Mary Moore at the Criterion, we cannot but see that the time is ripe for the advent of the actress-manager-ess, and that we are on the verge of something like a struggle between the sexes for the dominion of the London theatres, a struggle which, failing an honorable treaty, or the break-up of the actor-manager system by the competition of new forms of theatrical enterprise, must in the long run end disastrously for the side which is furthest behind the times. And that side is at present the men's side.

The reader will now be able to gratify his impatience, and pass on to Mr Archer's criticisms (if he has not done so long ago), with some idea of the allowances that must be made for circumstances in giving judgment on the curious pageant which passes before the dramatic critic as he sits in his stall night after night. He has had to praise or blame, advocate oppose, always with a human and reasonable re-

gard to what is possible under existing conditions.
Most of his readers, preoccupied with pure ideals of
the art of the theatre, know nothing of these conditions
and perhaps imagine that all that lies beyond their
ken is the working of the traps and the shifting of the
scenery. Perhaps these few hints of mine may help
them to understand that the real secrets of the theatre
are not those of the stage mechanism, but of the box-
office, the acting-manager's room, and the actor-manager's soul.

How to Lecture on Ibsen

(Letter to Janet Achurch in Ashley Dukes, "A Doll's
   House and the Open Door," *Theatre Arts* XII, January
   1928; also in *Nash's,* February 1928)

29, Fitzroy Square, W.
23rd April 1895

Charrington has just been here, with the dire news
that you want to lecture on Ibsen. Now if you get a
chance of making a speech under auspicious circumstances in New York, by all means do so. If there is
any artistic club that you can address, get them to ask
you to address them. Don't let it be a dinner, because
after-dinner speaking is difficult and inconvenient; and
the audience is always half drunk. But don't get a lecture agent to announce you as a lecture with a charge
for admission; and don't let yourself be put into the
position of a professional lecturer for a moment. There
must be no money in the transaction.

Suppose, then, that you are in for a speech, what
had you better do? To begin with, don't write your
speech. If you attempt to read a lecture on Ibsen, you
will embarrass yourself and bore your audience to dis-
traction. If you haven't sufficient courage and simplicity
of character to chatter away pleasantly to an audience
from a few notes and your own experience, then let
the platform alone. You can, without much prepara-

tion, get a very entertaining turn on some such lines
as the following.

First, you hope nobody expects that you are going
to deliver a lecture. For that, it is necessary to be a
critic, an essayist, a student of literature, like the
clever gentlemen who write about the drama for the
New York papers. Besides, you are not conscious of
your art as these gentlemen are. You took to the stage
as a duck takes to water. When people want a lecture
on swimming they don't go to a duck for it, but to
a professor who probably doesn't know how to swim
at all. In the same way, if people want a lecture on
the drama or the stage, they must not come to you
for it, but to one of the dramatic critics. Not that you
mean to suggest that they cannot act; on the contrary,
it is clear from the way they write that they are all
accomplished actors; and you would go a long way to
see a performance of a classical play with all the parts
filled by critics. The subject that you are really going
to talk about is yourself—a favorite subject of yours.
Perhaps they (the audience) think that an impertinence—oh, it is very kind of them to disclaim that
feeling; but you are sure some of them think so; and
if they don't they ought to. But you have a justification
ready.

The justification is that the actress really does take
a very important part in the history and development
of the drama. The drama progresses by a series of
experiments made on the public by actors and actresses with new plays. The public may determine
the result of the experiment; but the public never
makes the experiment. It does not come to you and
say, "Produce a play of Ibsen's, and see how we will
like it." The initiative comes always from the actor or
actress, who says, "I do so long to play Nora, or
Hedda Gabler; and I must try whether the public will
support me in it. If Ibsen had not interested *us,* the
actors, his plays would still be on the book shelf; and
I should have been celebrated for my impersonations
of Pauline Deschapelles, and Adrienne Lecouvreur,

and all sorts of nonsensical heroines instead of for
my Nora in A Doll's House." So you see it really does
matter what *we* like and what *we* think; and that is
my excuse for getting up here today to give you a
piece of my mind. If any lady or gentleman present
will write a play with a part in it which I feel I *must*
play, that play will be performed some day, even if
everyone else in Europe or America said worse things
of it than Herr Max Nordau says of Ibsen (Here
endeth the exordium).

Now you (the audience) perhaps want to know
why I am bent on thrusting plays like Ibsen's on the
public when there are so many excellent plays, by
Shakespear and other clever people, which were good
enough for Mrs Siddons and ought to be good enough
for me. Well, I can't tell you why any more than I
can tell you why I have different ideas from my
grandmother. Perhaps the change may be for the
worse; but that doesn't alter the fact that there is a
change, and that the change is taking place in you as
well as in me. If I were to revive some of Mrs Siddons's
popular parts for you, you would be the most astonished audience in America before it was half over. You
would find the sentiment of the play as much out of
date as its rhetoric, so much so that you would think
me mad in producing such a work at the present
day. Now what all the world feels about the plays of
a hundred years ago, a few people feel about the
plays of twenty-five years ago. I need not tell you that
an actress has to play parts in many plays of which she
has no very high opinion. Sometimes the author has
not written one single line right: the actress has to
invent the part for herself and play it *between* the
lines, or else speak her words with a pathetic intensity
that makes you forget that the actual words do not
mean anything pathetic at all, affecting the public as
Sarah Bernhardt affects people who do not know a
word of French or Duse people who do not know a
word of Italian. Sometimes the author had only
succeeded in a single scene, though that scene may be

worth producing the play for. Then some bits of a play wear out faster than others. In Shakespear there are parts—like that of Helena in All's Well for instance—which are still too genuine and beautiful and modern for the public; but there are also many passages which are tedious and impossible, though we all pretend to like them. These are terrible bits to get over on the stage when they cannot be cut out; when I come to them I am only *pretending to act,* which is the most horribly dishonorable feeling you can have on the stage, though perhaps that will not be easily understood by people who think that acting is all pretence. But I assure you that is how I feel; and the result is that a part that I can play from beginning to end with conviction attracts me more than the most popular play in which my faith is imperfect. Consequently I get strong preferences for one play over another; and I will try to make the nature of my preferences clearer to you by comparing certain passages in those modern plays which show the influence of the great movement of the past half century for the better education and freedom of women, with passages from other plays which date in feeling from before that movement.

Now here I (G.B.S.) must leave you (Janet) to make up the real stuff of your speech for yourself. The idea is to quote the sham womanly stuff from The Lady of Lyons, Adrienne, and so on, and contrast it with passages from Ibsen's plays. A comic performance of the death scene from Adrienne would be good. Do it exactly as you do it on the stage, telling them previously that they must not laugh, and assuring them that what you are going to do is to the eighth of an inch what you have so often set the house weeping with. They will probably laugh like anything. Then give them the sharp, businesslike death scene at the end of Hedda Gabler. Allude to Dickens's Edith Summerson and Agnes Wickfield as the sort of thing that women dislike, and show how the women on the stage are making constantly for the sort of work which, even when it makes them unamiable, at least makes them unamiable human beings, which is better than making them amiable impostors.

You might then, very carefully and slyly, point out, on the lines of my preface to Archer's book (proof of preface enclosed in lecture of C.C.'s which goes to you by book post this mail), how the men on the stage dislike the plays in which the women's parts are real parts, and how women are being driven into management by this, with the likelihood that we shall presently have half the theatres managed by actor-managers, with no chance of a good woman's play being produced, and the other half managed by actress-manageresses, with the men at the same disadvantage, and the drama thus worse off than ever. The moral ought to be desirability of management with artistic aims, the object being the production of the best plays and not the exhibition of this or that performer. And be sure to disclaim, in as amusing a way as possible, any pretence on your part to be fit to be trusted with management on those lines. Say that wherever you are in charge, they may depend on having actress-management at its worst.

If you can get an invitation to address a society of women, speak on acting as a profession for women, and show them as many stage tricks as possible. Remember, you cannot give yourself away too completely to please an audience; nor is there any method by which you can convey so strong an impression of modest amiability, of unconscious strength. You must honestly not try to make a success in the stage sense on the platform.

The post hour is come; and—thanks to this confounded project of yours, which you will have abandoned before this reaches you, probably, I have not had time to say a word to please myself. You are a hard taskmistress for an unfortunate literary man.

I went to Battersea Park yesterday to bicycle; and Nora came to see me fall. Florence Farr was there, caracoling on her machine with surpassing elegance, to the admiration of all the park. The Webbs also struggled with their new machines. But I must stop.

G.B.S.

The Problem Play—A Symposium

Should social problems be freely dealt with in the Drama?
(*The Humanitarian* VI, May 1895)

I do not know who has asked the question, Should social problems be freely dealt with in the drama?— some very thoughtless person evidently. Pray what social questions and what sort of drama? Suppose I say yes, then, vaccination being a social question, and the Wagnerian music drama being the one complete form of drama in the opinion of its admirers, it will follow that I am in favor of the production of a Jennerian tetralogy at Bayreuth. If I say no, then, marriage being a social question, and also the theme of Ibsen's Doll's House, I shall be held to contemn that work as a violation of the canons of art. I therefore reply to the propounder that I am not prepared to waste my own time and that of the public in answering maladroit conundrums. What I am prepared to do is to say what I can with the object of bringing some sort of order into the intellectual confusion which has expressed itself in the conundrum.

Social questions are produced by the conflict of human institutions with human feeling. For instance, we have certain institutions regulating the lives of women. To the women whose feelings are entirely in harmony with these institutions there is no Woman Question. But during the present century, from the time of Mary Wollstonecraft onwards, women have been developing feelings, and consequently opinions, which clash with these institutions. The institutions assumed that it was natural to a woman to allow her husband to own her property and person, and to represent her in politics as a father represents his infant child. The moment that seemed no longer natural to some women, it became grievously oppressive to them. Immediately there was a Woman Question, which has produced Married Women's Property Acts, Divorce Acts, Woman's Suffrage in local elections, and the curious deadlock to which the Weldon and Jackson cases have led our courts in the matter of conjugal rights. When we have achieved reforms enough to bring our institutions as far into harmony with the feelings of women as they now are with the feelings of men, there will no longer be a Woman Question. No conflict, no question.

Now the material of the dramatist is always some conflict of human feeling with circumstances; so that, since institutions are circumstances, every social question furnishes material for drama. But every drama does not involve a social question, because human feeling may be in conflict with circumstances which are not institutions, which raise no question at all, which are part of human destiny. To illustrate, take Mr Pinero's Second Mrs. Tanqueray. The heroine's feelings are in conflict with the human institutions which condemn to ostracism both herself and the man who marries her. So far, the play deals with a social question. But in one very effective scene the conflict is between that flaw in the woman's nature which makes her dependent for affection wholly on the attraction of her beauty, and the stealthy advance of age and decay to take her beauty away from her. Here there is no social question: age, like love, death, accident, and personal character, lies outside all institutions; and this gives it a permanent and universal interest which makes the drama that deals with it independent of period and place. Abnormal greatness of character, abnormal baseness of character, love, and death: with these alone you can, if you are a sufficiently great dramatic poet, make a drama that will keep your language alive long after it has passed out of common use. Whereas a drama with a social question for the

motive cannot outlive the solution of that question. It
is true that we can in some cases imaginatively recon-
struct an obsolete institution and sympathize with the
tragedy it has produced: for instance, the very dramatic story of Abraham commanded to sacrifice his
son, with the interposition of the angel to make a
happy ending; or the condemnation of Antonio to
lose a pound of flesh, and his rescue by Portia at the
last moment, have not completely lost their effect
nowadays—though it has been much modified—
through the obsolescence of sacrificial rites, belief in
miracles, and the conception that a debtor's person
belongs to his creditors. It is enough that we still have
paternal love, death, malice, moneylenders, and the
tragedies of criminal law. But when a play depends
entirely on a social question—when the struggle in it
is between man and a purely legal institution—nothing
can prolong its life beyond that of the institution. For
example, Mr Grundy's Slaves of the Ring, in which
the tragedy is produced solely by the conflict between
the individual and the institution of indissoluble marriage, will not survive a rational law of divorce, and
actually fails even now to grip an English audience
because the solution has by this time become so very
obvious. And that irrepressibly popular play It's Never
Too Late to Mend will hardly survive our abominable
criminal system. Thus we see that the drama which
deals with the natural factors in human destiny,
though not necessarily better than the drama which
deals with the political factors, is likely to last longer.

It has been observed that the greatest dramatists
shew a preference for the non-political drama, the
greatest dramas of all being almost elementarily
natural. But so, though for a different reason, do the
minor dramatists. The minor dramatist leads the literary life, and dwells in the world of imagination
instead of in the world of politics, business, law, and
the platform agitations by which social questions are
ventilated. He therefore remains, as a rule, astonishingly ignorant of real life. He may be clever,

imaginative, sympathetic, humorous, and observant of such manners as he has any clue to; but he has hardly any wit or knowledge of the world. Compare his work with that of Sheridan, and you feel the deficiency at once. Indeed, you need not go so far as Sheridan: Mr Gilbert's Trial by Jury is unique among the works of living English playwrights, solely because it, too, is the work of a wit and a man of the world. Incidentally, it answers the inquiry as to whether social questions make good theatrical material; for though it is pointless, and, in fact, unintelligible except as a satire on a social institution (the breach-of-promise suit), it is highly entertaining, and has made the fortune of the author and his musical collaborator. The School for Scandal, the most popular of all modern comedies, is a dramatic sermon, just as Never Too Late to Mend, the most popular of modern melodramas, is a dramatic pamphlet: Charles Reade being another example of the distinction which the accomplished man of the world attains in the theatre as compared to the mere professional dramatist. In fact, it is so apparent that the best and most popular plays are dramatized sermons, pamphlets, satires, or bluebooks, that we find our popular authors, even when they have made a safe position for themselves by their success in purely imaginative drama, bidding for the laurels and the percentages of the sociologist dramatist. Mr Henry Arthur Jones takes a position as the author of The Middleman and The Crusaders, which The Silver King, enormously popular as it was, never could have gained him; and Mr Pinero, the author of The Second Mrs. Tanqueray and The Notorious Mrs. Ebbsmith, is a much more important person, and a much richer one, than the author of Sweet Lavender. Of course, the sociology in some of these dramas is as imaginary as the names and addresses of the characters; but the imitation sociology testifies to the attractiveness of the real article.

We may take it then that the ordinary dramatist only neglects social questions because he knows noth-

ing about them, and that he loses in popularity, standing, and money by his ignorance. With the great
dramatic poet it is otherwise. Shakespear and Goethe
do not belong to the order which "takes no interest in
politics." Such minds devour everything with a keen
appetite—fiction, science, gossip, politics, technical
processes, sport, everything. Shakespear is full of little
lectures of the concrete English kind, from Cassio on
temperance to Hamlet on suicide. Goethe, in his
German way, is always discussing metaphysical points.
To master Wagner's music dramas is to learn a philosophy. It was so with all the great men until the present
century. They swallowed all the discussions, all the
social questions, all the topics, all the fads, all the
enthusiasms, all the fashions of their day in their non-
age; but their theme finally was not this social question
or that social question, this reform or that reform, but
humanity as a whole. To this day your great dramatic
poet is never a socialist, nor an individualist, nor a
positivist, nor a materialist, nor any other sort of "ist,"
though he comprehends all the "isms," and is generally quoted and claimed by all the sections as an
adherent. Social questions are too sectional, too topical,
too temporal to move a man to the mighty effort which
is needed to produce great poetry. Prison reform may
nerve Charles Reade to produce an effective and
businesslike prose melodrama; but it could never
produce Hamlet, Faust, or Peer Gynt.

It must, however, be borne in mind that the huge
size of modern populations and the development of
the press make every social question more momentous
than it was formerly. Only a very small percentage of
the population commits murder; but the population is
so large that the frequency of executions is appalling.
Cases which might have come under Goethe's notice
in Weimar perhaps once in ten years come daily
under the notice of modern newspapers, and are
described by them as sensationally as possible. We are
therefore witnessing a steady intensification in the hold
of social questions on the larger poetic imagination.

Les Misérables, with its rivulet of story running through a continent of essays on all sorts of questions, from religion to main drainage, is a literary product peculiar to the nineteenth century: it shows how matters which were trifles to Æschylus become stupendously impressive when they are multiplied by a million in a modern civilized state. Zola's novels are the product of an imagination driven crazy by a colossal police intelligence, by modern hospitals and surgery, by modern war correspondence, and even by the railway system—for in one of his books the hero is Jack the Ripper and his sweetheart a locomotive engine. What would Aristophanes have said to a city with fifteen thousand lunatics in it? Might he not possibly have devoted a comedy to the object of procuring some amelioration in their treatment? At all events, we find Ibsen, after producing, in Brand, Peer Gynt, and Emperor and Galilean, dramatic poems on the grandest scale, deliberately turning to comparatively prosaic topical plays on the most obviously transitory social questions, finding in their immense magnitude under modern conditions the stimulus which, a hundred years ago, or four thousand, he would only have received from the eternal strife of man with his own spirit. A Doll's House will be as flat as ditchwater when A Midsummer Night's Dream will still be as fresh as paint; but it will have done more work in the world; and that is enough for the highest genius, which is always intensely utilitarian.

Let us now hark back for a moment to the remark I made on Mr Grundy's Sowing the Wind *: namely, that its urgency and consequently its dramatic interest are destroyed by the fact that the social question it presents is really a solved one. Its production after Les Surprises du Divorce (which Mr Grundy himself

* Evidently a slip for Slaves of the Ring, mentioned above. This play was the subject of Shaw's first contribution to The Saturday Review as dramatic critic (January 5, 1895). He had printed on March 23, 1895 a comment on a revival of Sowing the Wind, which he found better than Grundy's usual product.

adapted for England) was an anachronism. When we
succeed in adjusting our social structure in such a
way as to enable us to solve social questions as fast
as they become really pressing, they will no longer
force their way into the theatre. Had Ibsen, for instance, had any reason to believe that the abuses to
which he called attention in his prose plays would
have been adequately attended to without his interference, he would no doubt have gladly left them
alone. The same exigency drove William Morris in
England from his tapestries, his epics, and his masterpieces of printing, to try and bring his fellow-citizens
to their senses by the summary process of shouting at
them in the streets and in Trafalgar Square. John
Ruskin's writing began with Modern Painters; Carlyle
began with literary studies of German culture and the
like: both were driven to become revolutionary pam-
phleteers. If people are rotting and starving in all
directions, and nobody else has the heart or brains to
make a disturbance about it, the great writers must.
In short, what is forcing our poets to follow Shelley
in becoming political and social agitators, and to turn
the theatre into a platform for propaganda and an
arena for discussion, is that whilst social questions are
being thrown up for solution almost daily by the
fierce rapidity with which industrial processes change
and supersede one another through the rivalry of the
competitors who take no account of ulterior social
consequences, and by the change in public feeling
produced by popular "education," cheap literature,
facilitated travelling, and so forth, the political machinery by which alone our institutions can be kept
abreast of these changes is so old-fashioned, and so
hindered in its action by the ignorance, the apathy,
the stupidity, and the class feuds of the electorate,
that social questions never get solved until the pressure becomes so desperate that even governments
recognize the necessity for moving. And to bring the
pressure to this point, the poets must lend a hand to
the few who are willing to do public work in the

stages at which nothing but abuse is to be gained by it.

Clearly, however, when the unhappy mobs which we now call nations and populations settle down into ordered commonwealths, ordinary bread-and-butter questions will be solved without troubling the poets and philosophers. The Shelleys, the Morrises, the Ruskins and Carlyles of that day will not need to spend their energies in trying to teach elementary political economy to the other members of the commonwealth; nor will the Ibsens be devising object lessons in spoiled womanhood, sickly consciences, and corrupt town councils, instead of writing great and enduring dramatic poems.

I need not elaborate the matter further. The conclusions to be drawn are:

1.   Every social question, arising as it must from a conflict between human feeling and circumstances, affords material for drama.

2.   The general preference of dramatists for subjects in which the conflict is between man and his apparently inevitable and eternal rather than his political and temporal circumstances, is due in the vast majority of cases to the dramatist's political ignorance (not to mention that of his audience), and in a few to the comprehensiveness of his philosophy.

3.   The hugeness and complexity of modern civilizations and the development of our consciousness of them by means of the press, have the double effect of discrediting comprehensive philosophies by revealing more facts than the ablest man can generalize, and at the same time intensifying the urgency of social reforms sufficiently to set even the poetic faculty in action on their behalf.

4.   The resultant tendency to drive social questions on to the stage, and into fiction and poetry, will eventually be counteracted by improvements in social organization, which will enable all prosaic social questions to be dealt with satisfactorily long before they become grave enough to absorb the energies which

claim the devotion of the dramatist, the storyteller, and the poet.

The Censorship of the Stage in England

(*North American Review* CLXIX, August 1899)

In England, no play may be publicly performed until a certificate has been procured from the Lord Chamberlain that it "does not in its general tendency contain anything immoral or otherwise improper for the stage." The Lord Chamberlain, who must be distinguished from the hereditary Great Chamberlains of England, is not a democratic official. He has nothing to do with the great offices by which the British Empire is administered—such as the Home Office, the Colonial Office, the India Office, staffed by bureaucrats elected by competitive examination to posts which they hold irremovably, through all changes of government, under the command of the Secretary of State for their department, a cabinet minister resigning whenever his party, defeated in the House of Commons, goes out of office. He is only a member of the Queen's household retinue—the Malvolio of St James's Palace—responsible to nobody but the Queen, and therefore really not responsible at all, because the Queen's interference with the fantastic agglomeration of little dignities and functions which serve as excuses for the perquisites of her retinue, does not spread far beyond her presence and her residence (which is not St James's Palace), and is politically and conventionally limited even there.

The Lord Chamberlain does not condescend to read plays himself; and the Examiner of Plays, who does it for him, is perhaps the obscurest unit in the imposing procession of Pages of the Back Stairs, Pages of the Chambers, Pages of the Presence, Masters of the Music, Keepers of the Jewels, Keepers of the

Swans, Gentleman Usher Daily Waiters, Gentleman Usher Quarterly Waiters, Bargemasters, Grooms of the Privy Chamber, Gentleman Ushers of the Privy Chamber, and all the other breath-bereaving retainers of whom only one, the Poet Laureate, has succeeded in imposing the fact of his existence on the consciousness of the British public. The Lord Chamberlain himself, with all this pageantry to superintend, has no time to keep any check on his subordinate, even if he could pretend to know anything more than he about dramatic criticism and the foundations of morality. The result is that the Examiner of Plays, humble, untitled, "middle-class" though he be, is yet the most powerful man in England or America. Other people may make England's laws; he makes and unmakes its drama, and therefore also the drama of America; for no American dramatic author can afford to defy a despot who can, by a nod, cut him off from any English stageright worth possibly $20,000 in London alone. The monarchy is limited; the Cabinet, with tears of rage, cannot assert itself even against Anti-Vaccinators; the House of Lords, nominally omnipotent, puts down its foot only to emphasize the humiliation of having to take it up again; but the Examiner of Plays, greater than all these, does what he likes, caring not a dump for nations or constitutions, English or American. The President of the United States himself practically cannot see a new play without first getting the Examiner's leave.

It will be inferred that no pains are spared to secure the services of a very highly qualified and distinguished person to wield this astonishing power—say the holder of a University chair of Literature or Dramaturgy. The inference is erroneous. You are not allowed to sell stamps in an English post office without previously passing an examination; but you may become Examiner of Plays without necessarily knowing how to read or write. The post is held at present by one George Alexander Redford, said to have been a bank clerk, but not ascertained to have been anything except lucky enough to obtain a place at court with a salary of some fifteen hundred or two thousand dollars a year, and powers to exact from every author or manager producing a new play five dollars and a quarter for each one-act piece, and ten dollars and a half for each piece of two or more acts.

The resultant income must not be estimated merely by the number of English plays whose fame reaches the United States. In England the law of dramatic copyright, or stageright, is mere madness and confusion. Not long ago a popular novelist announced for performance a stage version of one of his books. He was promptly warned that his version was an infringement of the stageright of a version already made by a sharp country solicitor, and duly licensed by the Examiner of Plays and performed. The author had actually to buy back the stageright of his own story from the pirate who had stolen a march on him. In such a state of affairs, every prudent novelist whose book contains valuable dramatic material takes the precaution to put together some sort of stage version, no matter how brief or inept, and to have it furtively performed at a suburban hall with a theatrical license, the actors being a few friends who read their parts anyhow, and the audience a single confederate who complies with the law by paying for his seat. The price of admission is prohibitive to the casual student of the bill on the door—usually about five dollars and a quarter.

Further, the English stageright in a play is forfeited if the play is performed first in America. Consequently, the first thing a dramatic author has to do, when his play is not written for immediate production in England, is to give a copyrighting performance of the kind described above. The dramatic authors and the novelists between them thus keep up a series of theatrical performances of which the public knows nothing, but upon every one of which the Examiner of Plays levies his ten dollars and a half. What is more, these freaks of the law of copyright greatly increase his power, since not only the performance of the play in England, but the acquisition of valuable property rights elsewhere, is made dependent on his pleasure.

There is another way in which the Examiner can increase his emoluments. Formerly, if a play was susceptible of amendment, the Examiner specified the lines to which he objected, suggesting additions to alter the complexion of the moral situation in the play, and even altering expressions which were against his rules: for example, changing "as drunk as a Lord" to "as drunk as a Heaven," in pursuance of a rule, now fallen into disuse, that Heaven should always be substituted for the name of any of the Persons of the Trinity. Mr Redford's immediate predecessor, refusing to license a translation of a French play, on the ground that the heroine, a married woman, had been guilty of an indiscretion in early life, was visited by the actress cast for the part, who naturally used all her powers of persuasion to induce him to revoke his decision. Finally he consented, on condition that the words "I sinned but in intention" were introduced into her part. Accordingly, every night, during the burst of welcome which hailed her first entrance in the piece, the actress remarked confidentially to the conductor of the band, "I sinned but in intention," and thereby rescued her country from demoralization by French levity.* A little later, a gifted American actress wrote a painfully powerful piece in which a mother, to save her child from growing up a helpless cripple, kills it. To this the Examiner had no objection; but, unfortunately, the mother baptized the child before killing it, a proceeding incompatible with his rules. He refused the necessary license. The American lady, unaccustomed to be so oppressed, swooped down on the Examiner as he sat at breakfast, and demanded an explanation. He soon weakened so far as to ask what, exactly, the lady proposed to do with the infant. She thereupon

---

* The play was a translated adaptation of *La Tentation,* a play by Octave Feuillet (1821–1890); the actress Janet Achurch. (See "Theatres and Reviews Then and Now.")

made a rag baby of his napkin, and, with the help of
the hot water from his tea-tray, rehearsed the scene.
He admitted its propriety; and she went off in triumph
with her license. The very form in which the license
is issued provides for these contingencies by excepting
such passages as may be endorsed on the back of the
certificate.

But Mr Redford is a sharper man of business than
his predecessor. On his refusal to license a certain
play of mine, I asked the usual question as to the
particular passages objected to. Mr Redford replied
impressively that, if a new play were submitted to
him, he would endeavor to forget having read the
former one. This meant that if I would guess the
obnoxious passages, and send him another ten dollars
and a half, he would tell me whether my guess was
right. He thus extracted double fees from me, and if
I had required the license for an ordinary production
of the play, instead of for a mere copyrighting for-
mality, it might very well have taken half a dozen
minimum guesses at ten dollars and a half apiece to
ascertain the exact line drawn by his moral opinions
without needlessly going beyond it. As it was, I
simply deprived the play of the passages which explained its meaning (the residue being sufficient for
my purpose), and so secured my license without
further expenditure. This procedure on the part of
the Examiner is unquestionably both logical and businesslike. It must increase his fees and economize his
work very considerably. No wonder his post, with its
fees, its powers, its unassailable permanence, and its
unimpeachable gentility as a post in Her Majesty's
household, is much sought after.

The statutory penalty for defying the Censor is a
fine of fifty pounds, which can, theoretically, be levied
on any person connected with a forbidden performance, call-boy, checktaker, carpenter, bandsman, actor,
author, manager, stage-doorkeeper, and who not? No
attempt has been made in recent cases to recover this
penalty, ostensibly because the department has no

Discusses the production of the "Cenci".

funds with which to institute prosecutions, but really, one suspects, because the cases would have to be tried by jury, and the average British juryman, though usually a worm under the foot of the judge, can turn if he likes. Even judges have flashes of the constitutional spirit at odd moments. Here we have the weak place in the Examiner's powers which led to the famous evasion of him on the centenary of Shelley's birth. It was proposed to celebrate that occasion by a performance of The Cenci. The Examiner would not hear of it; but the performance was given for all that in the Grand Theatre, Islington (a northern suburb of London), before an audience of poets, headed by Browning, and a crowd of their disciples. Technically, this performance was not a public representation of the play; it was only a meeting of the Shelley Society. The spectators did not pay at the doors; they had all joined the Shelley Society for the season, and were attending this particular "private" meeting of it in the exercise of their ordinary right as members. For the moment the defeat of the Censor was complete. But the performance had taken place in a London theatre; and London theatres are subject to the Lord Chamberlain, who licenses them from year to year. The unfortunate lessee, having let his house to the Shelley Society (without any knowledge of the plot in hand), found himself at the mercy of the outraged Chamberlain when the time came for renewing his license. What passed between them is not known; but there is now a clause in the lease of that theatre stipulating that no performances of unlicensed plays shall be given in it. When the Shelley Society proposed to repeat The Cenci some years later, the Lord Chamberlain was master of the situation. With a single revolutionary exception, no manager dared lend or let his theatre for the purpose. The terror was so complete that a manager who, not realizing his risk, had discussed quite favorably the possibility of placing his house at the disposal of the Society, was compelled to write to the press vehemently denying that he had "the tsar of the drama."

ever contemplated such an enormity, although his letters were in the hands of the very persons he was publicly contradicting.

Since then, the blockade has been run only by the Independent Theatre, which succeeded in producing Ibsen's Ghosts on three occasions without a license. In this case, no license was applied for, its refusal being practically certain; and the first performance, which was technically "private," like that of the Shelley Society, was over before the lessee of the theatre knew that anything exceptional was happening. After this, the theatres were thoroughly on their guard, but, later on, the founder of the Independent Theatre, Mr Grein, invited his friends (including all the subscribers) to an "At Home," hiring for the purpose one of the numerous halls which are let in London for dances, minor political meetings, lectures, and the like. Here he entertained his guests with a second performance of Ghosts. A third was accomplished some years later, virtually in the same way. No attempt was made by the Lord Chamberlain, on any of these occasions, to enforce the statutory fine, restrain the projectors by injunction, or otherwise assert any right of interference with performances which are not opened to the public by taking money at the doors for admission. But it is evident, from the fact that nothing will now persuade any manager or proprietor of a licensed theatre to allow such a performance to take place in his house, that the power of closing theatres which the Lord Chamberlain wields as the licensing authority, makes him effectively the Tsar of the drama.

To Americans, who, as I have pointed out, are as much concerned in the Censorship as the English are, the drama being practically international, this state of things may seem so Russianly subversive of fundamental western rights as to stand condemned by the mere statement of it. In England, the only question that arises is: How does the institution work? The fact that it violates those Rights of Man which are expressly constitutional in America is to the English mind all in its favor. No doubt the Englishman is earnestly jealous for his religious liberty, and at least excitable about his political liberty. An attempt to force the Salvation Army to have their hymns licensed by the Archbishop of Canterbury, or the daily papers to have their political leaders licensed by the Queen's Lectrice, would produce an overwhelming agitation at once; though there is rather more to be said for either measure than for the censorship of the English dramatists by Mr Redford. But beyond this the Englishman does not go. Far from believing that either he himself or anybody else can be safely trusted with further liberties, he lives absolutely convinced that only by a strenuous maintenance of restrictive laws and customs, supported on every public occasion by the most reverent professions of faith and loyalty, feigned or sincere, can society be withheld from casting all moral considerations to the winds and committing suicide in a general Saturnalia of reckless debauchery. I do not pretend that this will be accepted in England as a sane statement of fact; for, if England were conscious of its own absurdity, it would cease to be absurd. Still less do I mean to suggest that it is a delusion at all peculiar to England or unknown in America. But I am concerned here only with an application of it which *is* peculiar to England. Nobody will deny that the normal assumption in England is that without a Censor the stage would instantly plunge to the lowest practicable extreme of degradation—an assumption quite undisturbed by the fact that Literature, without a Censor, behaves far more decently than Drama with one. For myself, as a dramatic author, I can say that few things would surprise me more than to meet a representative Englishman who regarded my desire to abolish the Censor otherwise than he would regard the desire of a pickpocket to abolish the police. To such an Englishman, it seems the most obvious piece of common sense that some respectable person should be made responsible for the propriety of the plays to which his daughters go; so that he may be

guaranteed against the natural propensity of the
theatre towards licentiousness. Accepting the court
standard of decorousness as absolute, he considers that
if a lord who is a member of Her Majesty's household
cannot be trusted to decide questions of propriety,
nobody can. No competitive examination, no profes-
sorship of Dramatic Literature, no control by an
elected representative body, could give him any greater
sense of security than the position of the Lord Chamberlain. And, I may add, they could give the dramatists no greater sense of security either.

Let us, then, embrace this apparently common-
sensible view of the institution, and inquire simply
how it fulfils, not its original purpose (it was instituted
by Walpole to prevent Fielding from exposing parliamentary corruption on the stage), but the purpose for
which it survives. What sort of plays does it license;
and what sort of plays does it suppress? A very con-
clusive answer to this question would be a description
of the most unpleasant play licensed within my experience by Mr Redford's predecessor, who refused
to license The Cenci, and of the most unpleasant play
licensed by Mr Redford himself.* But, fastidious
reader, suffice it to say that, were such an answer
attempted, the guaranteed morality of the Censor-
protected stage would appear as an outrage in the
columns of the free Press.

This is not the fault of the Censor. A moment's
consideration will show it to be so inevitable, that if
you or I, punctilious reader, were Examiner of plays, it
would not be altered in the least. Let us examine the
position. You take a commonplace official; confront
him with a play by a man probably cleverer than himself, possibly a genius destined to be remembered for
many centuries; and ask him to decide whether the

---

* The two plays were summarized by Shaw in his manuscript, as
they are in the "Author's Apology" in *Mrs Warren's Profession,*
q.v. Despite an editorial assurance that the manuscript would
not be edited, the synopses were replaced by the address to the
fastidious reader.

net effect of a performance of that play on the destiny of the human race will be helpful or harmful. The Delphic oracle itself would not have the impudence to pretend that it could answer such a question. Even the Roman Catholic Church does not profess to exercise its censorship without supernatural guidance; and the Roman Catholic Church, which is at least not less qualified for the task than Mr Redford, has admittedly made serious mistakes both through the Inquisition and in the compilation of the Index Expurgatorius; failing to add anything to the natural check of public opinion upon really licentious literature, whilst restricting popular access to the Bible, and missing its mark in the suppression of books so frequently that the placing of a work in the Index almost raises a European and American presumption in its favor. But, pray, do not be so unjust as to conclude, because the British citizen thoughtlessly expects Mr Redford to succeed where a great Church has failed, that Mr Redford himself puts forward any such pretension. When Mr Redford refuses to license Tolstoi's Dominion of Darkness, for example, he does not refuse on the ground that he, Redford, is a more high-minded man, or a philosopher with a greater power of distinguishing the conventions of propriety than the realities of moral evil, or a more disinterested public-spirited citizen of the world, a deeper seer into the future, a keener observer of the present, a wiser critic of life than Tolstoi. If he took that ground, a shout of laughter from the whole civilized world would be the answer. What Mr Redford and every such censor does say to Tolstoi (if he has sense enough to understand his own position) is: "You are a much cleverer and, no doubt, a better fellow than I am; and I cannot pretend to criticize you. But I must administer the rules of my office as a judge administers the laws; and your play is against my rules. It may be a very good play; and certainly lots of the plays that are inside my rules are shockingly bad ones; but I cant help that: if I were to discriminate outside my rules I should be setting myself up as a sort of Platonic philosopher-king, which I'm not, and which no official is at all likely to be. I do my best to march with the times, stretching the rules as much as possible, or even dropping one out when it becomes too ridiculous; but I must point out to you that there is one rule that never varies, and never can vary; and that rule is that a play must not be made the vehicle of new opinions on important subjects, because new opinions are always questionable opinions, and I cannot make Her Majesty the Queen responsible for questionable opinions by licensing them. The other rules are simple enough. You mustnt make fun of ambassadors, cabinet ministers, or any living persons who have influence in fashionable society, though no notice will be taken of a gag at the expense of General Booth, or a Socialist or Labor member of the County Council, or people of that sort. You mustnt have any love affairs within the tables of Consanguinity in the Prayer Book. If you introduce a male libertine in a serious play, you had better 'redeem' him in the end by marrying him to an innocent young lady. If a female libertine, it will not matter if she dies at the end, and takes some opportunity to burst into tears on touching the hand of a respectable girl. There are lots of little ways in which a play can disclaim any unusual views as to the relations of the sexes, even when it stretches our rules as to conduct. In farcical comedy and musical farce, you cannot come into conflict with us, because all the fun in them depends on the conventional view of bad conduct. The observance of these rules of ours constitutes a sort of technique which is easily picked up, which is in harmony with the common usages of gentlemen, and which is never objected to by anybody but the people who would be disqualified anyhow by having new views—the cranks, in short. That's how our place works. You owe me two guineas, please, for refusing to allow you to produce your play. Thank you. Good morning."

The rules here spoken of are not printed for the

guidance of dramatists. They are traditional and probably unwritten. They are not the invention of any individual Censor; they simply codify the present and most of the past prejudices of the class he represents. To write a play which complies with them in form whilst grossly violating their purpose is as easy as lying: it is the trade of the adapter of French farces. To write a play which holds their purpose as sacred as any Examiner can, whilst violating their form in every scene, is as difficult as the achievement of greatness: it is the fate of the man of genius, necessarily always defending humanity against plutocracy and reality against hypocrisy. Each successive Censor makes the best of these rules when he is young and elastic, and the worst of them when he is old and ossified; but, in the main, they bind him as tightly as they bind the public. He may admire The Cenci; but he dare not license it. He may feel as deeply as Matthew Arnold did the degradation of the English theatre, and may know quite well that English Literature towers high above English Drama because Literature is subject to no judgment but that of its natural masters, the authors. Not only Matthew Arnold, but Byron and Shelley, Ruskin and Carlyle, Dickens, Thackeray and Mark Twain, Darwin and Mill, Huxley and Tyndall, George Eliot and Sarah Grand, Meredith and Tolstoi—all those, in short, whose eminence makes the roll of acted dramatists so petty by contrast—must have been suppressed by an Examiner of Books, had such an official existed. Mr Redford cannot help himself: a Censorship cannot work in any other way, until a Censor can be found greater than the greatest dramatists. That being impossible, he is doomed still to put his hallmark on profligate farces and thinly sentimentalized tomcat love tales, and to shut the stage door against the great dramatic poets. For these poets must say to themselves what Carlyle said to himself: "One thing in the middle of this chaos I can more and more determine to adhere to: to clear myself of cants and formulas as of poisonous Nessus shirts;

to strip them off me, by what name soever they are
called, and follow, were it to Hades, what I myself
know and see." And the Censor must reply: "I really
cannot allow you to do anything so ungentlemanly.
My instructions are to allow nobody to go on the stage
without a complete Nessus suit on, in which he must
make-up his mind to face straight for Church Parade
in the Park and turn his back decisively on Hades,
no matter what he knows or sees."

And so, in the end, the public gets neither the
dramatist's view of life, nor the Examiner's view of
life, nor its own view of life, nor in fact any real view
of life at all. It does not get a clean stage, simple as
that seemed: there is always one theatre, at least, in
London where the fun consists of blackguardism under
a royal certificate of propriety. It does not even get
the laws against the exhibition on the stage of very
young children enforced: reproachful-eyed babies are
still tossed about from hand to hand in lewd farces;
and infamous ballets are danced at eleven o'clock at
night by tiny children kept awake only by unhealthy
excitement. This at least the Censorship might stop;
but it never does. No serious steps to make London
theatres safe were taken, until the responsibility was
transferred to the County Council. Desiring to give a
judicial air to this article, I have racked my brains
and searched my pretty exhaustive experience as a
critic of the theatre to find a single item to the credit
of the Censorship's account in the books of the
Recording Angel. I find none. Shame, folly, ridicule,
and mischief are the fruits of it, and the sole possible
ones, as, I repeat, they would equally be if I or Tolstoi
himself were Censor. Nobody profits by it except the
Examiner, who lives by it, and the Lord Chamberlain,
who is occasionally presented by the managers with
silver plate, which he publicly accepts as naïvely as
those Stuart Masters of the Revels (the original
Censors) who entered in their journals the presents
made to their wives by the actor-managers of the day.

What, then, is to be done with the Censorship?

Nothing can be simpler. Abolish it, root and branch, throwing the whole legal responsibility for plays on the author and manager, precisely as the legal responsibility for a book is thrown on the author, the printer, and the publisher. The managers will not like this: their present slavery is safer and easier; but it will be good for them, and good for the Drama. And transfer the authority to license theatres from year to year from the Lord Chamberlain to the London County Council, which already deals with music halls, and is jealously criticized by the Press and the electorate.

Alas! when we pass from the What to the How, the simplicity of the problem vanishes. Some years ago, when the London Playgoers' Club invited my opinion as to how the Censor could be got rid of, I had to reply that, as far as I could see, nothing short of abolishing the monarchy could touch him. But we are not going to burn down our house to roast our pig in that fashion. Besides, nobody, except Mr William Archer and a few dramatists whose plays have been suppressed, seems to object to the Censorship. There are no complaints in Parliament, none in the Press, no petitions from the Society of Authors or from the managers. A forgotten Royal Commission on the subject came to the unimpeachable conclusion that a perfect censorship is a desirable thing; and the consensus among the manager-witnesses as to the superhuman personal qualities of their master, the then Examiner, quite outweighed the display of petulant shallowness made by that gentleman when he was invited to shine on the Commission in person. The public is either satisfied or indifferent, because the class in England which feels social matters deeply does not go to the theatre, and the class which does go wants to be amused there, and not ossified or conscience-stricken. There is no money in the question, no vote-catching power, no popular interest in or knowledge or comprehension of it, and consequently no political capital to be made out of it. The censorship will probably outlive the House of Lords and the supremacy of the Es-

tablished Church, as quietly as it has outlived the
Metropolitan Board of Works and the Irish Church.
In England this article will be entirely wasted: no
English editor has ever dreamt of asking me to deal
with the subject. In America, it may be useful, in view
of the likelihood of attempts to set up State Censorships in that country. In which case, O my friends
across the sea, remember how the censorship works in
England, and DONT.

On Being a Lady in High Comedy

(Letter to Janet Achurch on playing Lady Cicely in *Captain Brassbound's Conversion*, Stage Society production,
December 1900; in Ashley Dukes, "A Doll's House and
the Open Door," *Theatre Arts* XII, January 1928; also
in *Nash's*, February 1928)

> *Piccard's Cottage, St. Catherine's
> Guildford. Xmas Day 1900.*

My dear Janet,

I saw the performance at the greatest possible disadvantage from the back of the worst box in the house.
However, perhaps I am none the worse able to tell
you about it for having seen the thing too close.

There is no doubt that you did, in a sort, begin to
act high comedy for the first time in your life in the
sense of carefully composing a picture instead of
merely looking into a mirror in a volcanic manner, and
saying: There! there's your Nora, Candida, etc. And
you were so excited at finding the thing coming off,
that each laugh produced the effect of a tablespoonful
of brandy and soda; so that, if the graver touches had
not brought you back to your seriousness, dignity, and
power, you would finally have made Lady Cicely an
exceptionally obstreperous mænad. You made points,
rammed them home, and rollicked and clowned in a
way that would have scandalized John Nash.* Of

* A music hall star of mid-century (1828-1901) whose exuberant manner of putting over a song got him the sobriquet Jolly
John Nash.

course the audience liked it; but they knew no better; their delight was the measure of your condescension. A well trained French audience—say an aristocratic Gluck and Molière XVIII-century audience—would have been shocked. There were moments which you enjoyed amazingly, at which Sir Howard and Lady Cicely quite vanished, and what remained was "a Christian dorg and his woman."

The fact is, you tumbled to the trick of comedy acting suddenly and luckily; but the mere trick of it will carry you no further than —. You can save the situation by falling back, in *my* plays where the opportunities are mixed and the comedy tissue is shot with reality and tragedy, on the great Janet; but in a St James's fashionable comedy you wouldn't get the chance. And that is why you would not suit the St James's, because your comedy is not delicate enough, and your heavy qualities not wanted.

Before you can play Lady Cicely perfectly, you will have to do what the author did, and do it much more minutely and personally than he; that is, make a careful study of the English lady. Mind: I don't mean the English bourgeoise, nor the English artist-Bohemian; I mean the great lady. It is very difficult to say a thing like this to a charwoman, because she immediately flushes indignantly and says, "I ham a lidy." And as every human being has something of the charwoman's vanity and folly left, especially in their haughty youth, it is probable that the real reason that you have never dispassionately studied the great lady as an Icelander might study an elephant is that you have concluded that one lady is like another, and that since your father kept a gig (so to speak) you have nothing to learn. As a matter of fact there are no two animals in the whole human fauna more completely different in every trick and touch than a great lady and Janet Achurch.

I am like Molière in point of always consulting my cook about my plays. She is an excellent critic; goes to my lectures and plays; and esteems actors and ac-

tresses as filthy rags in comparison to the great author
they interpret. Consulted as to Lady Cicely, she at
once said: "No: she wasn't right: when she sat down
she got her dress tucked in between her knees: no
high lady would do that." Now that is an excellent
criticism. You played the whole part, as far as the
comedy went, with your dress tucked between your
knees. Of the dress itself I say nothing; for we must
do what we can afford in that way, not what we like;
but although you solved the difficulty of looking well
on artistic lines—on *Liberty lines*—on simple, sensible
lines, such lines are quite wrong for Lady Cicely,
who would associate that sort of dressing with Fitz-
john's Avenue and professional people who don't go to
church. The directions in the play, to the effect that
Lady C. does not wear a tailor-made tourist's suit, and
that she dresses as she would in summer in Surrey,
mean that she is too conventional to regard dress as
a wholly adaptable-to-circumstances matter. She would
wear petticoats and drawers, just as she would say her
prayers, for half a century after all the working
women in the country would have taken to knicker-
bockers and agnosticism.

She would hardly ever show real excitement, or lose
her distinction and immense self-complacency and
habit of patronage. She wouldn't, for instance, if a
fly bit her, go for it with a cat-o'-nine-tails as an
Australian drover goes for a fly on the flank of the
furthest off bullock with his stockwhip. She might have
plenty of tricks, and silly tricks too; she might be
childish, and make little jokes and puns that only
courtiers laugh at; she might even go on with men in
a way which in a shop-girl would lead to overtures and
be understood to have that intention; she might do
forty thousand things that no woman who was not
either above or below suspicion would do (the co-
incidences between the tramp and the aristocrat are
very interesting); but in everything external she would
be distinguished from the middle-class woman, who
lives her whole life under suspicion and shortness of

cash. Until you have mastered all these marks of caste, and can imitate them as easily as you can change a number five stick of grease paint for a number ten, you will not be able to do Lady Cicely as finely as a very obvious housemaid at the Théâtre Français can do the Queen in Ruy Blas. It is not that court ladylikeness is difficult; but it is antipathetic to the free Bohemian middle-class *revoltée:* the essence of it is flunkeyism, upper-servantism; and you will have to become as heartless as I am before you can study it quite dispassionately and put it on quite mechanically. But it is worth doing, as it involves a good deal of technical refinement along with its moral slavery.

Meanwhile, to be able to do Eyolf's mother and not a commonplace comedy is to have something of Laurence Irving's fault of never being able to strike less than twelve, which means being out of an engagement for 22 hours out of 24. Lady Cicely is the first sign you have given of reaching the wise age of comedy and being able to play the fiddle as well as the trombones and drums.

I went out of town dead beat, immediately after the Sunday performance, and did not see the Thursday one, nor get your letter in time to act on it. Was the Thursday performance worse than the Sunday one? I expected it would be. You may have observed that the critics have shaken down at last into something like a firm opinion about me, the favorable ones playing up strongly and the unfavorable ones saying boldly that the thing is a failure. That's a great advance on the help-a-lame-dog-over-a-stile business.

Barker was *very* good. We must stick to Barker.

Yrs, dear Janet

G.B.S.

Why Cyril Maude Did Not Produce
You Never Can Tell

(Chapter XVI of *The Haymarket Theatre*, by Cyril Maude,
   London, 1903)

(At the end of Chapter XV Maude wrote:)

I must now crave the indulgence of my readers, and
beg his or her leave to address them. It is in reference
to the next chapter of this book. On the face of it it
would seem that it were written by me. I deny the
impeachment—absolutely. In the first place, I would
not for one moment lay claim to such knowledge of
style as is therein betrayed; in the second, I would
not aspire to the bluntness, to put it mildly, therein
shown. The chapter was sent to me as an aid to the
completion of this work. It professes to deal with that
period of our management when we rehearsed a piece
by the brilliant Mr. Bernard Shaw. The writer, I am
assured, is well fitted to deal with that period. I leave
it to the reader to judge, and to guess its authorship.
Were I the proprietor of a popular penny journal I
would offer a prize in this connection; but, unhappily,
I am only part-manager of a theatre. With the supposed facts, the sentiments, the whole trend of this
chapter I and my collaborator entirely dissociate ourselves. But we confess that we have heard it whispered
that we would never print it.

(Here is Chapter XVI:)

I now come to an episode in the history of the
theatre which might have wrecked our enterprise had
not Providence, which has never yet disappointed our
humble trust in it, caused the danger into which we
had stumbled to withdraw itself at the eleventh hour.

I think it must have been in the year 1895 that the
devil put it into the head of a friend of mine to tempt
me with news of a play called Candida by a writer

named Bernard Shaw, of whom until then I had never heard. I wrote to him suggesting that he should let me see the play. He instantly undertook the management of our theatre to the extent of informing me that Candida would not suit us, but that he would write a new play for us—which I protest I never asked him to do. As I learnt subsequently, he then took a chair in Regent's Park for the whole season, and sat there in the public eye writing the threatened play.

In the winter of 1897 this play, which was called You Never Can Tell, came to hand. Some of our friends thought well of the author, and Harrison (who, as my readers have doubtless already gathered, is a perfect ignoramus in all matters connected with plays and acting) liked the play. In short, I allowed myself to be overpersuaded, and we actually put the play into rehearsal.

From the first the author showed the perversity of his disposition and his utter want of practical knowledge of the stage. He proposed impossible casts. He forced us into incomprehensible agreements by torturing us with endless talk until we were ready to sign anything rather than argue for another hour. Had I been properly supported by my colleagues I should not have tolerated his proceedings for a moment. I do not wish to complain of anybody, but as a matter of fact I was not so supported. I expected nothing better from Harrison, because with all his excellent qualities he is too vain—I say it though he is my best friend— to be trusted in so delicate an undertaking as the management of a theatre. The truth is, Shaw flattered him, and thus detached him from me by playing on his one fatal weakness.

The world knows, I think, that whatever my faults may be, I am an affectionate and devoted husband. But I have never pretended that my wife is perfect. No woman is, and but few men. Still, I do think she might have supported me better than she did through our greatest trial. This man from the first exercised a malign influence over her. With my full consent and approval she selected for herself a certain part in his play. He had privately resolved—out of mere love of contradiction—that she should play another. When he read the play he contrived to balance the parts in such a way that my unfortunate and misguided wife actually there and then gave up her part and accepted the one he had determined to throw upon her. I then recognized for the first time that I had to deal with a veritable Svengali.

Our mistake in admitting an author of this type to our theatre soon became apparent. At the reading, that excellent actor, Jack Barnes, whose very name calls up the idea of sound judgment, withdrew, overpowered by fatigue and disgust, at the end of the first act, and presently threw up the part with which we proposed to insult him—and I now publicly apologize to him for that outrage. Miss Coleman soon followed his example, with a very natural protest against a part in which, as she rightly said, there were "no laughs and no exits." Any author with the slightest decency of feeling would have withdrawn in the face of rebuffs so pointed as these. But Mr Shaw—encouraged, I must say, by Harrison—persisted in what had now become an intolerable intrusion.

I can hardly describe the rehearsals that followed. It may well be that my recollection of them is confused; for my nerves soon gave way; sleep became a stranger to me; and there were moments at which I was hardly in possession of my faculties. I had to stage-manage as well as act—to stage-manage with that demon sitting beside me casting an evil spell on all our efforts!

On one occasion Mr Shaw insulted the entire profession by wanting a large table on the stage, on the ground that the company would fall over it unless they behaved as if they were coming into a real room instead of, as he coarsely observed, rushing to the float to pick up the band at the beginning of a comic song. This was a personal attack on me, as my vivacity of character and *diable au corps* make me specially impatient of obstacles.

Mr Shaw was one of those persons who use a certain superficial reasonableness and dexterity of manner to cover an invincible obstinacy in their own opinion. We had engaged for the leading part (I myself having accepted an insignificant part as a mere waiter) no less an artist than Mr Allan Aynesworth, whose reputation and subsequent achievements make it unnecessary for me to justify our choice. Mr Shaw had from the first contended that one of the scenes lay outside Mr Aynesworth's peculiar province. There can be no doubt now that Mr Shaw deliberately used his hypnotic power at rehearsal to compel Mr Aynesworth to fulfil his prediction. In every other scene Mr Aynesworth surpassed himself. In this he became conscious and confused; his high spirits were suddenly extinguished; even his good-humor left him. He was like a man under a spell—as no doubt he actually was—and his embarrassment communicated itself most painfully to my dear wife, who had to sit on the stage whilst Svengali deliberately tortured his victim.

At the same time I must say that Mrs Maude's conduct was not all I could have desired. I greatly dreaded an open rupture between her and the author; and the fiend somehow divined this, and used it as a means of annoying me. Sometimes, when he had cynically watched one of her scenes without any symptom of pleasure, I would venture to ask him his opinion of it. On such occasions he invariably rose with every appearance of angry disapproval, informed me that he would give his opinion to Miss Emery herself, and stalked up the stage to her in a threatening manner, leaving me in a state of apprehension that my overstrained nerves were ill able to bear. Not until afterwards did I learn that on these occasions he flattered my wife disgracefully, and actually made her a party of his systematic attempt to drive me out of my senses. I have never reproached her with this, and I never shall. I mention it here only because it is the truth; and truth has always been with me the first consideration.

At last Aynesworth broke down under the torture.
Mr Shaw, with that perfidious air of making the best
of everything which never deserted him, hypnotized
him into complaining of the number of speeches he
had to deliver, whereupon Mr Shaw cut out no less
than seventeen of them. This naturally disabled the
artist totally. On the question of cutting, Mr Shaw's
attitude was nothing less than Satanic. When I suggested cutting he handed me the play, begged me to
cut it freely, and then hypnotized me so that I could
not collect my thoughts sufficiently to cut a single
line. On the other hand, if I showed the least pleasure
in a scene at rehearsal he at once cut it out on the
ground that the play was too long. What I suffered
from that man at that time will never be fully known.
The heart alone knoweth its own bitterness.

The end came suddenly and unexpectedly. We had
made a special effort to fulfil our unfortunate contract,
of which even Harrison was now beginning to have
his doubts. We had brought back Miss Kate Bishop
from Australia to replace Miss Coleman. Mr Valentine
had taken the part repudiated by Mr Barnes. The
scenery had been modelled, and a real dentist's chair
obtained for the first act. Harrison, whose folly was
responsible for the whole wretched business, came
down to the rehearsal. We were honestly anxious to
retrieve the situation by a great effort, and save our
dear little theatre from the disgrace of a failure.

Suddenly the author entered, *in a new suit of
clothes! !*

I have little more to say. Nobody who had not seen
Mr Shaw sitting there day after day in a costume
which the least self-respecting carpenter would have
discarded months before, could possibly have understood the devastating effect of the new suit on our
minds. That this was a calculated *coup de théâtre* I
have not the slightest doubt. That it fulfilled its purpose I cannot deny. With distracted attentions, de-
mented imaginations, and enfeebled reasons we made

a bewildered effort to go through the first two acts. I saw with inexpressible aggravation that Harrison's face grew longer and longer as he contemplated our company blundering through a rehearsal like disconcerted amateurs (as if it were anybody's fault but his own). Talma himself would have broken down before the famous pit of kings if that new suit had been in the house.

I neither know nor care how it all ended. I remember Svengali privately informing Harrison and myself that he felt that our ruin and disgrace could only be averted by a heroic sacrifice on his part. If Harrison had had a spark of manhood he would have kicked him then and there into the Haymarket. But Harrison's deplorable weakness of character again allowed our enemy to pose as our benevolent rescuer. As for me, the man was in some sort my guest; besides, I was too unspeakably relieved by the prospect of being rid of him and his absurd play to make any difficulties.

In concluding this sickening record of a disastrous experience I desire to say that I have the greatest admiration for Mr Shaw's talents and the sincerest esteem for his personal character. In any other walk of life than that of a dramatic author I should expect him to achieve a high measure of success. I understand that he has made considerable mark as a vestryman, collecting dust with punctuality and supervising drainage with public-spirited keenness. I do not blame him for imposing on Harrison, for Harrison's credulity simply invites imposture. I wish him well in every way, and I am glad to hear from time to time that he is prospering. I met him in Garrick Street not long ago, and noticed that he still wore the suit which he purchased in 1897 in anticipation of the royalties on You Never Can Tell.

His name is never mentioned in my household.

How to Make Plays Readable

(*The Author* XII, London, December 1901. Reprinted in
The Author's Year Book and Guide for 1904, edited by
W. E. Price, New York, 1904)

Five years ago every publisher who was approached
with a view to publishing a play at once said, "No
use: people won't read plays in England." This was
unfortunate, because the economic conditions of theatrical enterprise had by that time made it impossible
to ask a manager (except with a deliberate view to
his ruin) to produce any but very widely popular
plays; and if neither the managers nor the publishers
will touch the higher stratum of dramatic art, what
is to become of the unfortunate authors whose gifts lie
in that stratum? Must they relapse into novel writing,
or depend on the fact that though the production of
really philosophic plays at the commercial theatres is
an economic impossibility in the present state of popular culture, yet the thing may actually occur from
time to time, either as a pure error of judgment on
the manager's part, or in one of those emergencies
created by the failure of the supply of popular plays,
when, having to choose between an experiment in
high art or the closing of his theatre, the manager accepts what is to him the less of the two evils? I have
dissuaded managers from committing these acts of desperation with plays of my own often enough to convince me that a capable dramatic author can get any
sort of play, however excellent (or the reverse), produced at one time or another, provided he is ready to
take advantage of the manager's infatuation, his artistic
enthusiasm, his ambition to be regarded as an intellectual connoisseur, or his occasional destitution in
the matter of new plays. But as no honorable author
will take up dramatic work seriously on the chance of
being enabled, by accident at some uncertain date, to
add to the losses of a cornered or too appreciative
manager, immediate acceptance and success at the

commercial theatres may be left out of the question
by the writer of plays which are "above the head of the
public"; that is, the sort of head represented by the
greatest common measure of, say, 75,000 metropolitan
playgoers.

On the other hand, 2,000 purchasers or so, at six
shillings, less threepence in the shilling, will pay for
the publication of a volume of plays, and leave, perhaps, £100 for the author, which sum, eked out with
a little journalism, will at least save him from the
starvation threatened by the unmarketable nature of
his genius. The play, once published, will probably get
performed by the Stage Society or by Mr Grein, and
thus procure for the author some practical experience
of the stage, and give him a good advertisement into
the bargain, leading possibly to a commercial commission for a popular play "as you [the populace] like
it," as soon as he has learnt to write one.

A striking contemporary instance of this process is
Hauptmann, who came to the front as a dramatist
through single performances of his plays in Germany
by dramatic clubs like the Stage Society, and by their
publication. I myself have published ten plays. Seven
of them may be classed commercially as unacted. But
of these seven, five have been performed at London
theatres with the same ceremonies of first-night cele-
bration, press notices, and—what is far more important
—the same experience of the stage gained by the
author at rehearsal as if they had been built by Mr
Pinero, Mr Jones, or Mr Cecil Raleigh to run a thousand nights. Through that experience and advertisement
I was enabled to write and find a manager for a melodrama which brought me in from America alone more
money than I could have earned at journalism in the
time it took me to write all my ten plays. My two unperformed plays are in that condition for special reasons which do not affect the argument. I chronicle
these matters as business facts for our business paper,
not as "green-room gossip."

Of course, if I had foolishly and snobbishly stood

sneering at Ibsen, at the Independent Theatre, at the New Century Theatre, at the experiments of Charrington, Grein, Waring, Miss Farr, Miss Robins, and the other pioneers, instead of seizing the opportunity to help dramatic literature and train myself as a practical playwright at the same time, all this would not have happened to me. But the fact that it did happen, not only to me, but to others in proportion to their activity as uncommercial playwrights, seems to me to prove that it is quite worth any young author's while to peg away at the super-popular drama with a reasonable certainty of gaining sufficient stage experience and newspaper renown to ensure him a place among the commercially successful dramatists, if he chooses afterwards to turn his apprenticeship to account by writing what the managers and the public want.

But since this road to fame lies partly through the publication of plays, of what use is it to point it out if the publishers say, "No use: in England people don't read plays"? Well, of course they don't; but pray, whose fault is that? I suggest that it is the fault of the playwrights who deliberately make their plays unreadable by flinging repulsive stage technicalities in the face of the public, and omitting from their descriptions even that simplest common decency of literature, the definite article. I wonder how many readers Charles Dickens would have had, or deserved to have, if he had written in this manner—

Sykes *lights pipe—calls dog—loads pistol with newspaper—takes bludgeon from R. above fireplace and strikes* Nancy. Nancy: Oh, Lord, Bill! (*Dies.* Sykes *wipes brow—shudders—takes hat from chair O.P.— sees ghost, not visible to audience—and exit L.U.E.*).

This sort of thing, in which literary people trying their hand at the drama for the first time revel as ludicrously as amateur actors revel in flagrant false hair, misfitting tunics, and tin spears, is not a whit less dishonoring to literature and insulting to the public than an edition of Shakespear would be if it were cut down in this fashion:

Sc. 2. *Change to carpenter's scene and set room in the Tower behind.* Richard *on prompt to centre.*

> RICHARD. Now is winter of our discont't
> Made glorious summer by sun of York;
> And all clouds th. lowered, &c.,
> In deep bosom of ocean buried.

If the reader's imagination may be quenched, his taste offended, and his good sense revolted merely to save the author's time in describing the action of a piece, why should not the same thing be done in handling the dialogue?

But there is another party to be considered besides the author and the reader. There is the actor (who is nowadays the manager also), an exceptionally susceptible, imaginative, fastidious person, easily put out by the slightest incongruity, easily possessed by the slightest suggestion. His work is so peculiar and important; its delicacy depends so much on the extent to which a play can be made real to him and the technical conditions reduced to unnoticed matters of habit; above all, it is so necessary to his self-respect that the obligation he is under to make himself a means to the author's end should not be made an excuse for disregarding his dignity as a man, that an author can hardly be too careful to cherish the actor's illusion and respect his right to be approached as a professional man and not merely ordered to do this or that without knowing why. Imagine, then, the effect of handing an actor a part, or an actor-manager a play, drawn up exactly like a specification for a gas-fitter! How can any man or woman of letters be so foolishly inconsiderate as to suppose that an actor-manager, at the moment when he is full of curiosity and hope as to the opportunity of striking the public imagination offered him by a writer whom he can only judge according to his or her power of imaginative and vivid description, really likes to receive a silly amateur attempt to imitate a flyman's scene plot and a prompter's memorandum of positions and list of "props"? When I read the prompt copies that are not only sent in to managers for acceptance, but actually to the printers for the delectation of the unprofessional public, I often wonder how many managers or readers would ever get as far as the second page in Hamlet if it were presented to them in so loathly a fashion.

Let me give an example of a stage direction of my own which has been rebuked as a silly joke by people who do not understand the real relations of author and actor. It runs thus: "*So-and-So's complexion fades into stone-grey; and all movement and expression desert his eyes.*" This is the sort of stage direction an actor really wants. Of course, he can no more actually change his complexion to stone-grey than Mr Forbes-Robertson can actually die after saying, "The rest is silence." But he can produce the impression suggested by the direction perfectly. *How* he produces it is his business, not mine. This distinction is important, because, if I wrote such a stage direction as "*turns his back to the audience and furtively dabs vaseline on his eyelashes,*" instead of "*his eyes glisten with tears,*" I should be guilty of an outrage on both actor and reader. Yet we find almost all our inexperienced dramatic authors taking the greatest pains to commit just such outrages. The fact is, the actor and the reader want exactly the same thing, vivid strokes of description, not stage manager's memoranda of impertinent instructions in the art of acting from literary people who cannot act. It is true that most authors consider themselves born actors, and that most actors consider themselves born authors; but these weaknesses should be confessed under seal of rehearsal, not proclaimed to a derisive world. To do the actor justice, he tries not to carry the stage about with him wherever he goes, whereas the would-be playwright never lets you escape from it, even in print. If the reader attempts to forget that what he is reading is fiction, he promptly has a pin stuck into him by the statement that such and such a piece of furniture is R. or L., or "near the front of the stage," or that the masterpiece of painting on the easel, which the villain or adventuress will presently slash with a knife, is "turned away from the audience." It is just as if a novelist were to write, "A keen pang shot through the mother's heart; for she saw at a glance that her child had not many chapters to live," or "When we left Grimwood, he had just dealt the coward's blow that stretched young Alton Dale a corpse three lines from the foot of the first page of signature C." A dramatist's business is to make the reader forget the stage and the actor forget the audience, not to remind them of both at every turn, like an incompetent "extra gentleman" who turns the wrong side of his banner towards the footlights. Every such reminder is a betrayal in art and a solecism in manners. Why should novices advertise their inexperience by sedulously committing them on every page, and even clinging to the "exits" and "exeunts" which survive from the time when dramatists like Chapman wrote all their stage directions in Latin, perhaps to avoid spoiling the illusion by them, perhaps only to show off their scholarship?

The safe rule is, Write nothing in a play that you would not write in a novel; and remember that everything that the actor or the scene-painter *shows* to the audience must be described—not technically specified, but imaginatively, vividly, humorously, in a word, artistically described—to the reader by the author. In describing the scene, take just as much trouble to transport your reader there in imagination as you would in a narrative. Your imaginary persons must not call "off the stage"; you must not tell the public that "part of the stage is removed to represent the entrance to a cellar." It will often strain your ingenuity to describe a scene so that a stage-manager can set it from the printed description, yet not a word is let slip that could remind the reader of the footlights. But it can be done: and the reward for the trouble is that people can read your plays—even actor-managers, who suffer just as much from the deadening, disillusioning, vulgarizing effect of the old-fashioned stage direction as other people do.

The Dying Tongue of Great Elizabeth

(*The Saturday Review* XCIX, February 11, 1905; issued as
a pamphlet, London, 1920, by the London Shakespear
League)

Much as the Shakespearean orgies at His Majesty's
Theatre have interested and amused me from the first,
it was not until I witnessed Much Ado the other night
that it struck me that Mr Tree's detachment from
Shakespear was a phenomenon less personal and more
national—or, at least, more metropolitan—than I had
supposed. That detachment is certainly very complete.
We all know the actor-managers to whom Shakespear
is an august convention, conferring intellectual eminence, scholarship, and professional primacy on his
exponents; but however honorary the degree, however
imaginary the scholarship, however precarious the
primacy, there has always been between the author
and actor a genuine bond of stage method, of rhetoric,
of insistence on exceptionally concentrated personal
force and skill in execution, of hammering the play
in by ceaseless point-making. Far be it from me to pretend that these things were achieved always, or even
often; but they were aimed at; and the result was a
performance which, on its technical side, had at least
some relation to Shakespear, even when it was only
the relation of failure.

But even that bond is now broken. Among the managers who are imaginative and capable enough to
count seriously, Mr Tree is the first within my experience for whom Shakespear does not exist at all. Confronted with a Shakespearean play, he stares into a
ghastly vacuum, yet stares unterrified, undisturbed by
any suspicion that his eyesight is failing, quite prepared to find the thing simply an ancient, dusty,
mouldy, empty house which it is his business to fur-
nish, decorate, and housewarm with an amusing entertainment. And it is astonishing how well he does it.
Totally insensible to Shakespear's qualities, he puts his

own qualities into the work. When he makes one of
Shakespear's points—which he does extremely seldom
—it is only because at that particular moment Shakespear's wit happens to coincide with his own: for instance, in Much Ado he makes a point of the famous
"Love me! Why, it must be requited"; but you can
see by his colloquial alteration of the line to "Love
me! Oh! This must be requited," that he did not feel
the point in the original more rhetorical version, and
that it was his own dramatic instinct that prompted
him to re-invent it and introduce it as a pure inter-
polation, ingeniously using as much of the bard's
language as could be made to convey anything to himself or the audience. He is always papering the naked
wall, helping the lame dog over the stile, putting a
gorgeous livery on the man in possession, always, like
Nature, abhorring a vacuum, and filling it with the
treasures of his own ingenuity and imagination and
fun, and then generously giving our Shakespear the
credit. Think back a little on his achievements in
Shakespear's characters. Can you not remember some
telling stroke in all of them? But it is never one of
Shakespear's strokes. No doubt his Falstaff, being a
sin against nature, had all the atrocity peculiar to such
sins: still, one remembers, as an audacious but quite
credible character-quip, the knight who was impecu-
nious enough to take fifteen pence from Pistol as his
share of the price of the stolen fan, yet riding up to
his pothouse on a valuable white nag. Shakespear never
thought of that. You remember Caliban taking a huge
bite out of a raw gurnet, catching flies to prevent them
teasing his god Stephano, and lying on a promontory
with heaven knows what melancholy at his heart,
watching the ship that is taking away Prospero and
Prospero's daughter for ever into the unknown. You
remember Richard the Second, though moved only to
futile sarcasm by Bolingbroke's mastery of him, turning away with a stifled sob when his dog deserts him
and licks Bolingbroke's hand. You remember, too, how
Richard munches sweetmeats whilst his peers are com-

ing to blows in his presence, and how, after his disgrace
in Westminster Hall, instead of making the conventional pathetic exit, he clasps his hands affectedly behind him, cocks his chin pettishly in the air, and struts
out, not as an accomplished actor would go out, but—
he convinces you—as Richard himself probably did go
out on that occasion. And you will remember his Benedick up a tree, shying oranges at the three conspirators,
and finally shaking the whole crop down on them when
they accuse him of "a contemptible spirit," quite content to exploit the phrase in its modern sense, though
Shakespear means, not contemptible, but contemptuous.

Now some of these indelible remembrances are of
strokes of genius, and some are of inconsiderate tomfooleries (for you really should not, like Crummles's
comic countryman, catch flies when another actor is
trying to hold the audience); but they are all pure
original Tree and not Shakespear. They could only
have occurred to one whose mind was completely free
from all preoccupation with Shakespear. And that is
only possible to one who can see nothing in Shakespear except what must be obvious to any person of
normal senses.

Now I am quite aware that I here seem to be con-
demning Mr Tree in the most severe manner. Mr
Churton Collins, Mr Sidney Lee, Mr Swinburne will
say that if all this be true, then Mr Tree is not papering
a blank wall but barbarously whitewashing a fresco,
not helping a lame dog over a stile, but breaking the
leg of a lion. And they would be partly right. It cannot
be denied that Mr Tree takes unheard-of pains to
manufacture "business" to help out scenes that positively bristle with missed Shakespearean points. His
occasional crimes against literature are positively blas-
phemous. Let me give one example from Much Ado.
In the masked ball scene, when the Prince flits across
the stage with Hero, the little scrap of their conversation that reaches us is exquisitely caught up at the
end into a little trill of verse.

PRINCE: My visor is Philemon's roof;
   Within the house of Jove.
HERO: Why then your visor should be thatched.
PRINCE: Speak low if you speak love.

When, at His Majesty's, the first two lines were omitted, and "Speak low if you speak love" tacked suddenly on to "God defend, the lute should be like the case," I staggered to my seat as if a dart had been struck through my liver. Had I not been under a strong and recent personal obligation to Mr Tree for a service rendered to me in the production of a play of my own, I declare I should have risen and addressed the audience, and moved a resolution. Only once before in my life have I had such a shock. That was at Covent Garden one night at the end of Don Giovanni, when the statue, without a word of warning, lit on a note so utterly foreign to the key, that I sprang to my feet in the midst of the stalls and uttered a most fearful imprecation, as remote from the ordinary channel of my conversation as the statue's error was from the score of Mozart.

Now it is clear that Mr Tree's valuation of Shakespear's graces of language must be widely different from my own, or he would not make cuts of this kind, or modernize and interpolate as he does so freely throughout the play. And this brings me to the main object of my criticism, which is to defend Mr Tree by calling attention to a phenomenon which is being acted on in practice before we have learnt to allow for it.

Some time ago I received a copy of a book called The Twentieth Century Bible. It was a copy of the New Testament translated into such modern English as we find in the leading article of a respectable newspaper. Nobody who remembers the outcry that arose against our official revised version of the Scriptures— the very corrections of the errors of the authorized version being denounced as sacrilegious, and as exposing their makers to the curse in the last chapter of Revelation—can doubt that this Twentieth Century

version would never have been undertaken by a body
of devout Protestant believers (in America, too, of all
countries) under any pressure short of daily experience of the fact that the authorized version is no
longer intelligible to the common people: in short,
that Jacobean English is a dead language. And I
confess, not without an afterblush of amazement and
humiliation, that I myself, who have never lost touch
with the Jacobean language, who, as an Irishman, have
for my mother tongue an English two centuries earlier
than twentieth century cockney; who have all my life
had my head full of the Bible and Shakespear, did
nevertheless find that as I read this new vernacular
Testament (quite with the proper amused contempt
at first for its Philistine journalese) I gathered at once
from it numbers of important points that I had never
got from the authorized version, and saw others in
quite a new and highly suggestive light. And I said,
"If this is the case with me, who found George Eliot's
English thirty years ago a jargon of awkward neol-
ogisms, how must it be with cockneys who might be
my sons and daughters, and to whom George Eliot is
now quainter and more old-fashioned than ever Fielding has been to me?"

Now let us return to Much Ado.

The performance went on in the usual manner up
to the point at which Shakespear rescues the play from
collapse through the exhaustion of its wretched plot,
and through the impossibility of keeping up the pretence that Beatrice and Benedick are delightfully witty
and genuine creatures, by falling back on his old joke
a male Malaprop, and making Dogberry the savior
of the play. Before Mr Louis Calvert was half through
Dogberry's charge to the watch, I felt that something
had begun which was quite on a new plane. Mr Calvert, as I have some special reason to know, is an extraordinarily good actor; but after all, there were other
actors in the cast. If you come to that, Mr Tree can
act, and sometimes, when the work in hand suits his
genius, act very well indeed. No: the difference was

not the difference between good and ordinary acting: it was a difference in kind. And it flashed on me presently that the secret was that the language of Shakespear was a live language to Mr Calvert, whereas to Mr Tree and the rest it was more or less a dead one. Allowing as much as possible for the difference between a steady professional skill that never blurs a syllable nor drops the end of a line into the orchestra, and a whimsical carelessness that lets even such a line as "Come! I will have thee; but by this light I take thee for pity" fall flat because the word "pity" does not reach even the third row of the stalls, much less the gaping bardolatrous pit, still, no mere technical accomplishment on Mr Calvert's part could have dug the huge gulf that separated his utterance from that of the others. It is not perfect articulation, but perfect intelligence, that finds the nail in every phrase and hits it on the head unerringly. Now there is nothing to tax anybody's intelligence in Much Ado. Like all Shakespear's comedies it contains nothing beyond the capacity of a child except the indecencies which constitute the staple of its badinage. Mr Tree is as capable of understanding it as Mr Calvert, if only he knew the language of the seventeenth century as Mr Calvert does. But he only knows it as a scholar knows Coptic: he cannot really speak it. When he can neither frankly modernize it, as in his "Oh! This must be requited," nor confine his acting to those phrases which still survive in our speech, he is beaten by it. To Mr Calvert it is as natural as his native speech: he makes it clear, expressive, and vivid without the least preoccupation; whereas to Mr Tree, and indeed to all the rest, more or less, it is a continual embarrassment.

Now we are in a position to do Mr Tree justice. Here he is, confronted with a play in a dead language. What the language is to him, it is, *a fortiori*, to a public much inferior to him in culture. One has only to open a spare ear to hear the occupants of the stalls, presumably not the least literate section of the audience, giggling at such phrases as "Fair and softly" and the like, evidently taking them to be Dogberryisms, as if John Gilpin himself was too archaic for them. What can the manager do, playing to please such an audience at the huge hazards that a vast theatre involves, but treat Shakespear's language as a drawback only feebly counterbalanced by its reputation? The consequences are startling to those who have not analytic faculty enough to understand how much of Shakespear's magic is created by the beauty and fancy of his word-music. Paraphrase the dialogue of Much Ado in mere utilitarian prose, and you will find speech after speech awkward, superfluous, dragged in by the ears, and consequently irritating and tedious, fatal to the crispness of the action. The characters lose their glamor: one sees that the creator of the merry lady with her barmaidenly repartees and the facetious bachelor with his boarding-house funny man's table talk, was no Oscar Wilde. The three gallant companions in arms no longer bear thinking of in comparison with Athos, Aramis, and d'Artagnan. Dogberry is seen to be a cheap performance in comparison with the best comic figures of Cervantes, Scott, and Dickens. The subtler strokes of character are wasted because they could be made amusing and intelligible only by the method of comedy; and Shakespear, great at "drama," farce, and fairy extravaganza, had no idea of comedy. For instance, Claudio is a well-observed and consistent character; childishly selfish, cruel, and affectionate; without judgment or reflection; always rushing at a word of suggestion from one extreme of infatuation and credulity to the other. Labiche would have made him irresistibly amusing and interestingly instructive by the modern comedic method. Shakespear, for want of comedic faculty, gets no dramatic value out of him whatever, and fails to convey to the audience anything except a disagreeable impression of a conventional hero who is driven by the mere letter of the plot into an unconvincing misunderstanding and a dastardly revenge, in the meanness of which his gallant friends grovel as vulgarly as himself. The story is a hopeless one, pleasing only to lovers of the illustrated police papers. It was all very well for Shakespear to say "It does not matter what the story is, provided I tell it; and it does not matter what the characters say provided I turn the phrase for them." He could make that boast good only to people with an ear for his music and a born habit of thinking in his language. That habit once lost, the garden of Klingsor withers; Much Ado becomes what Don Giovanni or Die Zauberflöte would become if Mozart's music were burnt and the libretto alone preserved.

Mr Tree has to find substitutes for the lost charm; and he does so with a fertility that would do credit to a professed playwright. Much Ado is not only bearable at His Majesty's, it is positively pleasant to the disillusioned, and, I should think, enchanting to the young. All the lovely things that Shakespear dispensed with are there in bounteous plenty. Fair ladies, Sicilian seascapes, Italian gardens, summer nights and dawns (compressed into five minutes), Renascential splendors, dancing, singing, masquerading, architecture, orchestration tastefully culled from Wagner, Bizet, and German, and endless larks in the way of stage business devised by Mr Tree, and carried out with much innocent enjoyment, which is fairly infectious on the other side of the footlights. And then, since Shakespear's words are still the basis of the dialogue, there are moments when the bard enjoys his own again; for all the players are not as completely swanproof as Mr Tree; and sometimes the star dances and silence is *not* the perfectst herald of joy. On the whole, my advice is, go and see it: you will never again have the chance of enjoying such an entertainment.

The company is a strong one. Mr Henry Neville, as Leonato, is of course hampered at first by the violent make-believe which is necessary to face out the enormous lie that Beatrice and Benedick are providing (I am going to quote the program—a shameless document) "a brilliant encounter of wits by which the audience is perpetually confronted but never wearied."

He has also to pretend that the trick on Benedick is credible in proportion to its over-acting. So far Mr Neville is rather the benevolently mellow veteran, helping the play and the young people, than the deeply stirred actor; but in the church scene he will be remembered longer than most of our Leonatos. Mr Sidney Brough, agreeably to Mr Tree's historical conception of Don Pedro as a Spanish prince, makes up as Philip II, but repudiates the character of that gloomy monarch by a levity of deportment which verges on the comic relief to which Mr Brough's early years were dedicated. His luckless kinsman, Mr Lionel Brough, has been given the part of Verges after Mr Tree had first erased Verges from the book of life. The really exasperating stupidity of cutting out the scene of the visit of Dogberry and Verges to Leonato has been made traditional on the London stage ever since Sir Henry Irving (who will have an extremely unpleasant quarter of an hour if he is unlucky enough to come across the Bard in the heavenly Pantheon) ingeniously discovered that means of reducing Dogberry to a minor part. In the omitted scene we become acquainted with Verges as an intelligent old man enfeebled by age, whose straightforward attempts to explain things are baffled by the lusty pigheadedness of Dogberry. Deprived of that opportunity, poor Mr Lionel Brough can do nothing but echo Dogberry's words, and pretend to be a greater fool than he. It is infuriating to see a good actor treated in this fashion. How would Mr Tree like it himself? Mr Basil Gill cannot make Claudio a man to be thought about sympathetically; but he makes him pleasant and poetic to look at and listen to; and Mr Haviland, an admirable speaker, is irreproachable as the friar. Mr Laurence Irving, as Don John, wallows in wickedness as only a very amiable man can, and makes this most costive of villains inappropriately exuberant. It is when his part is over, in the church scene, that he suddenly begins to play silently, thoughtfully, and well.

As to Benedick, I defy anybody not to be amused
by him. When he is not amusingly good from Mr Tree's
point of view he is amusingly bad from the classical
Shakespearean point of view; and when you add that
arboreal personality of which I for one never tire, you
get a total result which it would be mere pedantry to
cavil at, and which I would not change for the most
perfectly classical Benedick the School of Dramatic
Art will ever turn out. It is, in its way, colossal.

Miss Miriam Clements, quite unconsciously, perhaps,
and all the better for that, is a classic Hero. I have
never seen the interrupted wedding played with such
perfect discretion. Anybody else would have torn it to
pieces. Really a most excellent piece of work. Miss
Winifred Emery plays Beatrice. I am afraid I was
guilty of the impertinence of being prepared to sympathize with her on account of her late illness; but the
first glimpse of her corrected that. I never saw anybody look so well. She was not like a sixteenth century
Italian, nor, thank goodness, a Shakespearean merry
lady. She was like an eighteenth century queen. Her
acting struck me as capricious and even grudging. Her
unbending walk across the choir before the altar in
the church scene was almost an anti-Ritualist demonstration. There were moments, notably in the overhear-
ing scene, when she seemed quite in earnest. There
were other moments when she seemed to stand aloof
from the play with infinite disparagement, and to be
on the point of losing her patience and going home,
leaving us to finish our nonsense as best we might
without her. Then she would take a sudden fancy to
a passage and dash into the play like a bird into a
fountain; and a delightful minute would ensue. It was
better, far better, than the usual hard-working Beatrice,
desperately determined to be "piercingly keen and
exquisitely apt" (program again) at all hazards, and
saying things that a flower-girl would spare a bus-
driver as if they were gems of delicate intuition. In
short, she was clever enough to play Lady Disdain

instead of playing for sentimental sympathy; and the effect was keenly good and original. And, happier than Verges, she had the *carduus benedictus* scene restored, to the great benefit of the play.

The scenery—for once, we have Italian scenery adequately lighted—is a vital organ, the only failure being the commonplace church, which will not bear comparison with Mr Gordon Craig's suggestion of a lofty nave. On the whole, a very bad play, but a very enjoyable entertainment.

Letters to Louis Calvert on Playing Undershaft*

(Calvert played in the original 1905 Court Theatre production of *Major Barbara*. These first appeared in *Vanity Fair*, February 1916, under the heading "Letters to His Leading Man.")

(From Derry Roscarberry, Ireland, July 23, 1905)

Dear Calvert—

Can you play the trombone? If not, I beg you to acquire a smattering of the art during your holidays. I am getting on with the new play scrap by scrap; and the part of the millionaire cannon founder is becoming more and more formidable. Broadbent and Keegan rolled into one, with Mephistopheles thrown in; that is what it is like. Business is Business will be cheap melodrama in comparison, Irving and Tree will fade into third class when Calvert takes the stage as Andrew Undershaft. It will be TREMENDOUS, simply. But there is a great scene at the end of the second act where he buys up the Salvation Army, and has to take part in a march to a big meeting. Barker will play the drum. You will have a trombone—or a bass-horn if you prefer that instrument—and it would add greatly to the effect if you could play it prettily. Besides if you took to music you could give up those confounded cigars and save your voice and your memory (both

* Shaw created the role of Andrew Undershaft expressly for Calvert, who had played Broadbent in 1904.

wrecks, like Mario's,* from thirty-seven cigars a day) for this immense part. It is very long, speeches longer than Keegan's, and dozens of them, and infinite nuances of execution. Undershaft is diabolically subtle, gentle, self-possessed, powerful, stupendous, as well as amusing and interesting. There are the makings of ten Hamlets and six Othellos in his mere leavings. Learning it will half kill you; but you can retire the next day as pre-eminent and unapproachable. That penny-plain and twopence-colored pirate Brassbound will be beneath your notice then. I have put him off for another year, as I cannot get the right Lady Cicely. ————, unluckily, has read my plays at Margate and is now full of the most insane proposals—wants Brassbound instantly. With you and Kate Rorke for one thing. But the trombone is the urgent matter of the moment.

By the way, trombone players never get cholera nor consumption—never die, in fact, until extreme old age makes them incapable of working the slide.

G. Bernard Shaw.

(Letter concerning a rehearsal, November 18)

My Dear Calvert—

I hope I did not worry you too much today at rehearsal. The fact is you are ruining the end of the second act by your enormous, desolating, oblivious-to-everybody absent-mindedness. The reason I put on an understudy for Barbara was that you had driven Miss Russell almost out of her senses by letting the scene drop when she was doing her hardest to get hold of it. She did not complain; but I saw what was happening and acted on my own initiative. You see, it is all very well for you; you know that you can wake up at the last moment and do the trick; but that will not help out the unhappy victims who have to rehearse with you. And you forget your own weight. The

* Giovanni Mario (1810–1883) was a great but erratic mid-century tenor frequently referred to in Shaw's music criticism.

moment you let the play go, it drops. You sit there, greatly interested (except when you are asleep) by the way to manage the play and the mistakes that all the rest are making, and trying to make out what is wrong with the whole scene. Of course, what is wrong is you. There is that frightful speech where Undershaft deliberately gives a horrible account of his business, sticking detail after detail of the horrors of war into poor bleeding Barbara to show her what Mrs Baines will stand for for £5000. Cusins, who sees it all, is driven into an ecstasy of irony by it; it is sort of a fantasia played on the nerves of both him and Barbara by Machiavelli-Mephistopheles. All that is needed to produce the effect is steady concentration, magnetic intensity. Irving, who could not do lots of things that you can do, could have done this superbly. But, you are evidently thinking of Lord knows what— the returns of your Sweet Nell Companies, or how Barker always drops his voice when he ought to raise it and emphasizes the wrong word, or what a monstrous thing it is that an idiot of an author should produce a play when he doesn't know the first rudiments of his business or—then you suddenly realize that the stage has been waiting for you for ten minutes. There are moments when if we were not in a conspiracy to spoil you, we should rend you to pieces and wallow in your blood. Miss Russell has been working at the thing with the greatest enthusiasm, and when she tries to get into the rush of it, and is slacked down every time by your colossal indifference, she almost gives up in despair. If you were an insignificant actor it would not matter; they could run away from you; but they are not strong enough for this; the piece takes its time and intensity from you in spite of all they can do.

Mind, I quite appreciate your heroic study of the lines; and I don't complain of anything except the end of the second act; but for that I have no words strong enough to describe your atrocity; you will scream through endless centuries in hell for it, and implore me in vain to send you ices from heaven to cool your burning tongue. We have only one week more; and I have set my heart on your making a big success in the part. And you are taking it as easy as if Undershaft were an old uncle in a farce. Spend tomorrow in prayer. My wife was horrified at my blanched hair and lined face when I returned from rehearsal today. And I have a blinding headache and can no more.

Your unfortunate,

G.B.S.

(From Adelphi Terrace, November 29, day after opening)

My Dear Calvert—

I see with disgust that the papers all say that your Undershaft was a magnificent piece of acting and Major Barbara a rottenly undramatic play, instead of pointing out that Major B is a masterpiece and that you are the most infamous amateur that ever disgraced the boards.

Do let me put ———— into it. A man who could let the seven deadly sins go for nothing could sit on a hat without making an audience laugh. I have taken a box for Friday and had a hundredweight of cabbages, dead cats, eggs, and gingerbeer bottles stacked in it. Every word you fluff, every speech you unact, I will shy something at you. Before you go on the stage I will insult you until your temper gets the better of your liver. You are an impostor, a sluggard, a blockhead, a shirk, a malingerer, and the worst actor that ever lived or that ever will live. I will apologize to the public for engaging you. I will tell your mother of you.* Barbara played you off the stage; Cremlin dwarfed you; Bill annihilated you; Clare Greet took all

---

* Calvert's parents, Mr. and Mrs. Charles Calvert, were the proprietors and leading actors of the Queen's Theatre, Manchester, one of the finest stock theatres in late nineteenth-century England. Shaw had long admired them; he had persuaded Mrs. Calvert after her retirement to return to the stage to play Catherine Petkoff in *Arms and the Man* in 1894.

eyes from you. If you are too lazy to study the lines
I'll coach you in them. That last act MUST be saved
or I'll withdraw the play and cut you off without a
shilling.

Yours,

G.B.S.

What Is the Finest Dramatic Situation?

(*The Strand Magazine* XXXI, February 1906)

I cannot answer the question, as my mind does not
work in superlatives. Even if it did I should still have
to point out that plays with detachable situations in
them are comparatively cheap, simple, mechanical
products—melodramas, in short. The most effective
situations on the modern stage occur in my own play,
The Devil's Disciple, but The Devil's Disciple is a
melodrama. There is a very ingenious situation in Mr
Gillette's Secret Service (another melodrama), in
which the hero, having either to arrest his own brother
as a spy or be himself arrested on the same fatal
charge, is saved by the brother shooting himself. The
Merchant of Venice is the most famous English play
written round a situation. It must have been tremendously effective at the first performance, when the audience did not know the solution of the pound of flesh
difficulty, and did not begin to suspect that the young
lawyer was Portia until they detected Nerissa in the
disguise of his clerk.

A first-rate play seems nowadays to have no situation, just as Wagner's music seemed to our grand-
fathers to have no melody, because it was all melody
from beginning to end. The best plays consist of a
single situation, lasting several hours. Mr Granville-
Barker's play, The Voysey Inheritance, which shows
a mastery that threatens to put us all on the shelf, is a
single situation in five acts, maintaining itself for three
hours at the pitch that an ordinary "constructed" play

attains for about five minutes at the end of the last act but one. My own play, Candida, is a single situation in three acts. The masterpieces of Greek tragedy were single situations in a single act. Mr St John Hankin's Return of the Prodigal, an unpretentiously light-handed comedy, is essentially a single situation in four acts. This expansion of the old momentary claptraps, introduced by tedious explanations between servants, and followed by a final act which was seldom more than a more or less adroitly covered up collapse into episodes of sufficient significance, richness, and variety to form whole plays, is the most hopeful sign about our modern drama. It is a pity it is not more generally understood. I am constantly praised—as all our leading playwrights are praised—for old professional tricks that we do no better than Robertson or Charles Reade, or Tom Taylor or Bulwer Lytton, or Plautus or Terence; whilst the real advances we make are either missed altogether or complained of as "undramatic," or some such nonsense.

Mr. Trench's Dramatic Values*

(To the Editor of *The Saturday Review* CX, July 2, 1910)

30 June 1910.

Sir,—Mr Trench's article is the best that has yet been written on the present dramatic crisis; but I think he has given the devil somewhat more than his due when he says that the public for his Class A seems wholly unlimited in numbers, whilst Mr Barker's Waste is unpopular. He also says that The Bad Girl of the Family will outrun a thousand Candidas. This is true, within certain time limits, just as it would be true,

* F. H. Trench (1865–1923), mainly remembered as a poet, had written and produced plays. The article on which Shaw comments was "Dramatic Values and a Suggested Solution," in *The Saturday Review* of June 25, 1910.

within similar limits, if I said that Bill Bailey would outsell a thousand such poems as Mr Trench's Apollo and the Seaman. But to all wildly popular things comes, suddenly and inexorably, death without hope of resurrection. All the king's horses and all the king's men cannot set the street pianos playing Nancy Lee again, though the tune is as good as ever it was, and they once played nothing else. No book within our recollection had so made a vogue in America as Du Maurier's Trilby; the elders of Trilby's day said there had been nothing like it since Uncle Tom's Cabin. But the American booksellers still talk of the miracle of Trilby's death. They aver that the demand stopped in one day. When La Fille de Madame Angot was new, audiences used to encore the Conspirators' Chorus (borrowed from an old tune on which Beethoven wrote variations) half a dozen times. When Sir Charles Wyndham tried to revive the work, that chorus passed without the slightest notice. The street-piano men of the East End will tell you that this psychological phenomenon repeats itself with every music-hall song that becomes the rage. For weeks and sometimes months nothing else will be listened to: there is no limit to the number of repetitions people will not only stand but clamor for. Then in one day they will not tolerate it on any terms; it would be safer to play a Bach fugue.

Now this does not happen to the higher works of art. The masterpiece begins by fighting for its life against unpopularity, by which I do not mean mere indifference, but positive hatred and furious renunciation of it as an instrument of torture. Beethoven's Ninth Symphony did not "catch on" like the Intermezzo in Cavalleria Rusticana: it was described even by eminent musicians as an outrage by a madman. But in the long run Beethoven leaves Mascagni nowhere even as a money-maker. And the same is true of all the masterpieces. Apollo and the Seaman will make more money than Bill Bailey; and though I dare not say that Candida will make more money than The Bad Girl of the Family (for that, too, may be a master-

piece: I have not seen it and cannot pretend to judge);
yet I put it to Mr Trench whether he would not rather,
on purely commercial grounds, revive Candida than
The Worst Woman in London. If you bring authors
to the test of how much money from first to last the
public had paid for witnessing representations of their
plays, you will find Shakespear first and the rest nowhere in England; and if you take all Europe you will
probably find Ibsen already far beyond many prime
commercial favorites.

It has to be considered, further, that in gambling
for a "catch on," prodigious sums of money are lost.
Managers who have to take off plays because they
draw "only" £800 a week, or, in some cases, "only"
£1500 a week, and who would not touch Ibsen or
Granville-Barker with a pair of tongs, often lose more
money in one week with "popular" plays than the entire capital with which Messrs Vedrenne and Barker
entered upon and carried on their campaign at the
Court Theatre. When we say that the higher art does
not pay, all that we mean is that it will not make sudden fortunes for speculators. But that is no reason why
high art should be classed as commercially impracticable, much less given up as impossible. Ruskin's
Stones of Venice and Spencer's Synthetic Philosophy
were not driven out of the bookshops by The Mystery
of a Hansom Cab. It does not pay so well pecuniarily
to be an Inspector of Education in the public service
as to be a Jay Gould, a Vanderbilt, a Barnato, or a
Colonel North; but that has not prevented the State
from procuring the services of two men of extraordinary ability in poetic and critical literature—
namely, Matthew Arnold and Mr Trench himself—to
fill that modestly paid post. In Arnold's case the Barna-
tos might have said that he had no choice, as he could
not have succeeded in business if he had tried; but
Mr Trench has tried, with the result that he has not
only held his own easily and triumphantly in theatrical
management after about a fortnight's experience (as
I told him he would when he felt diffident about it

on the brink of his plunge), but left most of them far behind as to the onerousness of the artistic conditions he is prepared to accept.

The time, also, has gone by for pretending that the appreciation of a work of any weight, whether it be a play, an opera, or a symphony, is a matter of one performance. Even when the author raises no hostility or misunderstanding by breaking new ground, as Beethoven did, yet it is not in the nature of things possible for a person to take in a play fully until he is in complete possession of its themes; or, to put it in another way, nobody can understand the beginning of a play until he knows the end of it: a condition which cannot be fulfilled at a first hearing, and one which explains the fact that plays are often much worse received on their first night than later on, when newspaper notices and dinner-table discussion have made the audiences familiar beforehand with the main upshot of the story. In music this goes without saying: no one pretends to be able to follow the Ninth Symphony until he knows all the themes as well as he knows God Save the King. Now probably there are many more people who can pick up and remember a new tune at one hearing than can master a new idea at its first utterance. Ibsen's plays may fascinate at the first hearing: they may convince the people capable of them that they are worth persevering with; but you may see them ten times without getting near the end of them. Familiar as I am with Mr Granville-Barker's methods and ideas, I find that until I have been through his plays at least six times I have not got fairly hold of them; and though in my own plays I tell my story and fling my meaning at the audience with an old-fashioned violence which seems downright barn-storming in contrast with the subtler ways of Mr Barker and Mr Galsworthy, yet the verdicts founded on a single hearing of my plays are absurd enough to have become one of the standing jokes of the modern theatre; and I have never met any real expert who professed to get on easy terms with, say, Major Barbara, in less than four visits.

The moral of all this is that Mr Trench must make an additional category of the plays which required to be nursed as they were nursed at the Court Theatre, where some of the most popular plays in the repertory began by playing to about one-twentieth of the gate-money that Mr Frohman demands as the price of a play's existence.

Another category is that of the "great plays" which depend on great acting. In putting The Blue Bird in the same class as Cyrano and Hamlet, Mr Trench has left this out of account. In London there will never be any difficulty in casting The Blue Bird adequately without paying a single exceptional salary. Cyrano or Hamlet, similarly cast, will collapse in ruin. On the other hand, very poor plays may keep the stage solely because some great actor has shown the way to interpolate a display of great acting between their lines. There is far more histrionic talent available in England than anyone would suppose from our theatrical routine; but when it comes to "great plays," the authors and managers must cut their coats according to their cloth.

I put forward these considerations not in opposition to Mr Trench, whose conclusion that the higher art of the theatre needs endowment I endorse, but because I do not think that the possibilities of commerce are exhausted by the existing system. I think that a manager who would be content with the ordinary income of a professional man or upper division civil servant, could do, not everything that ought to be done, but at least a very great deal more than is being done at present by the managers who are playing the ordinary game of hazard. That was the real secret of the solvency of the Court Theatre; and though nobody knows better than I and Messrs Vedrenne and Barker that the Court Theatre could not do the work that the Shakespear National Memorial Theatre aims at, yet I think it will not be denied that Messrs Vedrenne and Barker did a great deal of public service which the ordinary theatre had given up as commercially im-

possible. I see no reason why that service should not
be continued if anybody can be found able and willing to take it in hand. All that is needed is a comparatively modest guarantee to enable the new adventurer
to retreat with honor in case of failure.

Yours truly,

G. Bernard Shaw

On the Principles that Govern the Dramatist

(Letter to *The New York Times*, June 2, 1912; reprinted
  in Barrett H. Clark, *European Theories of the Drama*,
  Cincinnati, 1918)

I am asked to define the principles that govern the
dramatist in his selection of themes and methods of
treatment. But pray, who told you, gentlemen, that
the dramatists are governed by principles, or that they
have any choice in their selection of themes and
methods?

I am not governed by principles; I am inspired,
how or why I cannot explain, because I do not know;
but inspiration it must be; for it comes to me without
any reference to my own ends or interest.

I find myself possessed of a theme in the following
manner. I am pushed by a natural need to set to
work to write down the conversations that come into
my head unaccountably. At first I hardly know the
speakers, and cannot find names for them. Then they
become more and more familiar, and I learn their
names. Finally I come to know them very well, and
discover what it is they are driving at, and why they
have said and done the things I have been moved to
set down.

This is not being "guided by principles"; it is hallucination; and sane hallucination is what we call play
or drama. I do not select my methods: they are imposed upon me by a hundred considerations: by the
physical considerations of theatrical representation, by
the laws devised by the municipality to guard against

fires and other accidents to which theatres are liable, by the economics of theatrical commerce, by the nature and limits of the art of acting, by the capacity of the spectators for understanding what they see and hear, and by the accidental circumstances of the particular production in hand.

I have to think of my pocket, of the manager's pocket, of the actors' pockets, of the spectators' pockets, of how long people can be kept sitting in a theatre without relief or refreshments, of the range of the performer's voice, and of the hearing and vision of the boy at the back of the gallery, whose right to be put in full possession of the play is as sacred as that of the millionaire in the stalls or boxes.

I have to consider theatrical rents, the rate of interest needed to tempt capitalists to face the risks of financing theatres, the extent to which the magic of art can break through commercial prudence, the limits set by honor and humanity to the tasks I may set to my fellow-artist, the actor; in short, all the factors that must be allowed for before the representation of a play on the stage becomes practicable or justifiable; factors which some never comprehend and which others integrate almost as unconsciously as they breathe, or digest their food.

It is these factors that dictate the playwright's methods, leaving him so little room for selection that there is not a pennyworth of difference between the methods of Sophocles or Shakespear and those of the maker of the most ephemeral farce.

And withal, when the play is made, the writer must feed himself and his family by it. Indeed, there are men and women who are forced by this necessity to simulate inspiration, repeating its gestures and copying its tricks so as to produce artificial plays: constructed things with no true life in them, yet sometimes more amusing than real plays, just as a clockwork mouse is more amusing than a real mouse, though it will kill the cat who swallows it in good faith.

I could tell many other secrets of my trade, but

these are enough to put the wise inquirer on the track of the rest.

To Audiences at *Major Barbara*

(Prefatory note circulated to the press when Grace George produced the play in America, 1915 and 1916; the note was purportedly written by "a playwright whose work is well known in this country, in England, and in Germany. He prefers to keep his identity a secret, but it may be said without betrayal of confidence that he knows intimately and admires greatly Bernard Shaw.")

Major Barbara is the third of a group of three plays of exceptional weight and magnitude on which the reputation of the author as a serious dramatist was first established, and still mainly rests. The first of the three, completed in 1903, the author's forty-seventh year, was Man and Superman, which has never been performed in its prodigious entirety in America, nor in England until the present year. The second, John Bull's Other Island, followed in 1904, and was an immediate success. The third of the series was Major Barbara, which arrived in 1905. It made demands on the audience but the demands were conceded. The audience left the theatre exhausted, but felt the better for it and came again. The second act, the Salvation Army act, was a play in itself. Regarded in that way, it may be said to be the most successful of all the author's plays.

The possibility of using the wooing of a man's soul for his salvation as a substitute for the hackneyed wooing of a handsome young gentleman for the sake of marrying him had occurred to Bernard Shaw many years before, when, in the course of his campaigns for socialism, he had often found himself on Sunday mornings addressing a Socialist meeting in the open air in London or in the provinces while the Salvation Army was at work on the same ground. He had frequently, at the conclusion of his own meeting, joined the crowd round the Salvation lasses and watched their work and studied their methods sympathetically. Many of them sang, with great effect, songs in which the drama of salvation was presented in the form of a series of scenes between a brutal and drunken husband and a saved wife, with a thrilling happy ending in which the audience, having been persuaded by the unconscious art of the singer to expect with horror a murderous attack on the woman as her husband's steps were heard on the stairs, were relieved and delighted to hear that when the villain entered the room and all seemed lost, his face was lighted with the light of Heaven; for he too had been saved. Bernard Shaw was not at that time a playwright; but such scenes were not lost on him; the future dramatist was collecting his material everywhere.

Many years afterwards when he had acquired a considerable reputation as a critic of music, Bernard Shaw saw in a daily paper a silly remark describing some horrible noise as being almost as bad as a Salvation Army band. He immediately wrote to the paper pointing out that the Salvation Army bands were mostly good, and that some of them were of very conspicuous excellence. This compliment from an unexpected quarter made quite a commotion at the Army's headquarters in London. The general quoted it again and again in public, and the author was invited to attend one of the musical festivals of the Army. He did so and wrote an elaborate critical report on the bands, besides declaring that the performance of the Dead March from Handel's Saul at the great meeting at the Albert Hall in commemoration of Mrs Booth by the combined bands of the Army, headed by the International Staff Band, was incomparably the finest he had ever heard, and the only one which showed any understanding of the magnificent triumphal character of the closing section.

Shaw took advantage of the relations thus established to ask the Army staff why they did not develop

the dramatic side of their ritual by performing plays.
He even offered to write a short play as a model of
what might be done. The leaders of the Army, though
interested and not themselves hostile to the proposal,
could not venture to offend the deep prejudices
against the theatre that still form part of English
evangelism. They could only say rather doubtfully
that if the author of a play could guarantee that everything in it had actually happened, that "it was all
true," it might be possible to reconcile the stricter
Salvationists to it. Shaw put forward the old defence
made by Bunyan that parables were allowable; but
he was met with the assurance that the Salvationists
believed the parables to be records of facts as well
as vehicles of instruction.

Finally, Mrs Bramwell Booth told the author frankly
that a subscription would be more useful to the social
work of the Army than a model play; and so the
matter dropped. But it bore fruit in Major Barbara;
and during its run the spectacle was seen for the first
time of a box filled with Salvation Army officials in
uniform, sitting in a theatre and witnessing a play.
Their testimony was useful. Some of the critics, in an
inept attempt to be piously shocked, tried to present
the play as a gibe at the Army, on the ground that
the Salvationists were represented as being full of
fun, and that they took money from the distiller. The
Army received this with the scorn it deserved, declaring that Barbara's fun was perfectly correct and characteristic, and that the only incident that seemed
incredible to them was her refusal to accept the money.
Any good Salvationist, they said, would, like the com-
missioner in the play, take money from the devil himself, and make so good use of it that he would perhaps
be converted, as there is hope for everybody.

The play, however, raises larger issues than those
of popular Salvationism. Undershaft, with his terrible
trade—so grimly flourishing just now—and his doctrine
that money comes first, and that poverty is the worst

of crimes and the only unbearable crime, strikes the deepest note in the play as Barbara sounds the highest. It was the allusions to Nietzsche which he provoked that elicited from the author the well-known preface in which he protested against the habit of the English critics of referring every trace of intellect in the English drama to Norwegian and German writers when all the doctrines which so surprised them were to be found in the literature of the English language. His reference to Samuel Butler as the greatest English exponent of Undershaft's doctrine of the importance of money was the beginning of the vogue of that remarkable writer which has persisted and spread ever since.

It is an open secret that the part of Adolphus Cusins, the very unusual *jeune premier* of the play, owes its originality to the fact that Mr Gilbert Murray, the Regius professor of Greek at Oxford University, served the author as a very interesting model. He quotes his own famous translations of Euripides. Undershaft is perhaps the most exacting part that has fallen to the lot of an actor since Shakespear's big parts; it belongs thoroughly to the new drama in which a tragedy and comedy and even broad fun, are so intimately bound up that it needs the greatest versatility and flexibility on the part of the actor, and the most alert vigilance on the part of the audience, to avoid confusing them.

It is curious that ten years should have elapsed between the production of Major Barbara in London and its first appearance on the American stage. It has been the subject of many proposals, but until today the artistic conditions have never seemed to the author favorable enough to warrant him in venturing on an authorization. Miss Grace George's appearance in London has doubtless had its weight in his decision. But Shaw has always said that for plays of this class, the great question is whether the audience will be a failure or a success.

On Cutting Shakespear

(*Fortnightly Review* CXII, August 1919)

Mr William Archer has quoted me in support of the practice of performing selections from Shakespear's plays instead of the plays in their entirety as he left them.

Everything that Mr Archer says is very true and very sensible. Unfortunately, the results in practice are the productions of Cibber, Garrick, Irving, Tree, Augustin Daly, Sir Frank Benson, and the commercial managers generally, which may be highly entertaining productions, but are somehow not Shakespear, whereas Mr Granville-Barker's resolutely unreasonable shewing-up of Shakespear's faults and follies to the uttermost comma was at once felt to be a restoration of Shakespear to the stage.

The moment you admit that the producer's business is to improve Shakespear by cutting out everything that he himself would not have written, and everything that he thinks the audience will either not like or not understand, and everything that does not make prosaic sense, you are launched on a slope on which there is no stopping until you reach the abyss where Irving's Lear lies forgotten. The reason stares us in the face. The producer's disapprovals, and consequently his cuts, are the symptoms of the differences between Shakespear and himself; and his assumption that all these differences are differences of superiority on his part and inferiority on Shakespear's, must end in the cutting down or raising up of Shakespear to his level. Tree thought a third-rate ballet more interesting than the colloquy of Cassio with Iago on the subject of temperance. No doubt many people agreed with him. It was certainly more expensive. Irving, when he was producing Cymbeline, cut out of his own part the lines:

> " 'Tis her breathing that
> Perfumes the chamber thus. The flame o' the taper
> Bows towards her, and would underpeep her lids
> To see the unclosed lights, now canopied
> Under those windows, white and azure, laced
> With blue of heaven's own tinct."

He was genuinely astonished when he was told that he must not do it, as the lines were the most famous for their beauty of all the purple patches in Shakespear. A glance at the passage will shew how very "sensible" his cut was. Mr Archer wants to cut, "O single-soled jest, solely singular for the singleness," because it is "absolutely meaningless." But think of all the other lines that must go with it on the same ground! The gayer side of Shakespear's poetic ecstasy expressed itself in word-dances of jingling nonsense which are, from the point of view of the grave Scots commentator who demands a meaning and a moral from every text, mere delirium and echolalia. But what would Shakespear be without them? "The spring time, the only merry ring time, when birds do sing hey ding a ding ding" is certainly not good sense nor even accurate ornithological observation! Who ever heard a bird sing "hey ding a ding ding" or anything even remotely resembling it? Out with it, then; and away, too, with such absurdities as Beatrice's obviously untrue statement that a star danced at her birth, which must revolt all the obstetricians and astronomers in the audience. As to Othello's fustian about the Pro-pontick and the Hellespont, is this senseless hullabaloo of sonorous vowels and precipitate consonants to be retained when people have trains to catch? Mr Archer is credulous in imagining that in these orchestral passages the wit has evaporated and the meaning become inscrutable. There never was any meaning or wit in them in his sense any more than there is wit or meaning in the crash of Wagner's cymbals or the gallop of his trombones in the Valkyries' ride. The producer who has a head for syllogisms cuts such passages out. The producer who has an ear for music,

like Mr Granville-Barker, breaks his heart in trying
to get them adequately executed.

Then take my own celebrated criticisms of Shakespear, written when the Bard, like all the other dramatists, was staggering under the terrible impact of Ibsen.
Can men whose intellectual standards have been
screwed up to Goethe's Faust, Wagner's Ring, and
"deep revolving" Ibsen's soul histories, be expected to
sit and listen to such penny-reading twaddle as The
Seven Ages of Man, or even Hamlet's soliloquy on
suicide? Out with the lot of them, then: let us cut the
cackle and come to the 'osses.

I might pile Pelion on Ossa with illustrations of the
passages that might very well be cut out of Shakespear's plays on Mr Archer's grounds and on mine
and on Garrick's, Irving's, etc., etc., etc. It is clear
that you need only a sufficiently large and critical
committee of producers instead of a single producer to
cut out the entire play, a conclusion which most
managers reach without the assistance of a committee.
It is equally clear that to avoid this reduction to common sense the only workable plan is Mr Barker's plan,
which makes Shakespear, and not the producer, the
ultimate authority. That Shakespear is a bore and even
an absurdity to people who cannot listen to blank
verse and enjoy it as musicians listen to an opera
(Shakespear's methods are extremely like Verdi's);
that Mr George Robey, heroically trying to find jokes
crude enough for an audience of rustic Tommies,
would shrink from Touchstone's story about the beef
and the mustard; that we who think it funny to call
a man's head his nut remain joyless when Shakespear
calls it his costard (not knowing that a costard is an
apple); that Benedick cannot amuse or fascinate the
young ladies who have adored Robert Loraine and
Granville-Barker as Jack Tanner; that William's puns
are as dead as Tom Hood's or Farnie's; that Elizabethan English is a half-dead language and Euphuist
English unintelligible and intolerable: all these un-
deniable facts are reasons for not performing Shake-

spear's plays at all, but not reasons for breaking them up and trying to jerry-build modern plays with them, as the Romans broke up the Coliseum to build hovels. Businesslike and economical as that procedure seems (for why waste good material?), experience remorselessly proves that Shakespear making a fool of himself is more interesting than the judicious producer correcting him. The people who really want Shakespear want all of him, and not merely Mr Archer's or anyone else's favorite bits; and this not in the least because they enjoy every word of it, but because they want to be sure of hearing the words they do enjoy, and because the effect of the judiciously selected passages, not to mention injudiciously selected passages, is not the same as that of the whole play, just as the effect of the currants picked out of a bun is not the same as that of the whole bun, indigestible as it may be to people who do not like buns.

There are plenty of modern instances to go upon. I have seen Peer Gynt most judiciously and practically cut by Lugné-Poë, and The Wild Duck cut to the bone by Mr Archer. I have seen Wagner at full length at Bayreuth and Munich, and cut most sensibly at Covent Garden. I have actually seen Il Trovatore, most swift and concise of operas, cut by Sir Thomas Beecham. My own plays, notoriously too long, have been cut with masterly skill by American managers. Mr Henry Arthur Jones made a capital acting version of A Doll's House, entitled Breaking a Butterfly. I do not allege that the result has always been disastrous failure, though it has sometimes gone that far. A hash makes a better meal than an empty plate. But I do aver without qualification that the mutilation has always been an offence, and the effect different and worse both in degree and in kind from the effect of a remorselessly faithful performance. Wagner's remark when he heard Rossini's Barber of Seville performed for once in its integrity in Turin applies to all the works of the great masters. You get something from such a performance that the selections never give you. And I suggest that this is not wholly a mystery. It occurs only when the work is produced under the direction of a manager who understands its value and can find in every passage the charm or the function which induced the author to write it, and who can dictate or suggest the method of execution that brings out that charm or discharges that function. Without this sense and this skill the manager will cut, cut, cut, every time he comes to a difficulty; and he will put the interest of the refreshment bars and the saving of electric light and the observance of the conventional hours of beginning the performance before his duty to the author, maintaining all the time that the manager who cuts most is the author's best friend.

In short, there are a thousand more sensible reasons for cutting not only Shakespear's plays, but all plays, all symphonies, all operas, all epics, and all pictures which are too large for the dining-room. And there is absolutely no reason on earth for not cutting them except the design of the author, who was probably too conceited to be a good judge of his own work.

The sane conclusion is therefore that cutting must be dogmatically ruled out, because, as Lao-Tse said, "of the making of reforms there is no end." The simple thing to do with a Shakespear play is to perform it. The alternative is to let it alone. If Shakespear made a mess of it, it is not likely that Smith or Robinson will succeed where he failed.

Lord Grey, Shakespear, Mr Archer, and Others

(Letter in *The Nation*, London, XXV, September 6, 1919)

Now that Lord Grey has been sent to the United States to represent us there, I am moved by Mr Robert Dell's allusion to me to declare that though I have called the policy of our Foreign Office during Lord

Grey's secretaryship a Machiavellian policy, I do not regard Lord Grey as a Machiavelli. I heartily wish he were. I think Mr Dell has hit him off very accurately, except that when an English country gentleman is so "simple-minded" that he never knows what he is doing, and can, therefore, at any moment assure the country in all honor that he is not doing it, his simplicity is not of the kind called holy.

I should not myself have sent Lord Grey to America, or even, since our successes in the East, to Jericho. As an English country gentleman, Lord Grey regards Americans as outsiders, and Tsars as insiders. He made that clear in his dealings with Mr Morgan Shuster. He may have been right. But that is not the point, which is, that as our relations with America are extremely delicate just at present, and likely to become more so, and as the Americans do not regard themselves as outsiders (possibly again quite wrongly), the appointment of Lord Grey is hardly the masterpiece of tact it has been hailed as by the British press.

As to what Lord Grey will do in America, which is, after all, the important thing, he will be well received in American society. The conscious part of him will respond very agreeably to these attentions; and his speeches will be reassuring and quite intelligent and pleasant. And the unconscious part of him will fall into the hands of whoever the Japanese equivalent of Isvolsky may be, and will manoeuvre for a stranglehold on our most formidable rival now that Germany is disposed of. What else is there for Lord Grey to do, with his official traditions, and his instincts as "a simple-minded country gentleman"?

Now if there is one point more than another at which the Americans mistrust and dread our old diplomacy it is the Japanese point. The *Einkreisung* is too obvious. You will never persuade the American diplomats that Lord Grey has not a secret treaty with Japan in his pocket. And that is why I would not have sent Lord Grey to America.

I shall be asked, I suppose, whom I would send

instead of Lord Grey, the implication being that he
is the only diplomatist in the Empire. I reply, precisely
and without a moment's hesitation, that I should have
sent Mr H. L. Mackinder. Not so much because he is
a man of ability so distinguished that he may be
classed as one of our few geniuses, because that fact
is indiscernible in the House of Commons, which is
as unconscious of his being anyone in particular as it
was for thirty years of Lord Rhondda. I should send
him because he knows that North and South America
are only a couple of perilously situated islands, and
that it is dangerous for us to tomfool with island
security.

And now for a cheerful change of subject to my
friend Mr Archer, who, by being reasonable while Mr
Drinkwater and I and Mr Granville-Barker and Mr
Poel and the rest of us, have, as Mr Archer rightly
puts it, abjured the exercise of reason, produces an
impression of entire and perfect madness. One imagines Mr Archer at an orchestral concert, remonstrating with the audience, "What went ye out for to see?
Here is a man on a platform waving a stick threaten-
ingly at a herd of slaves in evening dress, who fran-
tically swallow and regurgitate lengths of brass tubing,
clash brass disks, thump the parchment covers of
monstrous jampots, and rub pieces of wood together
like the Swiss Family Robinson trying to light a fire,
to no apparent purpose but the combination of an
unseemly spectacle with a deafening din. Is this good
sense? Have you eyes? What do you mean by it?"

Mr Archer has not done full justice to his own
criticism of Shakespear. He says very truly that it is
not common sense to play Shakespear at full length.
But it is not common sense to play Shakespear at any
length. It is not common sense to act plays at all:
before such an absurdity is possible the actors and
the audiences have to make a tacit compact that good
sense is dethroned. Where is our common sense in
pretending that Sir Johnston Forbes-Robertson is the
Prince of Denmark when the very paper in our hands
tells us expressly that he is Forbes-Robertson, and

when we would walk out of the theatre if it told us that he was really Hamlet, who was only an amateur? Even if you agree to let this go, and only resume the exercise of your reason on minor points, what common sense is there in a melancholy Dane speaking English, and blank verse at that? Look at the man he addresses as father! Are ghosts common sense? Is Elsinore in Shaftesbury Avenue?

Fancy a man devoting forty years of his life to witnessing such lunacies, and writing grave articles in the papers discussing whether they are done efficiently or not! Such a man exists. His name is William Archer. And it is William Archer who lectures me for want of common sense!

When I said that I had seen Ibsen cut to the bone by Mr Archer, I should, perhaps, have mentioned that there is such a tremendous lot of bone in Ibsen that the phrase suggests more cutting than the actual operation involved. One of my early lessons in the erroneousness of cutting was a comparison of the first act of The Wild Duck, reasonably and sensibly cut by Mr Archer, and a subsequent senseless performance of it at full length by Mr Charles Charrington at the old Opera Comique. Mr Archer declares that I am in principle and by habit a liar for saying that he cut it, and then goes on to explain that the cuts were only little ones. I confess that I am not quite convinced of the accuracy of Mr Archer's memory; but I hope he is right, as nothing could strengthen my case more than a demonstration that the cuts which made such an astounding difference were in mere bulk so trifling that it is disingenuous of me to call them cuts at all. The impression produced on me was that about half the first act had been omitted, and that the play never really got on its legs after this act of mayhem. If I am wildly wrong, and Mr Archer's recollection is accurate, then all I can say is that I will never again consent to the omission of even half a comma from any play whatever. Let me add that I shall not be surprised if Mr Archer is right. It is amazing how a play can be altered and defeated by the omission of passages so slight that the author himself, failing to recapture the moment in which he wrote them, becomes a party to their slaughter. Mr Archer is full of praise for Mr Bridges Adams's Stratford uncut productions. Why does he think that the effect would have been improved by cutting? If he looks up some of his notices of heavily-cut performances in the past he will miss the note of genuine artistic satisfaction which rings in the article which began the controversy in your columns.

When Mr Archer says that the lines about the sneaping winds are "wholly incomprehensible to any human being," he tells a whopper so stupendous that the writing of it becomes a heroic gesture. Even of that individual human being called William Archer it is not true. I take the privilege of old friendship, and tell Mr Archer that he knows as well as I do, or as Mr Drinkwater does, that the lines mean quite plainly and unmistakably, "If I don't go home and look after my kingdom, I shall be getting all sorts of alarmist stories; and what's more, they will very likely be true." But even if the line meant nothing, its cadence is so familiar and charming that Mr Archer might just as well cut two bars out of a Mozart symphony as omit it. It is an exact echo of

> That nightly lie in those unproper beds
> Which they dare swear peculiar.

Mr Archer has an ear for verse; he has written some himself; and in his great work of translating Ibsen for us, which in any less barbarous country would be nationally acknowledged by a princely pension, the peculiar quality of his version, which so many brilliant writers have derided only to fail hopelessly when they tried their own hands, is produced entirely by a curious northern music which he has instinctively put into his phrases. I do not know whether he has ever heard idiots abusing his translations. I have; and the point they missed was exactly the point he is missing in Shakespear.

I Am a Classic But Am I
a Shakespear Thief?

(Letter in the *Arts Gazette*, London, II, January 31, 1920; also in *Hearst's Magazine* XXXVIII, September 1920)

In a recent issue of the London Arts Gazette Mr C. G. L. Du Cann has an article under the title, Bernard Shaw as Shakespear Thief, which is one of the most appreciative that has ever been written about me.

I have to correct Mr Du Cann on two points only.

It was I myself who first called attention to the fact that the so-called Shaw heroine is equally the Shakespear heroine. And the motto "Greater than Shakespear"—*Mr Shaw on himself*—is not as accurate textually as the hackneyed quotation from the Bible, "There is no God." There is a section of one of my prefaces headed with the question "Better than Shakespear?" But a question is not an affirmation, especially when it is answered as I answered it.

There are times when journalistic commonplace about famous authors becomes so absurd through journalists never reading their works, and hiding their unacquaintance by a pretence of idolatry, that it becomes necessary to throw in the public face the inevitable and enormous deficiencies of all creators of imaginary worlds, whether they dramatize mere reflections in a mirror held up to nature, or offer an interpretation behind evolution.

When critics assume that the differences between Giotto and Velasquez, Cimabue and Rembrandt, Shakespear and Ibsen, Walter Scott and Conrad, Dickens and Strindberg, Molière and Balzac, Handel and Hugo Wolf, are all superiorities, it is time to remind the public that in some respects the work of the juniors makes the work of the seniors childish by comparison.

Compare my play Arms and the Man with Chekhov's The Cherry Orchard, and if you do not at once perceive that the Russian play is a novel and delicate picture whilst the pseudo-Bulgarian one is a simple theatrical projection effected by a bag of the oldest stage tricks, then I shall form a very poor opinion of your taste.

It does not follow in the least that Chekhov is a better playwright than I, or The Cherry Orchard a greater play than Arms and the Man. The Endymion of Keats is a more exquisite work than the Iliad of Homer or the Divine Comedy of Dante; but the rashest gusher that ever called himself a modernist dare not back it to survive them.

But this business of giving orders of merit to artists as if they were boxing for points is silly.

For stage purposes there are not many types of character available; and all the playwrights use them over and over again. Idiosyncrasies are useful on the stage only to give an air of infinite variety to the standard types. Shakespear's crude Gratiano is Bene-dick, Berowne, and Mercutio, finally evolving through Jacques into Hamlet. He is also my Smilash, my Philanderer, my John Tanner.

Take Falstaff's discourse on honor; and how far are you from Alfred Doolittle's disquisition on middle-class morality?

I could multiply instances; but these glaring ones suffice for illustration. We are plagiarists one of an-other; and if Mr Du Cann will now pass on from me and my characters to Trollope and his Mrs Proudie, Lizzie Eustace, and Lily Dale (who, as forerunner to the young lady in Heartbreak House, wrote "Lily Dale, old maid" in her Bible), and then on to Thackeray, Dickens, Dumas *père,* and the rest of us, he will be able to elaborate his thesis with no more straining than his identification of Juliet with Ann Whitefield has cost him.

In short, Mr Du Cann is quite right.

I am a Classic.

I have never pretended to be anything else.

I play the old game in the old way, on the old

chessboard, with the old pieces, just as Shakespear
did. And the amazing fact that I have ever been mistaken for anything else is due solely to the ignorance of
literature prevalent among journalists who have no
time for reading, and, indeed, no taste for it: an
ignorance which enables managers to mutilate, travesty, and misrepresent Shakespear without detection
or rebuke, and to impose The Chocolate Soldier, in
which all the young men are cads and cowards, all
the old men *vieux marcheurs,* and all the women
prostitutes and nymphomaniacs, on the press as a
musical version of Arms and the Man, though it has
not one line or character to which I could have put my
hand.

The difference between comedy and pornography,
between tragedy and butcherly blank-verse bugaboo,
does not exist for popular criticism. And the funny
consequence is that when, bored by the artificial
"constructions" which supplanted genuine classic
drama on the Parisian stage in the nineteenth century,
I turned from the cat's-cradles in which some pitiful
"situation" was nursed into the semblance of a whole
play by the industrious apprentices of Scribe, and
went back to Shakespear, and finally even to the
Athenian theatre with its unities of time and place,
the journalists, never having seen anything of the kind
before, nor read a line of Shakespear or Sophocles,
classed me, first, as a Fabian who (of course) did not
know a play from a pamphlet, and was totally ignorant of stagecraft, and then, when that did not work,
as an innovator, an ultra-modernist, a scorner of all
rules and conventions, and a revolutionary practitioner of methods hitherto unheard of in the theatre.

Not until the younger generation, Shavians to a
man, demonstrated their Shavianity by scoffing at me
as a Back Number (that being the up-to-date way
to *épater le bourgeois* in the theatre) and even calling
me Roebuck Ramsden, did my own contemporaries
come to the conclusion, after taking a full quarter-
century to consider it, that Arms and the Man is a

classic, though they desire it to be distinctly understood that all my later works are Futurist extrava-
ganzas.

At last comes Mr Du Cann and declares that
"idolaters of Shakespeare and idolaters of Shaw (including the god himself) will be equally amazed to
hear that there is a good deal of Shakespeare in
Bernard Shaw's plays."

Of course there is; and of course the Bardolaters
will rend their garments and exclaim that Mr Du Cann
must be beside himself. But why should *I* be amazed?
I have entered into a great inheritance from the
Athenians, from Shakespear and Molière, from Goethe,
Mozart, and Wagner, and from the great novelists
who came to the rescue when the stage had fallen
into contempt, not to mention later legacies from
Ibsen and the Russians; and I have spent this magnificent fortune prodigally in the face of the world.

Where and when have I professed to be the most
ridiculous of frauds, a Self-made Man, that Mr Du
Cann should imagine that his communication must
amaze me?

I can only pay him the ironical Irish compliment,
"You would guess eggs if you saw the shells."

Letter to J. T. Grein

(Used as "Introductory" to *The World of the Theatre.
Impressions and Memoirs, March 1920–1921*, London,
1921)

My dear Grein: It is now very close on thirty years
since you madly began an apparently hopeless attempt
to bring the English theatre into some sort of relation
with contemporary culture. Matthew Arnold had suggested that step; but nobody in the theatre took the
slightest notice of him, because nobody in the theatre
knew of the existence of such a person as Matthew

Arnold. That was what was the matter with the theatre
then. There was nothing wrong with the acting: I cannot remember any actor or actress then occupying
a leading position who could be called an amateur or
a duffer: they had all been "through the mill," and
could make intruders who had not, look ridiculous.
The theatres were better managed than they are now:
the front of the house was not always controlled by
the bar; and at the best theatres all petty cadgings
like charges for programs and cloak room fees were
abolished. The public was so seriously interested in
the theatre that it booked seats months in advance:
in fact, it was by the booking that a manager knew
when his run was coming to an end. Photographs of
actors and actresses cost a shilling each; and at this
price the Stereoscopic Company did a big trade in
them. At every point except the one point of culture
and contact with the life of the time the theatre was
in a more dignified position than it occupies today.
If you and I could have set the Bancrofts, the Kendals,
the Rorkes, Hare and Wyndham and Irving and
Forbes-Robertson and Ada Rehan, to work in live
contemporary drama, the London stage would have
led Europe triumphantly. Forbes-Robertson's Caesar
proved it.

As it was, these artists were kept up to the mark
by the continual effort to pass off literary scarecrows
as heroes and heroines. The generation which succeeded them at the *fin de siècle* acquired this art and
acquired nothing else (never having had the chance);
so that you got actors and actresses who had an enchanting power of persuading you that they could say
and do the most wonderful things when the moment
came; but the author had to be particularly careful
to get the curtain down before it came; for when you
called on them, as Shakespear does for instance, not
for suggestion, but for execution, they knew better
than to give themselves away by trying. Shakespear
then became physically impossible. As the notion of
performing his plays as he meant them to be per-

formed never occurred to anyone but Mr William Poel, who was regarded consequently as the absurdest of cranks, the Bard had already become a mere stalking-horse for the scene painter, the costumier, and the spectacular artists generally. His plays were presented in mutilated fragments, divided into acts with long waits between, in which form they were so horribly boresome, being mostly unintelligible, that only the most powerful personal fascination could induce play-goers to endure him. As long as this fascination was associated with great executive power, Shakespear did not always "spell ruin," as the phrase went then. Whilst the actor could not only look as if he could say tremendous things, but could actually say them tremendously when he got the chance, it was possible for Barry Sullivan, who turned his back on London with disdain because he lost £800 in three months and was not used to such treatment, to die worth £100,000. But when the fascination was divorced from executive power, the Shakespearean game was up for the young of the old school. It was the young of the new school who discovered that Poel had really struck the trail. Then you got Granville-Barker, Drinkwater, Bridges Adams, and Fagan establishing genuine Shakespear on the English stage, and extracting from the play the fascination for which their fathers would have looked to the actor alone.

Now you may ask what this has to do with you, who never meddled with Shakespear. I assure you you had a great deal to do with it. When you first desperately stuck an advertisement into the papers to say that an unheard-of enterprise called the Independent Theatre would on a certain Sunday night and Monday afternoon perform an unheard-of play, totally unlike any play then current in the theatrical market; when the papers thereupon declared that the manager of the theatre ought to be prosecuted for keeping a disorderly house, and that you and the foreign blackguard named Ibsen who was your accomplice, should be deported as obvious undesirables, you made a hole in the dyke; and the weight of the flood outside did the rest. When you declared that you would bring to light treasures of unacted English drama grossly suppressed by the managers of that day, you found that there was not any unacted English drama except two acts of an unfinished play (begun and laid aside eight years before) by me; but it was the existence of the Independent Theatre that made me finish that play, and by giving me the experience of its rehearsal and performance, revealed the fact (to myself among others) that I possessed the gift of "fingering" the stage. That old play now seems as remote and old-fashioned as Still Waters Run Deep or London Assurance; but the newspapers of 1892 raged over it for a whole fortnight. Everything followed from that: the production of Arms and the Man by Miss Horniman and Florence Farr at the Avenue Theatre, Miss Horniman's establishment of Repertory Theatres in Dublin and Manchester, the Stage Society, H. Granville-Barker's tentative matinées of Candida at the Court Theatre, the full-blown management of Vedrenne and Barker, Edie Craig's Pioneers, and the final relegation of the Nineteenth Century London theatre to the dust-bin by Barrie. At present the cry in the papers is that the theatre is hopelessly out of date, that it needs fresh air, new ideas, scrapping of traditions and conventions. The most famous apostle of the new theatre has declared publicly that what has been holding the theatre back for twenty years past and making all reform impossible is not Sardou but Shaw. If only we could give the young lions a ride on Wells's Time Machine and take them back to 1892!

Well, more power to their elbows! I am always delighted to hear a clamor for new ideas, or indeed for ideas of any sort, in the theatre. So, I have no doubt, are you. But the clamorers will hardly see a revolution like the one you began by making the hole in the dyke. It is the second revolution that England owes to a Dutchman.   G.B.S.

Shakespear: A Standard Text

(To *The Times Literary Supplement*, Thursday, March 17, 1921; reprinted as "Knots in Shakespeare's Handkerchief," *Hearst's Magazine* XXXIX, June 1921)

Sir,—May I, as a publishing playwright, point out to Mr William Poel (who knows it already) that it is at present impossible to write or print a play fully or exactly in ordinary script or type? And it never will be possible until we establish in popular use a fixed and complete notation, such as musicians possess. No such notation exists in a shape intelligible to the general reader. Therefore the first flat fact to be faced is that the printers of the Shakespear Folio and the Quartos could not indicate how the Elizabethan actor spoke his lines, whether they were trying to do so or not. No doubt, when the Elizabethan punctuation of plays is more than usually crazy, as where, for instance, an unaccountable colon appears where there should be no stop at all, it may not be a mere misprint: the compositor may have set up some mark made in his copy by somebody in the theatre for some purpose. It does not follow that it was a stop written by Shakespear for publication. If we found one of Shakespear's handkerchiefs with a knot on it, we might reasonably conjecture that he had knotted it to remind him of something he was afraid of forgetting; but what sane producer of Othello would tie a knot in Desdemona's fatal handkerchief on the ground that all Elizabethan handkerchiefs were worn knotted? All actors and all producers and all prompters make marks on their parts and copies to indicate emphasis, strokes of stage business, signals, calls, and the like; but except in the matter of underscoring words, which is common practice, they each make different marks according to private codes of their own. Dots, strokes, crosses, angles indicating the position of the arms, crude footprints mapping the position of the feet, make memoranda perfectly intelligible to the actor who scrawls them, and inscrutable to anyone else. Every producer who knows his business, and does not merely fudge along at rehearsal from entry to entry by trial and error, sprinkles his copy of the play with a home-made shorthand which nobody but he can decipher. Even the prompter, whose copy should serve for his successors as well as himself, distractedly blackleads it until it is often difficult to make out the text, and impossible to understand the directions.

Now imagine manuscript copies treated in this way and then handed to a printer to set up, or to a scrivener to make fair copy for the printer. How is the scrivener to tell whether these dots and dashes and scriggles and crosses and clockhands and queries and notes of admiration are meant for stops or not? It is easy to say that he can use his common sense; but neither scriveners nor compositors are highly educated enough to understand everything they copy or set up: setting up Shakespear must often be very like setting up Einstein or Homer in the original. Thus what looks like a colon, and is set up as such in the Quarto, may mean, "emphasize the next [or previous] word," or "pause significantly," or "don't forget to pronounce the h," or merely the Elizabethan equivalent to "cur-tain warning" or "check your floats and take your ambers out of your number one batten." To cherish it as Shakespear's punctuation, or pretend to greater authenticity for it than for the colons of Rowe or Dr Johnson or Pope or Malone or the Cowden Clarkes or Q, or any modern editor, is next door to Baconian cipher hunting.

Let me recapitulate the process by which the plays got into print. First, Shakespear wrote a play. It may be presumed that he punctuated it; but this is by no means certain. I have on my desk a typed play by a clever young writer whose dialogue is very vivacious, and is that of an educated man accustomed to converse with educated people. It bristles with mad hyphens *à tort et à travers;* but there is not a stop in it from beginning to end except the full stops at the ends of the speeches; and I suspect that these were put in

by the typist. Oscar Wilde sent the MS of An Ideal
Husband to the Haymarket Theatre without taking the
trouble to note the entrances and exits of the persons
on the stage. There is no degree of carelessness that
is not credible to men who know that they will be
present to explain matters when serious work begins.
But let us assume that Shakespear punctuated his
script. From it the scrivener copied out the parts for
the actors, and made a legible prompt copy. That the
scrivener respected Shakespear's stops and "followed
copy" exactly is against even modern experience; and
in the XVI-XVII *fin de siècle*, when scriveners were
proud of their clergy and tenacious of their technical
authority, the scrivener would punctuate as he thought
Shakespear (whom he would despise as an amateur)
ought to have punctuated, and not as he did or did
not punctuate. The copies so produced were then
marked at rehearsal in all sorts of ways by all sorts
of people for all sorts of theatrical purposes. Thus
marked, they were fair-copied again by a scrivener
—possibly the same, possibly another—for the printer.
Now, as all authors know, the printer who does not
consider that punctuation is his special business, and
that authors know nothing about it (they mostly know
very little), has not yet been born. Besides, the printer
of that period would have the tradition that his page
should look well, and that the letterpress should not
be disfigured, as in modern books, by wide spaces
between sentences and words and letters, or by
awkward-looking stops. And so we get two opinionated
scriveners, a whole company of actors and stage
officials, and a tradition-ridden compositor, between
Shakespear's holograph and the printed page. Such
a process applied to an imperfect and inexact notation,
as to the use of which authors and even grammarians
are so little agreed that it cannot be used in legal
documents, leaves the punctuation of the Quartos
and the Folio practically void of authority. Even if it
could be proved that Shakespear corrected the proofs
of the best Quarto texts, I should still defy any

modern editor to follow them stop for stop without publicly washing his hands of all responsibility for them.

This does not mean that there is not a case, and a very strong case, for making facsimiles of the earliest printed texts. A glance through any of the facsimiles already published will discover points at which changes made by modern editors are changes for the worse. But when the utmost has been said that can be said for the readings of the Quartos and the Folio, no middle course is open to a modern editor between a photographic reproduction and a text doctored precisely as the conventional editions have been doctored. If the editor be Mr Granville-Barker, so much the better: he will test the questionable passages on the stage, and retain readings that a mere man of letters would tamper with. If the editor be Mr William Poel, he will print the text in the way that best suggests his divination of its proper delivery. He will run the words together in rapid passages, and bring out keywords in ways undreamt of by Heming and Condell. Such editions would be much more valuable and interesting than superfluous repetitions of existing editions made in the study; but they would not be a whit more "standard" or authentic.

Besides, they would introduce more controversial new readings than any merely literary editor dare venture. For example, take the following ranting and redundant utterance of Macbeth:

> Hang out your banners on the outer walls.
> The cry is still they come.

Barry Sullivan cured both the rant and the redundancy very simply. He entered at the back of the stage throwing an order over his shoulder to his subalterns, and then came down to the footlights to discuss the military situation. Thus we got the reading:

> Hang out your banners. On the outer walls
> the cry is still they come.

This, tested on the stage as Mr Granville-Barker would test it, is a convincing improvement. But the authority for it is not the text as it has come down to us, but Barry Sullivan's conjecture submitted to Mr Barker's test. And Barry Sullivan went further than that. Instead of saying, as Hamlet, "I am but mad north-north-west: when the wind is southerly, I know a hawk from a handsaw," he said, "I know a hawk from a heron. Pshaw!" This may read strainedly; but when acted with appropriate business it is so effective that Mr Barker's stage test would favor its adoption. Such readings, however, would compel Mr Barker to interpolate scores of stage directions for which there would be no authority but his own artistic instinct.

As to Mr Poel, there is no living enthusiast more firmly convinced than he that he knows the mind of Shakespear; and this conviction has nerved him to do yeoman's service to his master. It would nerve him equally to feats that Dr Johnson would have funked. The liberties he would take with the text to square it with his own original and vivid conception of character, theatrical technique, and Elizabethan political history and social structure would rouse a cry of controversy. On that very account a Poel Shakespear should be published, even if it were to consist of only a few specimen plays; and a Granville-Barker Shakespear should rival it. But neither edition could be called a standard edition except by the courtesy which allows every theatre to call itself the Theatre Royal. And the question which of the two famous Shakespearean producers were the more unscrupulous would never be settled.

Now may I be allowed a suggestion of my own? Why not try to make a record of our language as it is spoken today on the stage classically? We have in Forbes-Robertson an actor whose speech is unchallengeable in every English-speaking land, not only in Oxford and the West End of London, but in countries where the dialect of Oxford and the West End is received with shouts of derisive laughter. It does not matter how Forbes-Robertson pronounces this or that vowel: his speech will carry any Englishman anywhere. It is unquestionably proper for a king, for a chief justice, for an archbishop, or for a private gentleman; having acquired it, no one has anything more to learn to qualify himself as a speaker for the most dignified employment. Well, why not begin with an edition of Hamlet in which this Robertsonian speech shall be recorded by phonetic spelling? I am aware that this cannot be done completely except by using Bell's Visible Speech, which nobody but Mr Graham Bell and perhaps a few others can read; but by ekeing out the ordinary alphabet with a few letters turned upside down, and coming to a clearly stated understanding as to the meaning of those which remain right side up, it is quite possible to make a very useful record, supplemented by the existing phonographic records of which Sir Johnston can specify the defects exactly. Such a phonetic edition of Hamlet could be fairly described as a standard Hamlet, valid for its day. The Academic Committee of the Royal Society of Literature could justify its existence by undertaking this work.

As to the text, by all means let Mr Poel's points, and Mr Granville-Barker's points, be considered in making it. Both gentlemen might very well be co-opted to the editing committee. But I implore Mr Poel to dismiss from his mind the notion that there are two punctuations: a grammatical and an oral. The two are the same. Dr Johnson's punctuation of Shakespear's plays, far better on the whole than that of the Quartos or the Folio, is highly suggestive of the stage delivery of Garrick's day. The authorized version of the Bible, punctuated by preachers for preachers, is as oral as it is grammatical. What people call grammatical or literary punctuation is simply unskilled punctuation: the work of writers who pepper a page with commas, and disfigure it with dashes, leaving the printer to supply the semicolons, which he does with a convic-

tion that it is wrong to have two in the same sentence,
and that colons are of the nature of sacred music.
My own punctuation, which is as definite as the
multiplication table, is founded on the best Bible usage
(the Bible is not consistently stopped throughout) and
on the distinctions I find it necessary and possible to
make; and it is both grammatical and oral.

But I must repeat that the notation at my disposal
cannot convey the play as it should really exist: that is,
in its oral delivery. I have to write melodies without
bars, without indications of pitch, pace, or timbre,
and without modulation, leaving the actor or producer
to divine the proper treatment of what is essentially
word-music. I turn over a score by Richard Strauss,
and envy him his bar divisions, his assurance that his
trombone passages will not be played on the triangle,
his power of giving directions without making his
music unreadable. What would we not give for a copy
of Lear marked by Shakespear "somewhat broader,"
"always quieter and quieter," "amiably," or, less trans-
latably, "mit grossem Schwung und Begeisterung,"
"mit Steigerung," much less Meyerbeer's "con es-
plosione," or Verdi's *fffff* or *ppppppp,* or *cantando* or
parlando, or any of the things that I say at rehearsal,
and that in my absence must be left to the intuitions of
some kindred spirit?

It will be seen now, I hope, that this discussion about
the punctuation of the Shakespear Quartos raises the
much more serious question of making the great invention of reading and writing really effective and
educational. It is at present a wretched makeshift.
Children are taught to read at great expense; and
they cannot open their mouths without proving that the
sound of their noble native speech has never been
conveyed to them. They see on paper the words of
their poets, and repeat them in the voices of their
slums. Men whose noses were rubbed ruthlessly into
books and copybooks every day for nine years at
elementary schools are unemployable as butlers or
West End shop assistants because they cannot form a

grammatical sentence nor utter a sound that is admissible in cultivated society. Others, cultivated in country houses, and educated at Eton and Oxford, have their speech represented by Oxford's greatest phonetic experts as follows:

> Tell mii not in mɔnfl nambəz
> Laif iz bat ən emti driim
> Fɔ dhə sowl iz ded dhət slambəz
> aend thingz aa not whot dhei sijm.

To turn this into coster's cockney, all that is necessary is to change "tell" into "t'yoll," "laif" into "lawf," "aa" into "aw," and "dhei" into "dhy." Ask Forbes-Robertson to declaim the verse, and you will hear something quite different from either: to wit, the English language in the only form that has a right to call itself standard. But this English will be dead presently, unless we take the trouble and cultivate the artistic conscience to provide it with a notation. At most, I suppose, we shall continue to dispute whether "labour" or "labor" is the correct spelling, in crude ignorance of the fact that both inaccuracies are merely confessions of our inability to write the obscure vowel that is the commonest sound in our language. As to enabling me to hand down my plays as Sir Edward Elgar can hand down his Falstaff, I see no chance of that in literature. Perhaps the phonograph may be able to do something for me before I die; otherwise, like Shakespear, I shall take the secret of their performance to the grave with me, and with it almost all their artistic value, leaving posterity (if it troubles itself about them) to gnaw the cold bones of their intellectual skeletons.

Yours truly,

G. Bernard Shaw

(*Times Literary Supplement,* March 31, 1921)

Sir,—Professor Pollard challenges me. Well, if it comes to that, I challenge him. I challenge him to prove (1) that Shakespear knew how to write, and did not dictate his inspirations to the theatre scrivener; (2) that Shakespear ever used a comb before he became bald, or that Queen Elizabeth ever used hairpins; (3) that any mortar or scantling was used in the construction of the Globe Theatre; (4) that the lady at whose house Burbage found Shakespear on a famous occasion was ever baptized; and finally (not to go on like this for ever) that my own plays have not been studied and stage managed in the theatre from my own original manuscripts and subsequently set up by the printer from them.

He cannot do it.

A still better game than challenging is asking questions. I ask Professor Pollard has he ever seen Shakespear's handwriting; and would he like to study the part of Hamlet from it if he were an actor and the first night were only a fortnight off? I ask him has he ever written a play; and, if so, would anything induce him to sit down and copy out all the parts separately for the actors with his own hand when he could get somebody else to do it more legibly and tidily for the fiftieth part of the value of his own time?

In this, as in every other historical question, we must, in the absence of evidence, proceed upon normal assumptions, positive as well as negative. I contend that Professor Pollard can escape my positive assumptions only by advancing negative assumptions which are manifestly outrageous. There must have been somebody in the theatre whose business it was to keep the theatre library of prompt copies, and whose perquisite it was to copy out the parts and make fair copy for the prompter. In the same way, if there was a band, there must have been a music librarian (by tradition the drummer), who kept the band parts, and whose perquisite it was to copy them. To ask me to prove these things is like asking me to prove that Henry the Eighth had a bootmaker. To deny them is virtually to deny that there were any plays or any theatre at all, just as to deny the bootmaker is virtually to deny the boots. Surely Professor Pollard has had enough of the sort of controversy that, beginning with a demand for proof that Shakespear ever existed, has led to the crazy fictions known as "the man Shakespear," "Shaxper of Stratford" (both illiterate imbeciles acting as "ghost" to Bacon), proceeding to Shakespear the illegitimate son of Queen Elizabeth, and so on to no Shakespear at all, but to every Elizabethan peer who could knock a sonnet together. All that nonsense followed inevitably from the first suspension of common sense as something too vulgar to be applicable to an immortal. "Others abide our question: thou art free" was said of Shakespear, not of his commentators, though they have mostly assumed that privilege.

Having now dutifully kept up the readableness of the correspondence by this exhibition spar with the Professor, let me get to business and say, though he is satisfied (having given more attention to the subject and put more work into it than I have) that "there is a substantial body of evidence that many of the first editions of Shakespeare's plays were, as a fact, set up from prompt copies," there is no evidence at all that these copies were made by Shakespear. In fact, if they were prompt copies, meaning copies made for use at rehearsal, or made in the theatre in the same way and by the same official as if they were for use at rehearsal, they certainly were not made by Shakespear. And what other copies could they have been? Heming and Condell would naturally have had copies made for the printer in this way, and would not have used the copies actually wanted on the stage. There is just one barely credible alternative; and that is that Heming and Condell may have given the printer the original manuscript in Shakespear's handwriting from which the first prompt copies were made, and which Shakespear may have used himself at rehearsal as the author's copy. In the case of some of the quartos, Shakespear may have given the printer his own copy: in the case of others, the prompter, bribed by the pirate, may have given the original MS to save himself the trouble of copying it. These are pitifully thin conjectures; but they are not utterly incredible; and if Professor Pollard can substantiate them he may claim a little more authority for the printed texts than they can be allowed on the far more probable case as stated by me. But in any case the position as I have put it remains unshaken. There is no intermediate possibility between facsimiles of the folio and quartos and an edition edited as all the editions from Rowe's to Quiller-Couch's have been edited.

Yours truly,

G. Bernard Shaw.

(*Times Literary Supplement*, April 14, 1921)

Sir,—I gather from Professor Pollard's letter that I somehow managed in my last communication to assume that the theatres in which Shakespear's plays were first produced were equipped with revolving stage, hydraulic bridges, electric lights, Fortuny horizons, telephones, typewriters, and cinema lanterns. This was an unfortunate aberration on my part; for I protest I was perfectly sober when I wrote the letter, and meant to assume nothing beyond the barest necessities of the simplest theatrical establishment in the spacious times of great Elizabeth. I am sorry I did not make myself clear.

This time I hope it may emerge from the obscurity of my style that if Shakespear had wasted his time making legible copies of the parts in A Midsummer Night's Dream when he could have set himself free to write The Merchant of Venice by hiring some poor devil of a scrivener to make the copies for a few groats per folio, he would never have been able to buy the best house in the main street of his native town. Is that clear?

Ben Jonson complained that Shakespear could not be induced to read over his own plays when he had written them. Professor Pollard thinks that he sat down and laboriously fair-copied them word for word for the actors. Or can it be that Professor Pollard thinks that all that is necessary for the production of a play is one copy, from which a dozen actors learn their parts simultaneously? Here be "normal assumptions" indeed!

I take Professor Pollard's word for it that it was Massinger's autograph of Believe As You List that was submitted for license to the Master of the Revels. Of course it was. Surely the Professor does not believe that managers spend money on a play, whether for copying or dressing or scene painting or what not, until they know whether they are going to be allowed to perform it or not. The original manuscript must have been sent up for license whenever the author could write legibly enough. It was not until the license had been obtained that the rehearsals began, and with them the need for copies. It is possible that the original may have been used at rehearsal by the author or prompter or stage manager. If it was, it would get scrawled with such flowers of dramatic poesy as "whistle Boy," just as I explained so laboriously in my first letter. So what on earth is Professor Pollard nagging me about? Did I offer to say a word to the gentleman?

Finally, I assure Mr Dover Wilson that I have no doubt that the Cambridge University Press will follow the punctuation of the Folios and Quartos as closely as possible. Why shouldn't it? But how closely will that be without consigning the editor to an asylum for hopeless illiterates? Will the C.U.P. edition be virtually a facsimile of the Elizabethan printed texts or will it not? If so, I told Mr Dover Wilson so. If not, the editor will have to use his judgment just as Dr Johnson did. I told Mr Dover Wilson he would.

Is this correspondence about a standard text of Shakespear or is it about me? If the former, I suggest that future contributors should have the self-denial not to contradict me when they do not disagree with me.

G. Bernard Shaw.

On Clive Bell's Article

(*The New Republic* XXIX, February 22, 1922. In his article, "The Creed of an Aesthete," January 25, Bell said: "Mr. Bernard Shaw . . . is not an artist, much less an aesthete . . . he is a didactic.")

As will be seen in the above article, my friend Clive Bell is a fathead and a voluptuary. This is a very comfortable sort of person to be, and very friendly and easy and pleasant to talk to. Bell is a brainy man out of training. So much the better for his friends; for men in training are irritable, dangerous, and apt to hit harder than they know. No fear of that from Clive. The layer of fat on his brain makes him incapable of following up his own meaning; but it makes him good company.

A man out of condition muscularly not only dislikes rowing or boxing, but cannot conceive anyone liking them. A man out of condition mentally not only dislikes hard thinking, but cannot conceive anyone enjoying it. To Falstaff, Carpentier is an object of pity. To Clive, Einstein is the most miserable of mortals. So am I.

He is mistaken as to both of us. Intellect is a passion: and its activity and satisfaction, which can be maintained from seven years old to 107 if you can manage to live so long, are keenly pleasurable if the brain is strong enough for the exercise. Descartes must have got far more pleasure out of life than Casanova. Hamlet had more fun than Des Grieux, who tried to live on his love for Manon Lescaut, relieved by cheating at cards. Clive tells us how he poisons the clear night air of London with his cheroots after an evening of wine, woman, and song; and he is contemptuously certain that he has enjoyed himself far more than a handful of old gentlemen in a society of chemists, mathematicians, biologists, or what not, discussing the latest thing in quantums of energy, or electrons, or hormones. It is the interest of the tobacconist, the restaurateur, the theatrical manager, the wine merchant and distiller, to suggest that delusion to him. And what a silly delusion it is! No pleasure of the first order is compatible with tobacco and alcohol, which are useful only for killing time and drowning care. For real pleasure men keep their senses and wits clear: they do not deliberately dull and muddle themselves. I have not the smallest doubt that when the human mind is as fully developed as the human reproductive processes now are, men will, like the ancients in Back to Methuselah, experience a sustained ecstasy of thought that will make our sexual ecstasies seem child's play.

Clive is troubled—you know it when he cries Who cares?—because a rose grows out of manure. This comes of taking hold of things by the wrong end. Why not rejoice because manure grows into a rose? The most valuable lesson in Back to Methuselah is that things are conditioned not by their origins but by their ends. What makes the Ancient wise is not the life he has lived and done with but the life that is before him. Clive says why not live in the present? Because we don't, and won't, and can't. Because there is no such thing as the present: there is only the gate that we are always reaching and never passing through: the gate that leads from the past into the future. Clive, meaning to insist on static sensation, slips inevitably

into talking of "*the significance* of all that comes to
one through the senses." What then becomes of his
figment of sense without significance? "Whatever is
precious and beautiful in life," he says, "is precious
and beautiful irrespective of beginning and end."
Bosh! The only sensations intense enough to be called
precious or beautiful are the sensations of irresistible
movement to an all-important end: the only perceptions that deserve such epithets are perceptions of
some artistic expression of such sensation or pre-
figured ideal of its possibilities. The pain with which
a child cuts its teeth, though felt, is not suffered because the child feels it as Clive pretends to feel his
pleasures: that is, it cannot anticipate the next moment
of it or remember the last; and so, fretful as it may
seem, it does not suffer at all. If Clive ever gets his
pleasures down to the point at which he also does not
anticipate the future or remember the past, he will
not enjoy it in the least. In short, his imaginary present
and its all sufficing delight is unconsidered tosh.

The reason Clive enjoys his suppers is that he first
works hard enough to need relaxation—at least I
presume and hope he does. If he did not he would be
miserable, and would probably have to take to drugs
to enable him to bear his pleasant evenings at the
Russian Ballet. Even now he cannot get through them
without the aid of cheroots. I never eat supper; I
never smoke; I drink water; and I can sit out
Petrouchka and enjoy the starlight in Piccadilly all
the same. But clearly, if I could be persuaded that
Petrouchka, instead of being a relaxation, is as creative
as the Piccadilly starlight is recreative, I should enjoy
it a thousand times more. So would anybody.

No, my Clive: in vain do you sing

> Sun, stand thou still upon Gibeon,
> And thou, Moon, in the valley of Ajalon.

They will not stop for you. Lopokova will dance, as
you say; but when you stretch your arms to her and
cry

Verweile doch, du bist so schön

you cannot stop, either of you, any more than Paolo and
Francesca could stop in the whirlwind. You delight
in the music of Mozart; but does it ever stop? It ends;
but your delight ends with it. You are a destinate
creature, and must hurry along helter-skelter; so what
is the use of waving your cheroots at us and assuring
us that you are motionless and meaningless? There is
nothing in the world more ridiculous than a man
running at full speed, and shouting to everyone that
he is in no hurry, and does not care two straws where
he is going to.

The Art of Rehearsal

(A letter to an Irish colleague in response to a request for
advice and information. *Arts League of Service Annual,
1921–22;* also in *Collier's Weekly,* June 24, 1922, under
the title "Make Them Do It Well." Issued as a pamphlet
under its original title, Samuel French, New York, 1928)

My Dear McNulty:
As to stage technique, there are several stage tech-
niques; and people may be very clever in one or more
of them without being good at them all, and may
even—especially in acting—know bits of them and
not the rest. The beginning and end of the business
from the author's point of view is the art of making
the audience believe that real things are happening
to real people. But the actor, male or female, may want
the audience to believe that it is witnessing a magnificent display of acting by a great artist; and when
the attempt to do this fails, the effect is disastrous,
because then there is neither play nor great acting:
the play is not credible nor the acting fascinating.
To your star actor the play does not exist except as a
mounting block. That is why comparatively humble
actors, who do not dare to think they can succeed
apart from the play, often give much better representations than star casts.

Many star actors have surprisingly little of what I call positive skill, and an amazing power of suggestion. You can safely write a play in which the audience is assured that the heroine is the most wonderful creature on earth, full of exquisite thoughts, and noble in character to the utmost degree, though, when it comes to the point, you find yourself unable to invent a single speech or action that would surprise you from your aunt. No matter: a star actress at $1,000 a week will do all that for you. She will utter your twaddle with such an air, and look such unutterable things between the lines, and dress so beautifully and move so enigmatically and enchantingly, that the imagination of the audience will supply more than Shakespear could have written.

This art of suggestion has been developed to an abnormal degree by the emptiness of the mechanical "well-made play" of the French school. And you may be tempted to say: "If this woman is so wonderful when she is making bricks without straw, what heights would she not reach if I were to give her straw in abundance?" But if you did, you would be rudely disillusioned. You would have to say to the actress: "Mere suggestion is no use here. I don't ask you to suggest anything: I give you the actual things to do and say. I don't want you to look as if you could say wonderful things if you uttered your thoughts: I give you both the thoughts and the words; and you must get them across the footlights." On these conditions your star might be dreadfully at a loss. She might complain of having too many words. She would certainly try hard to get in her old suggestive business between the lines; to escape from the play; to substitute a personal performance of her own for the character you wanted to make the audience believe her to be; and thus your trouble with her would be in direct proportion to her charm as a fashionable leading lady.

The success of the Dublin Abbey Street Theatre was due to the fact that, when it began, none of the

THE ART OF REHEARSAL

company was worth twopence a week for ordinary
fashionable purposes, though some of them can now
hold a London audience in the hollow of their hands.
They were held down by Yeats and Lady Gregory
ruthlessly to my formula of making the audience believe that real things were happening to real people.
They were taught no tricks, because Yeats and Lady
Gregory didn't know any, having found out experi-
mentally only what any two people of high intelligence
and fine taste could find out by sticking to the point
of securing a good representation.

Now as to your daily business in the theatre. It will
be more laborious than you expect. If before you begin
rehearsing you sit down to the manuscript of your
play and work out all the stage business; so that you
know where every speech is to be spoken as well as
what it is to convey, and where the chairs are to be
and where they are to be taken to, and where the
actors are to put their hats or anything else they have
to take in their hands in the course of the play, and
when they are to rise and when they are to sit, and if
you arrange all this so as to get the maximum of effect
out of every word, and thus make the actors feel that
they are speaking at the utmost possible advantage—
or at worst that they cannot improve on your business
however little they may like it—and if you take care
that they never distract attention from one another;
that when they call to one another they are at a due
distance; and that, when the audience is looking at
one side of the stage and somebody cuts in on the
other, some trick (which you must contrive) calls the
attention of the audience to the new point of view
or hearing, etc., then you will at the first rehearsal get
a command of the production that nothing will shake
afterward. There will be no time wasted in fumbling
for positions, and trying back and disputing.

When you have put your actors through an act for
the first time in this way, go through it again to settle
the business firmly in their memory. Be on the stage,
handling your people and prompting them with the

appropriate tones, as they will, of course, be rather
in the dark as to what it is all about, except what they
may have gathered from your reading the play to them
before rehearsal. Don't let them learn their parts until
the end of the first week of rehearsal: nothing is a
greater nuisance than an actor who is trying to remember his lines when he should be settling his position and getting the hang of the play with his book in
his hand.

One or two acts twice over is enough for each pre-
liminary rehearsal. When you have reached the end
of this first stage, then call "perfect" rehearsals (that
is, without books). At these you must leave the stage
and sit in the auditorium with a big notebook, *and
from that time forth never interrupt a scene, nor allow
anyone else to interrupt it or try back*. When anything
goes wrong, or any improvement occurs to you, make a
note; and at the end of the act go on the stage and
explain your notes to the actors. Don't criticize. If a
thing is wrong and you don't know exactly how to
set it right say nothing. Wait until you find out the
right thing to do, or until the actor does. It discour-
ages and maddens an actor to be told merely that you
are dissatisfied. If you cannot help him, let him alone.
Tell him what to do if you know: if not, hold your
tongue until it comes to you or to him, as it probably
will if you wait.

Remember that when the "perfect" rehearsals begin,
the whole affair will collapse in apparent and most
disappointing backsliding for at least a week as far
as the long parts are concerned, because in the first
agony of trying to remember the words everything
else will be lost. You must remember that at this stage
the actor, being under a heavy strain, is fearfully irritable. But after another week the words will come
automatically; and the play will get under way again.

Remember (particularly during the irritable stage)
that you must not tell an actor too much all at once.
Not more than two or three important things can be

borne at one rehearsal; and *don't* mention trifles, such as slips in business or in words, in a heartbroken desperate way, as if the world were crumbling in ruins. Don't mention anything that doesn't really matter. Be prepared for the same mistake being repeated time after time, and your directions being forgotten until you have given them three or four days running.

If you get angry, and complain that you have repeatedly called attention, etc., like a schoolmaster, you will destroy the whole atmosphere in which art breathes, and make a scene which is not in the play, and a very disagreeable and invariably unsuccessful scene at that. Your chief artistic activity will be to prevent the actors taking their tone and speed from one another, instead of from their own parts, and thus destroying the continual variety and contrast which are the soul of liveliness in comedy and truth in tragedy. An actor's cue is not a signal to take up the running thoughtlessly, but a provocation to retort or respond in some clearly differentiated way. He must, even on the thousandth night, make the audience believe that he has never heard his cue before.

In the final stage, when everybody is word perfect, and can give his or her whole mind to the play, you must watch, watch, watch, like a cat at a mouse hole, and make very well-considered notes. To some of them you will append a "Rehearse this"; and at the end of the act you will ask them to go through the bit to get it right. But *don't* say when it doesn't come right: "We must go on at this until we get it, if we have to stay here all night": the schoolmaster again. If it goes wrong, it will go wronger with every repetition on the same day. Leave it until next time.

At the last two rehearsals you ought to have very few notes: all the difficulties should have been cleared away. The first time I ever counted my notes was when I had to produce Arms and the Man in ten rehearsals. The total was 600. That is a minimum: I have run into thousands since. Do not forget that though at the first rehearsal you will know more about the parts than the actors, at the last rehearsal they ought to know more about them (through their undivided attention) than you, and therefore have something to teach you about them.

Be prepared for a spell of hard work. The incessant strain on one's attention (the actors have their exits and rests; but the producer is hard at it all the time), the social effort of keeping up everyone's spirits in view of a great event, the dryness of the previous study of the mechanical details, daunt most authors. But if you have not energy to face all that, you had better keep out of the theatre and trust to a professional producer. In fact, it sometimes happens that the author has to be put out. Unless he goes through the grind I have described, and which I face with greater reluctance as I grow older, he simply bothers and complains and obstructs, either saying that he does not like what the actors are doing without knowing what he wants instead, or at the first rehearsal expecting a perfect performance, or wanting things that can't be done, or making his suggestions ridiculous by unskilful demonstrations, or quarrelling, or devil knows what not.

Only geniuses can tell you exactly what is wrong with a scene, though plenty of people can tell that there is something wrong with it. So make a note of their dissatisfaction; but be very careful how you adopt their cure if they prescribe one. For instance, if they say a scene is too slow (meaning that it bores them), the remedy in nine cases out of ten is for the actors to go slower and bring out the meaning better by contrasts of tone and speed.

Never have a moment of silence on the stage except as an intentional stage effect. The play must not stop while an actor is sitting down or getting up or walking off the stage. The last word of an exit speech must get the actor off the stage. He must sit on a word and rise on a word; if he has to make a movement, he must move as he speaks and not before or after; and the cues must be picked up as smartly as a ball is fielded in cricket. This is the secret of pace, and of holding an audience. It is a rule which you may set aside again and again to make a special effect; for a technical rule may always be broken on purpose. I once saw a fine play of Masefield's prolonged by half an hour and almost ruined because the actors made their movements in silence between the speeches. That does not happen when his plays are produced by Granville-Barker or by himself.

Remember that no strangers should be present at a rehearsal. It is sometimes expedient that strangers, and even journalists, be invited to witness a so-called rehearsal: and on such occasions a prearranged interruption by the producer may take place to affirm the fact that the occasion is only a rehearsal. But the interruption must be addressed to the mechanical staff about some mechanical detail. No direction should ever be given to an actor in the presence of a stranger; and the consent of every actor should be obtained before a stranger is admitted. The actor, of course, is bound to the same reticence. A stranger is a non-professional who is not in the theatre on business. Rehearsals are absolutely and sacredly confidential. The publication of gossip about rehearsals, or the disclosure of the plot of a play, is the blackest breach of stage etiquette.

I have tumbled all this out at express speed, as the best I can do for you out of my own experience, in reply to your innocent question about technique. I hope it is intelligible and may be helpful.

Shakespear and the Stratford-upon-Avon Theatre: A Plea for Reconstruction

(*Stratford-upon-Avon Herald*, April 23, 1923)

Very few of us understand what has happened to Shakespear in the twentieth century. We think of him as a famous playwright whose works have held the stage for 300 years continuously. We are quite mistaken. What has really happened is that the young men of the theatre of the twentieth century have found themselves plunged into a struggle to restore Shakespear to the stage after an exile of 250 years. During those 250 years we have had Betterton, Garrick, Kemble, Mrs Siddons, Kean, Macready, Barry Sullivan, Irving, Ada Rehan, and Tree (to name the dead only). They all put the name of Shakespear on their play-bills, and professed, and sometimes felt, a superstitious reverence for his genius even when they were taking the most grotesque and often the most ignorant and maladroit liberties with him. But they could not have given us Shakespear's plays as he meant them to be given even if they had wanted to and understood his intentions, because when the English theatre recovered from the suspension of the monarchy under Cromwell, it was transformed into a new sort of theatre that Shakespear's plays could by no means be fitted into. The Puritans, repudiating the playhouse, were all the more infatuated about music; and Cromwell, after extirpating the Shakespearean playhouses, welcomed the Italian opera-house, which was a quite different affair. What people looked to it for was not nature in Shakespear's dramatic mirror, but magic: the magic that changed speech into music by the art of the singer and changed the boards into Elysian fields by the art of the scene-painter. And the singer was never so popular as when singing the trills and roulades that are most remote from human speech and natural expression, while the scene-painter's triumph was the "transformation scene," radiant with a glory that never was on sea or land. The enchanted public would have nothing else, and soon could not even conceive that anything else was presentable in the theatre.

The magic of scenery put Shakespear on a Procrustean bed; and his torture grew worse and worse as audiences became more and more critical of scenic art, and demanded a more and more perfect illusion. The new opera theatre had a proscenium like a picture frame and a curtain to hide the stage while the scenes were being set. When two scenes, each occupying the whole depth of the stage, followed one another, the curtain had to descend between them and the audience had to wait in idleness and boredom until the carpenters were ready and the curtain went up again. Playgoers were broken in to enduring these interruptions four times in the course of a single play. Thus Shakespear's cinematographic method of presenting a play in an unlimited number of brief scenes, with the greatest possible variety and rapidity, became impossible. First, the time occupied by the four intervals, say three-quarters of an hour, had to be cut out of the play somehow. Next, what was left had to be patched and transposed and pieced so as to avoid having to change the scene too often during the acts.

Still, the mischief was not so great at first as it afterwards became, because certain simple changes of scene in full view of the audience were tolerated for two hundred years. In my youth I was accustomed to the closing in of flats, the withdrawal or protrusion of side wings, the descent of sky borders and front scenes, all carried out shamelessly under the eyes of a pit without stalls, which jeered mercilessly when the flats would not join, or when the trick of their withdrawal was betrayed by the twinkling heels of the carpenters running them off, or, greatest delight of all, when the pulling back of a side wing revealed some old gentleman who, immersed in study of the opera libretto or a copy of the play, would remain for a few delirious moments unconscious of the fact that he was on the stage, in full view, and that the roar of applause and laughter from the delighted house was a tribute to his incongruous self.

The odd thing was that the audiences who had this sort of fun more or less every night were great sticklers for illusion on the stage, and really believed that the ridiculous makeshifts they laughed at helped their dramatic imagination instead of destroying it. They were not subtle enough to distinguish between the pleasure of looking at a picture, which the best scenic artists gave them in a very high degree, and the interest of a drama, which is a very different matter.

But when they became more critical, the wings and flats and sky borders and front cloths had to go, and changes of scene in view of the audience were barred. Shakespear's plays had then to be aborted into five scenes, or else the number of intervals had to be increased, which meant an increase of boredom and interruption for the audience. Under such conditions Shakespear became unbearable: it was the actor that drew the audience (when there was any audience): and the actor had to spend absurd sums on scenery and stage pageantry to make up for the ruin of the mutilated play. All the plays that did not offer star parts to the actor or actress vanished from the stage. Hamlet and Benedick, Beatrice and Rosalind were torn to rags whilst thirty plays and three hundred characters lay on the shelf, dead as Tutankhamen.

A revolt against this was inevitable sooner or later. First came Mr William Poel, now a veteran of 70, with his Elizabethan Stage Society. Single-handed, in the face of misunderstanding and, worse still, no understanding at all, of ridicule, of the inadequate resources of a man of modest private means, he managed to give occasional and isolated performances which at best were interesting throughout both dramatically and decoratively, and at worst always provided at least a convincing sample or two of what he was driving at. Among the young actors who took part in these pioneer experiments was Mr Harley Granville-Barker; and in the fulness of time Mr Granville-Barker, as a full-blown London West End manager, astonished the capital by giving a series of Shakespearean performances in which not a line was omitted nor a scene transposed or altered in any way, without act divisions or waits or interruptions, and with a splendor of decorative beauty and an increase of dramatic illusion that left the pictorial devices of opera-house Shakespear nowhere.

And now, what has all this to do with Stratford-upon-Avon?

Well, just as Mr Granville-Barker in his prentice days was attracted by the ideas of Mr Poel and worked with him, so Mr Bridges Adams in his college days was attracted by the work of Mr Granville-Barker, and shared it as a professional training; and it is Mr Bridges Adams who has restored Shakespear to the Stratford stage, and made an end of the star system, and of the tedious waits for the carpenters to set the old sham scenery, and of the monstrous mutilations by which the plays were hacked to fit the proportion of an hour and a half of playing to an hour of sitting staring at the curtain or patronizing the refreshment bars. In short, of the bed of Procrustes.

But the Stratford audiences see only what Mr Bridges Adams has been able to do: they have no idea yet of what he could do if the Memorial Theatre had been built as a Shakespearean theatre instead of as an opera-house. It was built, unhappily, 16 years ago, when the last traces of the Shakespearean tradition had been lost, and the stage cut back to the proscenium and elevated and withdrawn to an extent which destroyed all the old intimacy between the actors and the audience. Mr Poel had got over this difficulty by giving his demonstrations, not in theatres, but in the old halls of the city companies or of the Inns of Court. Mr Granville-Barker, at great expense, had reconstructed the London and American stages on which he worked by building a forestage out into the auditorium. In the Stratford theatre this is not possible. The requisite space cannot be spared from the auditorium; and the elevation and remoteness of the stage floor are insurmountable obstacles to any sort of adaptation, temporary or permanent. All that Mr Bridges Adams can do is to pretend that the front of the existing stage is a forestage, and make the box office pretend; but successful as he has been, he is still reproached by the doctrinaires of genuine Shakespearean production for makeshifts that are forced on him by the construction of the theatre, which is the very worst possible for his purpose just because it was built to be the very best possible for operatic purposes. It will have to be completely redesigned and reconstructed before Shakespear's plays can be performed as they are now performed on the best modern stages of America and Central Europe. Until this is done all the other activities of the Shakespear Association of Stratford will be unable to realize the ideal of maintaining a model Shakespear theatre and a model school of Shakesperean acting and production for the whole world.

This reconstruction will cost money. The little town of Stratford, in which £50 would be quite a large sum to raise by public subscription, has from first to last put down in money and land upwards of £100,-000 for Shakespear; and the multi-millionaires of the rest of the world have contributed less than £15,000. Hardly fair, this distribution of the burden—which ought to be considered a privilege—of supporting the pleasantest and most intensely and happily English place of pilgrimage left in this island. Will no rich gentleman or lady oblige with the requisite funds? Or any poor lady or gentleman shame the rich ones by a modest subscription to the Association?

On Printed Plays

(*The Times Literary Supplement*, May 17, 1923)

Sir,—Your excellent article on The Printed Play last week left out one point of instruction to would-be playwrights (including probably 95 per cent of your readers) which the writer will forgive me for supplying.

In preparing a play for publication, the author's business is to make it intelligible to a reader. In preparing it for performance he has to make it intelligible to a spectator and listener. The last quality is the one in which a writer who has always worked for publication alone is likely to fail in direct proportion to his inveterate practice and his virtuosity. For example,

Henry James wished to succeed as a playwright. Not long ago the Stage Society performed an early attempt of his. It was quite successful, and helped to make the reputation of Mr Nicholas Hannen as a comedian. The same society tried one of James's fully matured attempts.* In spite of a representation by Miss Ellen O'Malley of the heroine which was as charming and delicate as even the fastidious James could have desired, it was a hopeless failure. Why?

The explanation is simple enough. There is a literary language which is perfectly intelligible to the eye, yet utterly unintelligible to the ear even when it is easily speakable by the mouth. Of that English James was master in the library and slave on the stage. At the last-mentioned performance I experimented on my friends between the acts by repeating some of the most exquisite sentences from the dialogue. I spoke fairly and distinctly, but not one of my victims could understand me or even identify the words I was uttering.

I cannot give any rule for securing audible intelligibility. It is not missed through long words or literary mannerisms or artificiality of style, nor secured by simplicity. Most of the dialogues that have proved effective on the English stage have been written either in the style of Shakespear, which is often Euphuistic in its artificiality, or in that of Dr Johnson, which is, as Goldsmith said, a style natural only in a whale. Ben Jonson's Volpone is detestably unreadable; yet, when spoken on the stage it is a model of vivid dialogue. The Jamesian passages with which I experimented did not contain any word of more than two syllables: word for word they were as simple as The Pilgrim's Progress. But they "came across" as gibberish. Speech does not differ from literature in its materials. "This my hand will rather the multitudinous seas incarnadine" is such a polysyllabic monstrosity as was never spoken anywhere but on the stage; but it is magnificently effective

* *The Outcry*, produced by the Incorporated Stage Society, July 1 and 3, 1917.

and perfectly intelligible in the theatre. James could
have paraphrased it charmingly in words of one syllable and left the audience drearily wondering what
on earth Macbeth was saying.

It is significant that many successful writers for the
stage have never written for anything else. Others have
excelled as public speakers or in conversation. There
is, of course, a born genius for dialogue which needs
no training. Molière, Goldsmith, Chesterton, Lady
Gregory are the first highly literary examples that occur to me. But the disastrous plays of James and the
stage failures of novelists obviously much more richly
endowed by Nature and culture than many of the successful playwrights with whom they have tried to compete, suggest that they might have succeeded if only
they had understood that as the pen and the *viva vox*
are different instruments, their parts must be scored
accordingly.

Possibly this hint may be of use to some of our
novelists. The scarcity of effective playwrights amid a
multitude of popular novelists is ridiculous and un-
natural.

Yours truly,

G. Bernard Shaw

John Barrymore's Hamlet

("A Letter to John Barrymore," *Ladies Home Journal*,
XLIII, February 1926; reprinted in *Confessions of An
Actor*, by John Barrymore, Indianapolis, 1926)

22nd February, 1925.

My dear Mr Barrymore:

I have to thank you for inviting me—and in such
kind terms too—to your first performance of Hamlet
in London; and I am glad you had no reason to complain of your reception, or, on the whole, of your press.
Everyone felt that the occasion was one of extraor-

dinary interest; and so far as your personality was concerned they were not disappointed.

I doubt, however, whether you have been able to follow the course of Shakespearean production in England during the last fifteen years or so enough to realize the audacity of your handling of the play. When I last saw it performed at Stratford-on-Avon, practically the entire play was given in three hours and three quarters, with one interval of ten minutes; and it made the time pass without the least tedium, though the cast was not in any way remarkable. On Thursday last you played five minutes longer with the play cut to ribbons, even to the breath-bereaving extremity of cutting out the recorders, which is rather like playing King John without little Arthur.

You saved, say, an hour and a half on Shakespear by the cutting, and filled it up with an interpolated drama of your own in dumb show. This was a pretty daring thing to do. In modern shop plays, without characters or anything but the commonest dialogue, the actor has to supply everything but the mere story, getting in the psychology between the lines, and presenting in his own person the fascinating hero whom the author has been unable to create. He is not substituting something of his own for something of the author's: he is filling up a void and doing the author's work for him. And the author ought to be extremely obliged to him.

But to try this method on Shakespear is to take on an appalling responsibility and put up a staggering pretension. Shakespear, with all his shortcomings, was a very great playwright; and the actor who undertakes to improve his plays undertakes thereby to excel to an extraordinary degree in two professions in both of which the highest success is extremely rare. Shakespear himself, though by no means a modest man, did not pretend to be able to play Hamlet as well as write it; he was content to do a recitation in the dark as the ghost. But you have ventured not only to act Hamlet, but to discard about a third of Shakespear's script and substitute stuff of your own, and that, too, without the help of dialogue. Instead of giving what is called a reading of Hamlet, you say, in effect, "I am not going to read Hamlet at all: I am going to leave it out. But see what I give you in exchange!"

Such an enterprise must justify itself by its effect on the public. You discard the recorders as hackneyed back chat, and the scene with the king after the death of Polonius, with such speeches as "How all occasions do inform against me!" as obsolete junk, and offer instead a demonstration of that very modern discovery called the Œdipus complex, thereby adding a really incestuous motive on Hamlet's part to the merely conventional incest of a marriage (now legal in England) with a deceased husband's brother. You change Hamlet and Ophelia into Romeo and Juliet. As producer, you allow Laertes and Ophelia to hug each other as lovers instead of lecturing and squabbling like hectoring big brother and little sister: another complex!

Now your success in this must depend on whether the play invented by Barrymore on the Shakespear foundation is as gripping as the Shakespear play, and whether your dumb show can hold an audience as a straightforward reading of Shakespear's rhetoric can. I await the decision with interest.

My own opinion is, of course, that of an author. I write plays that play for three hours and a half even with instantaneous changes and only one short interval. There is no time for silences or pauses: the actor must play on the line and not between the lines, and must do nine-tenths of his acting with his voice. Hamlet— Shakespear's Hamlet—can be done from end to end in four hours in that way; and it never flags nor bores. Done in any other way Shakespear is the worst of bores, because he has to be chopped into a mere cold stew. I prefer my way. I wish you would try it, and concentrate on acting rather than on authorship, at which, believe me, Shakespear can write your head off. But that may be vicarious professional jealousy on my part.

I did not dare to say all this to Mrs Barrymore on the night. It was chilly enough for her without a coat in the stalls without any cold water from

Yours perhaps too candidly,

G. Bernard Shaw.

Theatres and Reviews Then and Now

(*The Saturday Review* CXL, November 7, 1925, Seventieth Anniversary Supplement)

Thirty years ago I was the Saturday Reviewer in the theatres. D. S. MacColl was the Saturday Reviewer in the picture galleries. Cunninghame Graham was a Saturday Reviewer in the universe, with perhaps a slight specialization towards Spanish South America. Music was reviewed by J. J. Runciman, young, clever, and quite genuine, but, like many middle-class Bohemians, without a notion of public or private manners. He drank, died, and is forgotten; but he held his own among us for a time. The editor was Frank Harris, who had no quality of editorship except the supreme one of knowing good work from bad, and not being afraid of it.

People who did not understand the peculiar structure of English society were puzzled by weeklies like The Saturday Review when they thought about them at all. These weeklies were not Radical. They were snortingly aristocratic; and yet they were staffed (when they were lucky enough to find the right men) by writers of whom the perfect type today is Leo Trotsky, with his unbounded contempt for the bourgeoisie, his uncompromising repudiation of their prejudices, their tastes, and their religion, his ruthlessly candid self-criticism, his subtle analytical power as a critic, and his trenchant skill with the pen. He would have been an ideal Saturday Reviewer. What! you will say: a Socialist? A Communist? A Red? Why not? I was a

Socialist; Cunninghame Graham was a Socialist, militant to his spurs; Runciman was a Socialist; Harris was a Socialist. We never asked MacColl what he was: it was enough that he was an artist and a very fine critic and brilliant writer; let it suffice that if he had any conventional weaknesses he knew better than to betray them in the Saturday. No Liberal, Radical, or Labor paper would have dared to employ us; one whiff of our brimstone would have terrified their editors out of their senses. Only in unchallengeably aristocratic papers could we have been let rip as we were.

The explanation of this paradox of aristocratic papers manned (and to some extent womaned) by revolutionaries, is simply that England was governed by an oligarchy of aristocrats and plutocrats; and as Nature obstinately refused to conform to this arrangement by making every aristocratic or plutocratic baby a completely conventional Conservative, there was always a Left and Right in the party of privilege as there is in the party of Labor, except that the aristocratic Right was more prejudiced and the aristocratic Left much more seditious than the Labor Right and Left. The aristocratic Left constituted a nineteenth century Fronde; and the papers which appealed to it were those which, without saying a word against Church or State which could disqualify them for the tables of the most exclusive clubs, country houses, or even rectories, nevertheless criticized everything and everybody without the smallest respect for either. That was the secret of The World under the editorship of Edmund Yates when I was the critic of music; and it was the secret of The Saturday Review also. On both papers I was perfectly at home when the Radical and Socialist papers would have been partly shocked and partly terrified by my audacities.

Things have changed since this. The aristocratic Fronde is disabled by Inflation, Supertax, and Death Duties; and its place in modern culture has been taken by the bourgeois Intelligentsia. At the same time

Socialism, having become recognized and official, has also become straitlaced; and the weekly journals, instead of representing Freethought (in the general sense), now represent Capitalistic and Socialistic interests in definite opposition; while the old anti-bourgeois weeklies, representing really the descendants of the freethinking nobles of the eighteenth century, and always Frondeur and *épatant* no matter who was in power, have disappeared. There is still nominally a Saturday Review; but it no longer keeps a red flag under its mattress.

I am asked to compare the dramatic criticism of thirty years ago with that of today. But how can I? Thirty years ago I was myself a critic, which means that I never read any dramatic criticism except the proofs of my own articles. People used to accuse me of paradox because when Henry Irving, the leading actor of that day, was quoted as an authority on the theatres, I pointed out that he knew less about the theatres than anyone else in London, because he was on the stage—the same stage—every night. Only the other day my friend Walkley demurred to the account of modern criticism I have in the preface to St Joan. He forgot that I had read every English and American criticism of my play, and that he would have died rather than swallow such a dose. He may not even have read his own notice; certainly he did not read anyone else's. He has not the faintest notion of what criticism is in the lump; he knows it only by his own extremely flattering samples. Thirty years ago I was as ignorant as he: I read his criticisms when we were together on the Star, and Archer's when we were on the World; and we all three read Clement Scott's frantic denunciation of Ibsen; but it was not until I forsook criticism for playwriting, and had to read notices as a matter of business, that I got anything like a conspectus of theatrical journalism.

I know that to students of the British Schimpflexikon which Archer compiled to chronicle the Press reception of Ibsen in this country we must needs appear an obscene rabble throwing mud, screaming foul abuse at every great man who came our way. Our musical colleagues had cut an equally poor figure when confronted with Wagner. And I cannot pretend to consider my own reception as a playwright by my quondam colleagues as, on the whole, a critical success. But critics must be judged by their normal activities, and not by their convulsions when a new departure upsets them. The critics who declared that Wagner's music had no melody; that his harmonies were meaningless discords, his orchestration a hideous uproar, and the man himself a despicable charlatan, were quite good judges of Gounod and Arthur Sullivan. Those who yelled for the prosecution as disorderly houses of theatres in which Ibsen's plays were performed were sane enough about Robertson and Tom Taylor, Sardou and Dumas *fils;* and they could stand the advance led by Pinero, Jones, and Gilbert without losing their heads. Oscar Wilde had no more to complain of than is in the day's worries of any successful playwright.

On this plane I should say that there has been an improvement. Thanks to the development of the literary and artistic sides of the daily newspapers, to the gramophone, the pianola, and wireless, the supply of journalists with a knowledge and love of art, and a cultivated sensibility to refinements in artistic execution, is much greater than it was. Editors are no longer contemptuously ignorant of art; they may still be ignorant, but they are ashamed of their ignorance, and no longer dare to hand over the theatre with a snub to the least cultivated of their casual reporters. When, as a beginner, I got an introduction to Morley (not then Lord Morley), and he asked me what I thought I could do, I threw away the opportunity by saying that I thought I could write about art. In utter disgust he turned away, flinging over his shoulder a muttered "Pooh! ANYBODY can write about art." "O, CAN they???" I retorted, with a contempt equal to his own; and I honestly thought I was showing great self-restraint in not adding "you wretched Philistine second-hand Macaulay." That concluded the interview; and Morley missed his chance of becoming my editor. As to Stead, who succeeded Morley, and under whom I became a contributor to the old Pall Mall Gazette, he was an abyss of ignorance in part; a theatre was to him a sort of *maison tolérée* which God forbid he should ever enter.

Nowadays editors may be Philistines; but they know that they must find a specialist to write theatrical feuilletons for them, and think themselves lucky if they can find a good one. I gather from what I read that they get imposed on occasionally; for the theatrical feuilletons are sometimes as nonsensical as the city articles; but whereas nothing will teach an editor finance, he is more and more likely nowadays to know enough to criticize his art critics, as Massingham, for example, did. A first-rate critic like Desmond McCarthy would be snapped up eagerly today. When he made the first display of his powers in the theatre twenty years ago the editors were much slower in the uptake. And as the critic also is more and more likely to know his business, the level is rising.

As to the theatre itself, it is beginning to educate its critics, whereas in the old days it stultified them. I have no space left in which to describe how completely the theatre used to be divorced from the national life. It was more secluded than any modern convent, and much more prudish. It knew nothing of religion, politics, science, or any art but its own. It had only one subject, which the censorship did not allow it to mention. Janet Achurch was forbidden to produce a little play by Octave Feuillet, about a lady with what we called a past, until she gave the Censor her word of honor to say every night on the stage, "I sinned but in intention," which she accordingly whispered to the conductor most faithfully always on her first entry. The Censorship still blunders over Pirandello's famous Six Characters as it did over Mrs Warren's Profession and Blanco Posnet. But Mr

Noel Coward's heroines do not have to make matters
worse by explaining that though they did not sin, they
meant to. That will perhaps give a rough measure
of what the theatre was thirty years ago, and what
it is today.

The Colossus Speaks

Under this heading Mr. Bernard Shaw addresses an open
    letter to Mr. Gordon Craig. (One of Craig's many at-
    tacks on Shaw took the form of an article, "The Colos-
    sus," in his journal, *The Mask*, January 1926. Shaw
    replied in the April issue, Vol. XII.)

My dear Gordon Craig:

In so far as my colossiousness is not a legitimate
stage effect which you would be the last man to dis-
parage, it is something that I cannot help. I can only
apologize and plead that I was born so. How would
you alter me if you could?

You are quite right in saying that the contribution
I and my followers (in the chronological sense) have
made to the drama is not an artistic contribution.
Wycherley could say what he had to say as well as I,
and could put it on the stage with as much art. Congreve was as fine an artist as Granville-Barker. The
fact that Man and Superman leaves The Country Wife
so far behind that I cannot persuade people that the
two authors belong to the same species, and the stupendous superiority of The Madras House to The Way
of the World, is due wholly to the difference in the
subject matter and the mental capacity of the authors.
Wycherley and Congreve thought women over thirty
ridiculous, venereal disease funny, and the betrayal
of an old husband by a young wife screamingly
laughable. That covers their entire recorded body of
thought. I do not share these tastes; and if I did, I
have something more important to think about and
make an audience think about. I have nothing in com-

mon with Wycherley and Congreve except our art, and an indefensible love of acting for its own sake. And I daresay Granville-Barker would say the same.

But this is not what has drawn a reply from me to your sally. You have brought against me the unjust accusation that I have thrust everybody else off the stage. You specify our friend Henry Arthur Jones as a case in point. Now the truth is that I could not get my last play into the theatre until Henry Arthur gracefully made way for me by suspending the performance of a play of his which was still unexhausted after a long run. When, long before the war, Mr Jones renounced his London vogue and withdrew to America, he did so, not because he was crowded out, but because, like Shakespear, he fell into a mood of disillusion with English society which he expressed in plays compared to which Timon of Athens seemed a genial optimistic comedy. He went away because he could not stand us any longer, not in the least because we could not stand him. When he returned after the war he found himself for a time excluded from the London West End theatres; but so were we all. The war had raised theatre rents to a figure which no serious author's following could cover. When the situation was eased by the substitution of the sharing system for the renting system he made a triumphant return with the play that kept mine waiting. Your sympathies are due to me, not to him; all the more so as his misanthropy has taken a most unfortunate turn for me. He could not feel like Timon towards his country when the war smote it. He forgave it, but forgave it on the very unexpected ground that its faults were the result of having been misled by two fiends in human shape, tri-initialled and one-syllabled, by name H. G. Wells and G. B. Shaw. What could we say but that if the indictment he brought against his entire nation can be narrowed down to a gorgeous burst of his best invective against two harmless individuals, we will suffer meekly for the sake of reconciling him to his own people?

Thus Mr Jones's cause is not really your point. When next you are moved to accuse me of shutting the doors of the theatre on my fellow-playwrights just as Mr Jones accuses me of shutting the gates of mercy on mankind, pause and remember what the theatre was when I stormed it, and what it is now. As far as serious original work was concerned there were two men in possession, Pinero and Jones, and two new arrivals in the offing: Barrie and Carton. The others were translating from the French or writing comic operas, or complaining bitterly that they were being kept out of the theatre by an imaginary Ring. Today the first policeman you ask can, without mentioning Pinero, Jones, Carton, Barrie, or myself, reel you off a list of twenty established West End London playwrights, enjoying a liberty of subject and treatment, and a standing in literature (to say nothing of the fortunes they have in their film rights) which drive the aforesaid P, J, B, C, and G.B.S. to shake their fists at the heavens and ask despairingly why they were not born fifty years later. And you, Edward, have had a splendid share in this triumph over the Philistines. In the nineteenth century they did not know what you were talking about; today they may not know much better; but you are the most famous theatre man in Europe. Twenty years ago Charles Ricketts made a stage picture of the third act of Man and Superman which neither he nor any other artist in Europe has surpassed or can surpass. Nobody took the slightest notice of it then. Today it would make ten reputations. I am actually asked what would St Joan have been without Ricketts: and I am obliged to confess that it would have been a mere sketch in black and white.

And you have the face to tell me that I have closed the theatre to everyone but myself; that its wide walls encompass but one Man! Ungrateful Edward!

But I forgive you for the sake of your deftly implied flatteries.

Ever yours, a little the worse for wear,

G. Bernard Shaw

Playhouses and Plays

(*New York Herald Tribune*, November 14, 1926)

The following article was written by Mr. Shaw when the Guild opened its new theatre, and for some strange reason has lain buried under the masonry all this time. It has been exhumed, by a strange coincidence, just as the Guild is in the act of presenting Mr. Shaw's Pygmalion.

There is no doubt at all in my mind that the Theatre Guild should have a new theatre. And by a new theatre I mean a new theatre and not another old theatre. The nineteenth century has left our cities stuffed with pestiferous playgoer barrels in which the unfortunate playwrights and actors were expected by sheer force of entertaining power to set up an attraction that would counterbalance the greatest discomfort of the greatest number. There is a tradition of discomfort in the theatre dating back to a time when ground rents, which now make it compulsory, were comparatively negligible. In Shakespear's time it seemed a matter of course that playgoers should stand staring at the stage without a roof over their heads, as they do still at a Punch and Judy show. A seat was a privilege to be hired as one hires a trestle at a race to look over the heads of those in front. To this day in the Italian theatres you pay for ingress to the theatre and then pay for your seat in addition as a separate transaction. In Pepys's time the money was still collected from the spectators Punch and Judy fashion at the end of the first act. Within my recollection Shakespear's seatless groundlings were provided with plain wooden benches only, though, to be sure, they were roofed in. There were no stalls, and there was half price after 9 o'clock. In the old Theatre Royal, Dublin, a first-rate house of its kind, there was, besides the dress circle and the undress circle for the aristocracy and the bourgeoisie 4s and 3s, the pit at 2s, a middle gallery at 18d, and a top gallery of gods at sixpence. Nobody dreamed of comfort or expected it, though in the circles there was grandeur, consisting of red stuffed upholstery on the narrow benches. It was the business of the play and of the actors to hold you spellbound and forgetful. And this was not for a mere two and a half or three hours. The first time I was ever in a theatre the program consisted of a farce, Tom Taylor's drama, Plot and Passion, in three acts, a grand Christmas pantomime, and probably another farce which I was not allowed to wait for. Most of the spectators were seated on narrow planks, without cushions, sides, or backs; but they stuck it out like the French at Verdun, except that they did it voluntarily and paid for the privilege. Such feats of endurance are not things of the past. They are surpassed every season in London by infatuated people who wait at the theatre doors for eight, twelve, and sometimes actually twenty hours to secure front places on occasions like the return of Melba the other day, creating unmentionable problems of provision and sanitation. Every night the devoted theatre queues may be seen in London, beginning to form three hours before the opening without extraordinary provocation.

Having discovered that people will perform these feats of self-torture as resolutely as do the Indian fanatics who swing on hooks, or the early Christian ascetics, the theatre managers and the architects have naturally concluded that comfort is thrown away on playgoers. A theatre is therefore regarded as a palace of enchantment, but not as a prosaically comfortable place. If criminals were crowded together in our prisons without proper ventilation and elbow room, as playgoers are in our theatres, there would be an agitation against the cruelty of the authorities. In many London theatres the $3 stalls are so closely packed that the back of each stall overhangs the knees of the person in the stall behind it. The gymnastics of the later comers, who have to choose between pulling over the stall in front of them as they cling to it and crashing into the laps of those already seated behind them, are familiar to every playgoer.

I am in favor of making the playgoer comfortable. I admit that once you get him into the theatre he will endure anything, and that if you give him good drama and acting you give him, in effect, a chloroform that would make him forget St Lawrence's gridiron if he happened to be sitting on it. But the difficulty is to get him in. If a good play makes him forget his discomfort, a bad one makes him remember it and fear it next time. He craves for the comfort of the cinema theatres, the best of which are made very comfortable because, as they are seldom full, nor even expected to be full, and pay quite handsomely when they are what the manager of an ordinary theatre would call empty, the temptation to pack the seats together without regard to the comfort of the sitters is less strong than the desire to court their custom. Besides, the cinema relieves the spectator of all preoccupying and worrying self-consciousness—about his dress, for instance—whereas the ordinary theatre, the moment it takes its glaring lights off the actors, turns them full onto the blushing spectators. This factor in the success of the cinema is of enormous importance; but it is so little talked about that I should not be surprised if some idiot were to invent a means of making the screen visible in a fully lighted auditorium, and be hailed as a deliverer by the industry he was trying to ruin.

For the moment, however, people go to the picture palace oftener than to the theatre because they are more comfortable and less conspicuous there, and to meet this competition we of the regular theatre need to demolish most of our existing playhouses and replace them with structures in which the audience is comfortable and obscure and the stage blazingly conspicuous.

But there is another condition to be fulfilled. The cinema has restored to the stage the dramatic form used by Shakespear: the story told with utter disregard of the unity of place in a rapid succession of scenes, practically unlimited in number, uninterrupted by waits and just as short or as long as their dramatic interest can bear. In this free, varied, continuous manner, almost anyone who can tell a story well can also write a play. The specific ingenuity needed to force the story into the strait waistcoat of three or five acts, with one unchanging scene in each, is no longer needed. The classic unities have their value for those who can handle them and are indeed inherent in drama at its highest concentration, but they were originally only products of the mechanical conditions of the ancient Greek theatre, and to impose these conditions, or, still worse, the conditions of the scenic theatres of the XVII–XIX centuries on all playwrights is to deprive the theatre of the services of many most entertaining novelists and fabulists of one kind or another, and to put a premium on the mental defects of playwrights who have what is called a sense of the theatre, which usually means that they have lost all sense of anything in nature but the stage.

No theatre is likely to be generally useful in the future unless its stage is so constructed that it can present a play in fifty scenes without a break. I do not mean that there should be no break, as fifty scenes might be too much for the endurance of the audience; but I do mean that the suspension of the performance for ten minutes or so should be solely for the relief of the spectators, and not a mechanical necessity. If I am right, most of our existing theatres will become unlettable as playhouses. I hope they will; the sooner the better.

My next play will be a chronicle play which will be impracticable without a Shakespearean stage. I do not know whether it will be in fifty scenes or fifteen or five hundred, but in writing it I shall ignore the limitations of the nineteenth century scenic stage as completely as Shakespear did. I shall have to depend on the Theatre Guild of America for a performance of it, just as I had to depend on it for a performance of Back to Methuselah. But I want the Guild to build a new theatre for it, and I should hesitate to ask them to do so if I did not believe that the sort of theatre my next play needs will soon be the only sort easily saleable or lettable for popular theatrical purposes. The auditorium must combine the optics and acoustics of a first-rate lecture theatre and a first-rate circus. There must be a forestage extending on occasion to the occupation of all the floor level (what is called the ring in an equestrian circus), and the backstage must be easily curtained off and provided with modern machinery capable of doing its work noiselessly whilst the play is proceeding on the forestage. That the stage lighting should be modern, and if possible planned by persons who have never seen footlights, and wonder what on earth they can have been when they read about them in books, goes without saying. Lee Simonson knows all about that.

The general effect during a performance should be the reverse of the nineteenth century effect. In it the important spectacle was the evening dress and diamonds of the members of the acting manager's free list, occupying the stalls and boxes to the exclusion of the outsiders who get into a theatre by paying (a thing nobody can do), the stage being a mere hole in the wall at the narrow end, through which you peeped at a remote *tableau vivant* resembling a pictorial advertisement of the best rooms in the latest hotel. In the new theatre of the Guild, the audience must pay and not be seen, as good children should be seen and not heard; and it should be impossible for a person entering during the performance to have eyes for anything but the all-dominating stage. The stage must be in general conception a tribune, and not a ridiculous peepshow with painted canvas profiles pretending to be natural scenery.

Let me, however, warn all the vulgar theatre builders and planners—meaning mostly those who consider

the Theatre Guild an asylum for freaks and cranks—
that though they may possibly find many authors able
to write effectively for this new old sort of theatre who
cannot write for the theatre of Scribe and Sardou at
all, they must not imagine, as so many film companies
have done, that playing about with the latest lighting
systems and showing what hydraulic lifts and electric
turntables can do will interest any audience for more
than the first half minute. The old formula of two
trestles, four boards, and a passion still holds, and
will hold until we grow out of playgoing altogether,
provided the passion be passionate enough; for the
best in this sort are but shadows, and the worst no
worse if imagination mend them, as Shakespear found.

My own practice varies, as far as the mechanical
conditions allow me, from the ultra-classic to the ultra-
operatic. In certain plays of mine I have voluntarily
accepted the strictest unity of time and place for a
three hours' action, as if I were Sophocles; in others
I have thrown the unities to the winds, and not only
presented my play in three or five acts but divided
those acts into scenes. But that does not concern the
spectators, who neither know nor care how I do it:
it is the what, not the how, that they look to. Still,
though the mechanical conditions count for nothing
with them (for they can see a play as in a dream and
are only awakened and annoyed by having the physical
conditions of the uncomfortable place they are packed
into thrust on their notice), none the less the playwright and the actors must work subject to those physical conditions and know how to turn them to account.
The novelist, who writes in a dream almost as completely as the playgoer sees the stage in one, often
cannot write an actable play for this reason. If I were
to forget the physical conditions of the theatre and
the physical reality of the actor for a moment, my
plays would become partly ineffective, partly impossible. Thus I am tied down to what can actually be
done with the theatre as it stands, and if you perform
my plays in any sort of theatre but the one they were

written for, you may have to mutilate them more or less horribly to make them practicable. That is what happened to Shakespear when the Elizabethan stage was supplanted by the operatic scenic peepshow stage. The Shakespearicidal result of that proves that when you have to choose between mutilating the play and rebuilding the theatre you had better rebuild the theatre.

Also, it is evident that if the Theatre Guild can give me another sort of theatre I can write another sort of play, quite as good as and fresher in form than the old ones, but impossible of performance in the old nineteenth century theatres. Wagner, after composing operas for the old opera-houses, composed the Ring for a theatre that did not exist, and thereby forced it into existence. But his Bayreuth theatre would be of no use to me for my chronicle play, which I am writing for a theatre that does not yet exist in New York, but which the Theatre Guild will have to design and build for the purpose. Whether my play will have the compelling force of the Ring I do not know; but at least if my New York congregation will not provide the Guild with funds for the theatre the play shall be there to tantalize them; and they may find themselves in the almost inconceivable retrograde position of being behind London after leaving London nowhere by tempting the Guild to produce "Back to Methuselah," an exploit, still unique, which so amazed me that I have hardly yet recovered my breath after it.

Mr. Shaw on Mr. Shaw

(*The New York Times,* June 12, 1927)

In the following personal letter, published here with his permission, Bernard Shaw discusses his theories of play craftsmanship, as illustrated in his own works. The letter is a reply to Alexander Bakshy's analysis of

Shaw's plays in a book entitled The Theatre Unbound, *published in London by Cecil Palmer.*

Dear Mr Bakshy:

It is impossible for me to do more than send you a hasty note or two on your chapter concerning myself in your interesting and in some ways very acute book, The Theatre Unbound.

You will understand that my plays are not constructed plays: they grow naturally. If you "construct" a play: that is, if you plan your play beforehand, and then carry out your plan, you will find yourself in the position of a person putting together a jig-saw puzzle, absorbed and intensely interested in an operation which, to a spectator, is unbearably dull. The scenes must be born alive. If they are not new to you as you write, and sometimes quite contrary to the expectations with which you have begun them, they are dead wood.

A live play constructs itself with a subtlety, and often with a mechanical ingenuity, that often deludes critics into holding the author up as the most crafty of artificers when he has never, in writing his play, known what one of his characters would say until another character gave the cue.

I am not a Rationalist. I began, as everybody did in the nineteenth century, by writing novels. I wrote two (1879 and 1880) within Rationalist limits; and the hero of the second was a thorough Rationalist. I then discovered that Rationalism was an impasse, and that I could not get a step further with it. In my third novel I threw it over completely: my hero was a sort of Beethoven. By the time I began writing plays I had left Rationalism far behind me; what was mistaken for it in my plays was a very vigorous exercise of a power of reasoning which I had cultivated as a sociologist and economist. I could therefore reason on problems from which most writers of fiction took refuge in mushy emotionalism. I did not take refuge with Allah as long as I could help myself; but not for a moment will you find in my plays any assumption that reason is more than an instrument. What you will find, however, is the belief that intellect is essentially a passion, and that the search for enlightenment of any sort is far more interesting and enduring than, say, the sexual pursuit of a woman by a man, which was the only interest the plays of my early days regarded as proper to the theatre: a play without it was "not a play."

Neither have I ever been what you call a representationist or realist. I was always in the classic tradition, recognizing that stage characters must be endowed by the author with a conscious self-knowledge and power of expression, and, as you observe with genuine penetration, a freedom from inhibitions, which in real life would make them monsters of genius. It is the power to do this that differentiates me (or Shakespear) from a gramophone and a camera. The representational part of the business is mere costume and scenery; and I would not give tuppence for any play that could not be acted in curtains and togas as effectively as in elaborately built stage drawing-rooms and first-rate modern tailoring. Even Blanco Posnet and Feemy should be able to hold their own as Ishmael and Rahab.

You are right in saying that my plays require a special technique of acting, and, in particular, great virtuosity in sudden transitions of mood that seem to the ordinary actor to be transitions from one "line" of character to another. But, after all, this is only fully accomplished acting; for there is no other sort of acting except bad acting, acting that is the indulgence of imagination instead of the exercise of skill.

Again you are right when you say that my technique is classic and Molièresque (the *Commedia dell'Arte* was improvised Molière). Your word "kinship," too, to express the relation between me and Congreve and Sheridan is precisely correct. We are all three Irishmen: that is all. They had no part whatever in forming my habits. On the other hand, the fact that I was

brought up on Italian and German opera must have
influenced me a great deal: there is much more of Il
Trovatore and Don Giovanni in my style than of The
Mourning Bride and The School for Scandal; but it
would take me too far to pursue this.

Faithfully,

G. Bernard Shaw

10 Adelphi Terrace, London, W.C. 2
May 24, 1923.

Bernard Shaw Talks about Actors and Acting*

(*The New York Times,* January 6, 1929)

*Being excerpts from an address delivered before The
Royal Academy of Dramatic Art at the Academy
Theatre, London, on December 7, 1928.*

Ladies and Gentlemen:

The greatest number of listeners to this address of
mine have just been informed that what is happening
is "London calling the British Isles." What is actually

* A verbatim report of a radio address given by the B.B.C. to
the press. The Royal Academy of Dramatic Art was founded in
1904 by Beerbohm Tree at His Majesty's Theatre; a year later
it was moved to Gower Street, where in various places it has
remained. From 1909 to mid 1946 Sir Kenneth Barnes, knighted
in 1938, was its director. His successor is John Fernald. From
the beginning Shaw was interested in the work of the Academy,
which offers a two-year course of training in all branches of
theatre art, and he always gave generously of his time and labor
to help the young students. Among other things he edited and
wrote an introduction for a little booklet of practical advice and
encouragement, entitled *The R.A.D.A. Graduate's Keepsake and
Counsellor,* to be given to young people at graduation. His will
provided that if his desire to finance spelling reform were not
allowed legally, the R.A.D.A. should be one of three institutions
to share the money.

happening is Bernard Shaw calling the universe. I want
to emphasize that, because some of my audience consists of our young students here, and I want to remind
them at the outset that their parents might probably
hear them, no matter how remote may be the part of
the globe in which they happen to be at this moment.
So, if they feel tempted at any moment to interrupt me
with use of epithets or anything of that kind, I want
to remind them that their voices may be recognized. . . .

Being in the school, perhaps I had better talk about
it, because this Royal Academy of Dramatic Art is a
very peculiar place. The subject is difficult for me,
because the government is always very nervous, for
some reason or other, whenever I speak in public. I
do not know why, because, after the performance of
some of their own members in that way, I should imagine that they would not be afraid of anything. But
they are a little afraid of me, and they always appeal
to me not to deal with any controversial subject. But,
unfortunately, I am driven here to speak on one of
the most controversial subjects in the world, and that
is whether a member of a family shall go on the stage
or not. We are a school for training the member of the
family who wants to go on the stage, and the differences between ourselves and other schools will at
once occur to you. In the case of the other schools,
the parents want the child to go to the school to get
rid of it; the child does not want to go and would
rather stay at home. In our case, the child wants to
go very desperately and determinedly, and the parents
usually object very strongly indeed. They used to
object still more strongly than they do today, but,
nevertheless, there is the objection.

Before I come to the grounds of that objection,
which are reasonable enough, I want to remind you
how very strong it has been and still to a great extent
is in this country.

Take the example of Charles Dickens. He was a born

actor. He would have gone on the stage; he was trying to go on the stage at the very moment when a colossal and overwhelming literary success condemned him to be a writer instead of an actor. While he was pursuing his literary career he was never happy unless he was getting up some kind of acting performance, and finally he definitely became an actor in the most extreme and concentrated form—that is to say, the actor who plays all the parts in the play himself. He became one of the most famous dramatic reciters in the world, and he went on at that until he killed himself. You would not expect Charles Dickens to have any prejudice against the theatre of the ordinary kind—of the kind of the parent who imagines that the theatre is the gate of hell. And yet when Charles Dickens's daughter wanted to go on the stage, and when she had a very admirable opportunity of going on it, when she had been offered an engagement by a well-known manager of that time, Charles Dickens absolutely refused to allow his daughter to think of such a thing. He said it was impossible, it was out of the question; the theatre was a place into which his daughter could not go in a professional capacity.

At about the same time a very well-known French dramatic author, Alexandre Dumas *fils*—not *père*—wrote a public letter to a young lady of noble family in France who went on the stage, and he took the same line more strongly than Dickens. He said that no lady could go on the stage. I believe this was a princess, which ought to have made the matter easier, as it would have done today.

I can remember myself at a much later date, but no later than the beginning of the present century, when, perhaps, the best-known dramatic critic of that time was Clement Scott. He created an extraordinary sensation by saying that a woman could not be an actress and a respectable woman at the same time; and the controversy went on until the poet, the late Robert Buchanan, settled it. He said, "This is a monstrous calumny. No respectable woman on the stage! There are thousands of respectable women on the stage and only about six actresses!"

Nowadays, of course, matters have changed. We have come to a point at which we are seeing something that, I think, never existed in the annals of public life before, and that is persons who have not yet grown up becoming possessed of enormous fortunes. You find—well, I don't like to mention the name—but you find celebrated film stars, and you may say almost that these ladies have the governments of the world in their pockets and the banks of the world in their pockets; they are much richer than queens and kings, and some of them are quite young. . . .

The bearing of this on this school is this: that we have the parents who really think that the child's salvation has been imperilled by coming here. In that case the child usually has some strong artistic bent in opposition to its parents. But you are now getting the other sort of parent, who comes here with an entirely hopeless daughter without any artistic qualifications whatever, and insists on our turning a film star into a great actress, earning heaven knows what sums of money, on which her family will be enabled to retire from business for the rest of their lives.

That being our position, I want to come to the question whether the old prejudice has anything in it. What is it that we teach here? To begin with, perhaps I had better ask you, What does a parent desire its child to learn? Take the case of a daughter. Do respectable families in this country desire their daughter to spend a great deal of time in making herself attractive to men? I quite grant you that they all want her to make herself attractive to one man, with a pretty solid income and a good position; but when you come to the question of her absolutely and promiscuously making herself attractive to every man who sees her, no matter what his class may be, whether he is sitting in a stall which has cost 12s 6d or 13s 6d or whether he is in the gallery, admission to which is perhaps obtained for 2d, that is another story. That she is to paint herself, to dress herself, so as to make herself irresistibly fascinating to all these people—does any respectable family contemplate that lot for its daughter without recoiling in horror? But that is what we teach young ladies to do here. Even in the painting part of it we give them elaborate lessons. We teach them to wear wigs; we teach them every single art that can fascinate and attract large bodies of men. So that really there is some reason in the prejudice, after all, on the surface of it.

Take the case of a young man. His parents desire a big career for him. The very last thing that they desire is that he should go out into the world and be laughed at by everybody. We teach young men here to be laughed at. We take the greatest care, we spend incalculable pains in training them to be ridiculous, in training them to such a pitch that we consider we have done our very best when we have turned out a young man who the moment he appears on the stage provokes a roar of laughter, even before he opens his mouth.

Well, that is certainly a very questionable sort of school, I think you will admit. And yet we have a royal charter. You will say: "What on earth was the King thinking of?" When I tell you that this theatre of ours was inaugurated by the Prince of Wales, you will say, "What! has the royal family gone mad to countenance these proceedings, this sort of training of children?" Well, it is so; they do this kind of thing. We have got our charter, and I am speaking here without the slightest fear of it being revoked, although I am within hearing not only of this audience but of the government, who are probably anxiously listening.

Why do people want to go on the stage in spite of all these scandalous difficulties at the outset of the career? Well, partly because it is an eligible profession to some people, and partly because it is the satisfaction of a human instinct. Those two things operate, and I shall have, I think, to deal with them separately.

In the theatrical profession we have what are called theatrical families. They are old families, all the members of which have been actors or actresses; and they are usually most desolatingly respectable. Usually they are extremely skilled in their profession, and very satisfactory to work with, because they know their business, which is not quite so common as it ought to be on the stage. But they are there for some reason. Whether it is that they are brought up with much greater strictness than any other sort of families, the fact is that I have never been in a Quaker family which was anything like so strict as an ordinary theatrical family. But they produce the actor who is on the stage, and who very often has a distinguished career there; and yet, so far from being stage-struck is he or she that they positively do not enjoy acting; but they are driven into it by the fact that they can get a living more easily, they know how to go about getting a living more easily, in the theatre than anywhere else.

I could give you some quite noted examples. Take the case of Macready. The scion of a theatrical family, he did not want to go on the stage. He was educated, he was brought up to be a gentleman, not an actor. That distinction used to exist in his time. Now, of course, all that is completely changed. Nowadays if anybody asks me of a person, "Is he a gentleman?" I should say, "Oh, yes, he is an actor," and that would settle the matter at once. But in Macready's day it was not so. When he discovered that really the most evident opening, the one in which he was most certain to succeed, was that of an actor, he became the leading actor of his time in England. Yet if you read his diary you will find that it was very far from being a congenial occupation to him. In the first place, he always shuddered when he saw his name put in large letters on a bill anywhere, and ran away to the other side of the street. The modern actor shudders when he sees his name in small letters. . . .

The actor of my time who was most unquestionably

our leading classic actor in the special sense is Sir Johnston Forbes-Robertson. He was an artist by temperament; he was a painter; but he found matters so difficult as a painter that he went on the stage, solely because he could live as an actor more easily than he could in the other way. In his very interesting autobiography he makes a very curious statement: that he can only remember one period, one performance in his life which he enjoyed in which he was acting himself. There you see this curious thing, that it is not always the satisfaction of the instinct that settles a career; sometimes it is the economic pressure of the career.

I want to say a very interesting thing about that. Those people who are driven by this outside pressure onto the stage are very often the best actors, and the people who are most hopelessly stage-struck are sometimes impossibly bad actors. I simply state that as a general proposition, because there may be in this audience some person who has never dreamed of becoming an actor, who has been brought up perhaps to be a clergyman, and is contemplating that career with some doubt as to whether it is a quite eligible one—it is difficult to get people to go into the Church now. But I just want to say this to encourage such a person: Even if he has not the slightest desire to be an actor, he has just as good a chance to be a celebrated actor as people who devote all their lives to the theatre. I say that as a general encouragement.

But I am most interested when I come to that side of the matter which is the satisfaction of an instinct, because then it becomes psychologically very curious. Humanity produces two types occasionally. In their extreme form they are not very common; but these two types created the theatre originally. There must have been some man, probably in archaic Greece or anywhere you like, who, instead of earning an honest living as a carpenter or a mason or something of that kind, or even as a politician, although that might have satisfied his instincts— You find that this man—and the same thing applies to women, although it began with men—this man does not want to be himself. He wants to magnify himself, he wants to be a hero. You don't get opportunities every day of being what is called a real hero. You don't find battles ready for you in which to win Victoria Crosses. You may have no opportunity at all: and the result is that, not having an actual opportunity of being a real soldier, you have to pretend to be a soldier; so you develop your personality, you give yourself the air of a soldier. Your wear your hair, or sometimes do, of a length at which heroes were supposed to have worn it at whatever particular period it happens to be; and you pose before your fellow-creatures, you utter heroic sentiments. If you are in a difficulty as to improvising the heroic sentiments, you may possibly get another person to do it for you, and learn them off by heart: in which case you invent the dramatic author—you invent me, in fact. But still there is this type of man, and he has to entertain. He begins by reciting, by playing all the different characters himself, and that is a propensity which still lingers among actors.

There are many actors nowadays who, although they do not play all the characters themselves, regret that they cannot do so. I ought in fairness to say that sometimes the author regrets that he cannot play all the parts as well. But at last the man who has spouted, if one may put it that way, to a crowd gets up on a soapbox, if there is such a thing, or stands on a barrel; and then finally he gets something more permanent. He wants a sort of stage or tribune to speak from; he gets beautiful costumes; he exaggerates his height with buskins. He still plays all the parts himself, but although he begins in that way he finds it is necessary to present a sort of something like what we now call a drama. Yet at first the necessity for playing all the parts himself brings him to this curious point. He says to the author, "I want to play both Romeo and Juliet, or Tristan and Isolde, whatever the case may be; but you must understand that Romeo and Juliet must never be on the stage at the same time;

Romeo must come on and make love, and then he must go away; then Juliet must come on and express her sentiments." The author naturally says, "This is very awkward." I suppose that after a time the authors made a little struggle and said, "Well, would it not be nice to have somebody else to play the lady? I will not make her part very prominent, but still it would help you a great deal; and really it would make it more interesting to the public." And so you get your drama in that way.

But over against this particular actor who is the tragedian, and who dreads above everything else on earth being laughed at—the one terrible and fatal thing for him is ridicule of any kind—there, side by side, strangely enough, in order to restore that balance which Nature always appears to have in view, there arises the other sort of man, who is born with a tremendous desire to be laughed at and who will undergo the most extraordinary ignominy, who will paint his nose red, who will allow people to kick him about, who will have the most disastrous falls, if only he can make people laugh.

This is a curious psychological thing. It has prevented me from being a really great author. I have unfortunately this desperate temptation that suddenly comes on me, just when I am really rising to the height of my power, that I may become really tragic and great: some absurd joke occurs, and the anti-climax is irresistible. I am reminded that there is a very distinguished actress,* who is among you today, who, instead of speaking of me respectfully as Mr Bernard Shaw, in the manner that is befitting to my age and years, always addresses me as Joey, the name of the clown in the pantomime. I cannot deny that I have got the tragedian and I have got the clown in me; and the clown trips me up in the most dreadful way. The English public have said for a long time that I am not serious, because you never know when the red-hot

* Mrs. Patrick Campbell.

poker will suddenly make its appearance or I shall trip over something or other.

There is another thing. There is the desire that we all have to escape from reality. Now a very great actress, Ellen Terry, once told me of this, when speaking of a play which I had written for her. In writing the play I did the sort of usual thing that an author does. The author, in writing for a particular genius, a particular personality, instead of thinking of gratifying that personality and enabling her or him to escape for a moment from himself or herself, seizes on the personality and dramatizes it. I did this with Ellen Terry in a play which she played with great success. But she said to me on one occasion: "I wish somebody would write a part for me to act. In this play of yours I have nothing to do but go on the stage and be myself, and the thing is done." There, you see, there came in this curious desire, that she wanted to escape from herself; she wanted to be somebody else for a time.

You get that on the stage, and you also get very interestingly precisely the opposite. You get other sort of artists whose desire is not to escape from themselves. Their desire is self-intensification. They want to develop and intensify their own personality to a tremendously magnetic and overwhelming extent, and in doing so, pursuing this entirely egotistical aim, they sometimes attain a degree of fascination which is quite extraordinary, and then you see the influence that an actor or an actress may have. . . .

The relations which arise between authors and actors owing to this difference, of course, are very interesting, although they ought to be preserved exclusively for behind the scenes, because what the author would like to do is to combine the intensity of the one kind of actor with the curious dramatic imagination of the other kind of actor who wants to be somebody else, wants to change his personality. The extreme, for instance, is well represented by certain actors who are called character actors. I believe that the reason that they go on the stage is an unconquerable shyness. You may think that shyness is about the very last thing that would drive a person on to the stage. You imagine that if a person wants to obscure himself, to be in the background, not to be called forward to say anything, the very last thing he would want to do would be to walk on the stage and face the footlights and all the other lights. And yet it is the most complete refuge that you can possibly imagine. If only you are a character actor, you can go and be somebody else, you never need betray your own personality. . . .

From all this you will see how extraordinarily interesting the theatrical profession is to anybody who is behind the scenes, and perhaps the best way to get behind the scenes is to come to this school and get trained, to take up the profession of an actor. But it requires a great deal of character to hold your own on the stage. The impression which some people have that you require less character to be an actor than to be anything else is a most terrible mistake. You must get that out of your heads at all possible costs. The way in which the stage will find out every single weakness that you have got, every vanity that you have got, every folly that you have got, every little slip in self-control that you are subject to, is really very terrible. Therefore, to come back to the children whom parents may want to send to this school, they had better send us the pretty strong characters, even if those strong characters, by the way, have revealed themselves by kicking over the traces in every possible direction in ordinary domestic life. . . .

Now, as I am coming to the end of my case, I may inform you that, as I am broadcasting, I may be cut down to the last possible second, though my own propensity is when I once get on my legs to go on for three or four hours. But that is not possible on this particular occasion, and in five or six minutes there

will be an end of me and you will be able to go and
take your tea.

But I want to say again, Why, after all, is it that
this curious mad art of ours, this elaborate pretending
to be somebody else, this satisfaction of instincts
which are entirely irrational and many of them absurd
—why is it, after all, that it does enjoy a royal charter
and royal patronage and all the rest of it? and why is
it that the public will forgive almost anything to this
profession of ours except being bored, and that they
are quite right not to be? Well, it is because we really
render—the art of the theatre, like many other arts,
renders—very conspicuous public service.

In the old days Aristotle said that tragedy purged
the soul with pity and terror; and the old definition of
comedy was that it chastened morals, chastened manners—because the word expressed both—by ridicule.
I have never regarded that as a permanent definition.
Ridicule may be rather unkind. I think the worst kind
of play is the comedy in which the author sets you
laughing at one another. The old-fashioned comedy,
to take a simple example, always made fun of old
women, simply because they were old. Well, that was
abominable and detestable. And so on all through.

As to pity and terror, if people's souls could only
be set going right by pity and terror, then the sooner
the human race comes to an end the better. You cannot
pity unless you have misfortunes to pity. That is the
reason, by the way, why I am not a philanthropist,
why I do not like philanthropists—because they love
suffering of all kinds. They are never happy unless
some one else is unhappy, so that they can exercise
their philanthropy. I do not want there to be any more
pity in the world, because I do not want there to be
anything to pity; and I want there to be no more
terror because I do not want people to have anything
to fear.

But there are other things. You may throw pity and
terror on one side, and you can reveal life, and you can

stimulate thought about it, and you can educate people's senses. If you look on that life as it presents itself to you, it is an extraordinarily unmeaning thing. It is just as if you took a movie camera and went out into the Strand or Piccadilly and began to turn the handle, and afterward developed your film and then said, "Well, that is life—all those people moving about." Lots of them have tragic histories, some of them have comic histories; some of them are abounding with joy because they are in love, others are going to commit suicide because they have been disappointed in love. It is all very wonderful! But when you look at the film you say, "Well, I don't see anything there but a lot of people running about in a perfectly meaningless way." Now what the drama can do, and what it actually does, is to take this unmeaning, haphazard show of life, that means nothing to you, and arrange it in an intelligible order, and arrange it in such a way as to make you think very much more deeply about it than you ever dreamed of thinking about actual incidents that come to your knowledge. That is drama, and that is a very important public service to render. . . .

Speech as Guest of Honor at London Critics Circle Annual Luncheon, October 11, 1929

("Shaw Tells Critics They're Never Good," *New York Times*, October 12, 1929)

I used to be a critic. I still regard it as one of the professions I keep in reserve. I gave it up because the profession of playwright which I adopted is very much easier, very much more illustrious, and much more attractively remunerative. You will notice I don't say it was better paid.

After all, a critic's payment was modest when I was in the first flight. I only got £6 (about $30) a week. That's as much as I ever got, but it was regular and you got a forty years' engagement. . . .

Now I was a critic in those glorious times now

spoken of with enthusiastic admiration, especially by the younger members, as the "glorious '90s," the great days of those wonderful critics Archer and Walkley, Clement Scott, Thomas, Joe Nye, and so on. I sat with those men on first nights and was one of them, and I find that a writer the other day in a Liverpool paper, in commenting on the reception of my last play, said:

"Oh, what would the criticisms have been like in the really golden and palmy days of dramatic criticism? Think of what Archer would have written about it! Think of what Walkley would have written about it!"

Well, I do think, and I am rather glad—well, I cannot say I'm glad—that two very affectionate friends of mine are dead, but, still, there it is.

I do feel called upon as a survivor from that time to tell you that dramatic criticism today is not worse than the criticism of that time. It could not be. After all, there are limits to what can be done by incompetence, by ignorance, by carelessness, and by the irresponsible, and in those old days, several times a week, those limits were reached cheerfully. You may try as hard as you like. You can get no further.

The gentleman who has just been mentioned by the president—Hannen Swaffer—he went out the other day for the record, and I believe he thinks he actually made it. He must not flatter himself. Let him go to the British Museum and turn up the newspapers of the '90s and let him read the notice in which William Archer, our most enthusiastic and devoted worshiper of Ibsen—read the notice with which Archer received Ibsen's last play. He will read. Then you will hear about drivelling idiots, back numbers, and people who are making a miserable exhibition of themselves. Swaffer cannot get beyond that.

Criticism is, has been, and eternally will be as bad as it possibly can be. I am speaking as critic myself. I did it myself. I am criticizing myself. It never can be worse. It is always down to the limit.

I wonder why? That is well to begin with when you
become a dramatic critic—and, curiously enough, we
ourselves cannot tell you how you do become a dramatic critic. It happens to you in some extraordinary
way. But when you become a dramatic critic nobody
ever asks for your qualifications. I never was asked
whether I could read or write, still less whether I had
ever read Shakespear or any of the other great dramatists whose names begin with the same two letters.

I can, however, tell you why I became a critic. I
did not at first become a dramatic critic. Your first
steps in crime don't go as far as that. I started as a
musical critic, or rather as a critic of music, which is
not always the same thing. My first editor was T. P.
O'Connor, and he made me musical critic, quite
frankly and explicitly on the ground that he did it to
prevent my writing about anything else than music.
My other writings were ruining his paper.

The only instruction he ever gave me—and it was
very sound instruction—was, "For God's sake, don't
fill the paper with Bach in B minor."

Accordingly, I became a critic, and there was no
inquiry into my qualifications. I was never interfered
with by an editor. I remember on one occasion I
wrote a notice in which I referred to an old melodrama and gave a little description of how it used to
be acted. When my notice appeared I found this
passage had been cut, and I asked the editor what was
wrong with it. He said there was nothing wrong with
it, but that the actress whom I had mentioned was
his mother.

Then I remember a critic who was interfered with,
not on artistic, but on purely political grounds. Austin
Harrison was critic of The Daily Mail, and when I
began to make trouble in the theatre Austin Harrison
was interested and wrote long notices of my plays.
They were either not put in or they were cut extremely
short. When Harrison, not undertsanding why this
happened, asked Lord Northcliffe the reason, North-

cliffe said, "I am not running my paper to advertise a damned Socialist."

So you see, a dramatic critic is never interfered with as such. Interference is always on political grounds. So you see, also, we have no qualifications. We can say exactly what we like. Nobody will interfere with us at all, and we are irremovable.

We are entirely irresponsible. Whether we are qualified or not is pure accident. Under those circumstances—I'm sorry for it, but human nature is such that under those circumstances men always do their worst, and they always will do their worst. There is no remedy whatever for it.

The only consolation I have is that every notice I get advertises me. Also, you must remember there is one check on the badness of dramatic criticism, and that is the talent of the critic. He cannot always help its creeping in in spite of himself.

Many dramatic critics really are very clever, and when they are at their worst they cannot get quite as bad as their irresponsibility might prompt them to do. Sometimes you see an admirable notice—for instance, a notice of The Apple Cart which was written by your president [St. John Ervine]. I thought it really was an admirable conception and a most praiseworthy performance for one so young, and I would like to give a sort of general hint to the whole circle that if they want to know the sort of notice I like, that's it.

I hope I have not given away the show too much. I really want to do a service to critics, because I think the public expects a little too much from them. I think if you will understand their position, if you will consider all that irresponsibility, all that certainty of our posts, the fact that no matter how ghastly a mess we make of it nothing happens—I think you will admit that under those circumstances we probably do well; just as well as you would do if you were in the same position.

On Gordon Craig's *Henry Irving*

(From an interview recorded by G. W. Bishop in *The
    Observer*, London, October 26, 1930; also in *The New
    York Times*, November 30, 1930)

Mr Craig thinks that I, a very prominent theatre
critic in those days, offered plays to managers: that is,
invited bribes. I did nothing of the sort: I published
my plays and offered them to nobody. They were there
on the table *à prendre ou à laisser*. Irving made me
the usual offer to announce my play* as accepted by
him, and place it on his already well-stocked shelf for
future production, with, of course, any advance on
account of author's fees that might be convenient to
me. When the expected change in my criticisms did
not take place my play was withdrawn from the list of
future productions. It was a pity he did not venture;
I could have got a fine performance out of him, and
incidentally taught him what real production and real
team-work mean in the theatre.

Mr Craig, in his quaint innocence, thinks that Irving
was insulted by my stage directions, and that the stage
business these indicated was borrowed from Irving
himself. That would probably have flattered Irving
enormously; but the truth is that the elaborate strokes
with which Irving built up his parts—which, by the
way, were always his own inventions and never those
of the author—would have been of no use to any other
actor. I of course annexed everything I could from
every actor and actress who could teach me anything—
for instance, from Ellen Terry; but Irving's business
was useless to me; and, as a matter of fact, I never
saw him in any of the parts which Mr Craig specifies
as having added to my bag of stage tricks. Why, in
any case, Mr Craig should disapprove of my learning
my business in the theatre instead of in the air is a
question which I leave him to answer.

* *The Man of Destiny*, eventually first performed in the United
States by Arnold Daly.

(Answer to question did Shaw not consider Craig had been neglected:)

Neglected! Why are we talking about Mr Craig at such length today? Why are you not bothering me with questions about Charles Ricketts and Paul Shelving, about Albert Rutherston and Norman Wilkinson, about Granville-Barker, about the designers of Mr Cochran's revues, about all the other English artists who have actually done the work that Mr Craig says he wants to do?

If ever there was a spoilt child in artistic Europe, that child was Teddy Craig. The doors of the theatre were far wider open to him than to anyone else. He had only to come in as the others did, and do his job, and know his place, and accept the theatre with all its desperate vicissitudes and poverties and inadequacies and impossibilities as the rest of us did, and the way would have been clear before him for all the talent he possessed. But that was not what he wanted. He wanted a theatre to play with, as Irving played with the Lyceum; a theatre in which he could frame his pictures in the proscenium, and cut the play to pieces to suit them, and forbid the actors to do anything that could distract the attention of the audience from his pictures.

Such theatres are not to be had; that is not what a theatre is for. So he had to be content to have his pictures and figures classed as "good to steal from," until he found his feet as a literary propagandist of pictorial art on the stage, and now at last, as an irresistible sort of goose-genius in artistic biography and autobiography. So please do all you can to go on exploiting that charm of his; and let us hear no more of the neglected fairy prince who would have redeemed the theatre from nothingness if only he had not been cruelly hindered by wicked people who went in crudely and did what came to their hand in the theatre as best they could.

(Answer to question did Shaw defend his stage directions against Craig's denunciations:)

They need no defence. Do you realize that my plays are being kept alive by desperate little bands of enthusiasts, mostly very poor, who perform them in all sorts of out-of-the-way valleys and villages, and pay me author's fees which sometimes do not exceed ninepence? These people have to buy my plays in the printed book, and get up their shows from the directions in them.

My First Talkie

(*Malvern Festival Book,*° 1931)

To the uninitiated general patrons of the Talkies the little film entitled How He Lied to Her Husband is a talkie like any other talkie. To those behind the scenes it is an experiment. Like all playwrights, I have had many proposals from the great film corporations for the screening of my plays, some of them tempting enough commercially. In the days of the Movies the objection to these proposals was that my plays were made to be spoken and could be of no use as silent plays, no matter how ingeniously they were patched by scraps of printed dialogue thrown on the screen as "sub-titles." When the Talkies arrived the situation was changed. It became possible for the screen not only to shew my plays, but to speak them. The rejected proposals were renewed.

But when we came down to the tacks, I found that the film corporations were nearly as far as ever from real play screening. The only business they had mastered was the Movie business; and their notion of a screened play was really only a Movie with spoken sub-titles. The only use they had for a play was to

° The souvenir program published annually, 1929–39, for the month-long festival held primarily in honor of Shaw. Twenty of his plays were produced at the Festival, seven of them for the first time in England.

re-arrange it as a Movie in which the actors were occasionally heard as well as seen; and the movie stars, instead of putting drama into their voices, put it, as they were accustomed to, into their facial expression and gesture, and then repeated the words by rote, unmeaningly and often very discordantly. Though they had acquired to perfection the special art of moving for the lens, they had no idea of the equally special art of speaking for the microphone.

In this phase the talkie art was quite useless to me. My plays do not consist of occasional remarks to illustrate pictures, but of verbal fencing matches between protagonists and antagonists, whose thrusts and ripostes, parries and passados, follow one another much more closely than thunder follows lightning. The first rule for their producers is that there must never be a moment of silence from the rise of the curtain to its fall. Hollywood would not hear of such a condition: it was, they said, impossible. To cut out half my dialogue, in order to insert dozens of changing pictures between the lines of what was left, seemed to them quite indispensable. So we parted with reciprocal assurances of the highest consideration, but—nothing doing.

It was, I think, the great success of the talking films in which Mr George Arliss appeared that first shook the Hollywood superstition. Mr Arliss's performances proved that a good play could be a good play, and good acting good acting, on the screen exactly as on the stage. British International Pictures resolved to try an experiment in the new manner; and I placed How He Lied to Her Husband at their disposal for the purpose. Mr Cecil Lewis, a playwright and stage producer, keen on developing the talkie dramatically, and free from Hollywood superstitions, undertook the direction.

The result can be seen and heard at the Malvern Picture House during the Festival. The points for connoisseurs are (a) that the dialogue is continuous from end to end, except when Mr Gwenn purposely makes a silence more dramatic than words could be, and (*b*) that as the entire action takes place in the same room, the usual changes from New York to the Rocky Mountains, from Marseilles to the Sahara, from Mayfair to Monte Carlo, are replaced by changes from the piano to the sideboard, from the window to the door, from the hearth rug to the carpet. When the husband arrives he is not shewn paying his taxi, taking out his latchkey, hanging up his hat, and mounting the stairs. There is no time for that sort of baby padding when the action of a real play is hastening to its climax. Yet I do not think anyone will miss it. It will seem incredible that only the other day Hollywood declared that such things are the life and soul of the films.

When *How He Lied* was produced in London the young film fans complained that the conversation of my characters was such as had never been heard except in old-fashioned nineteenth century super-literary books. The poor fellows had never read anything but a Hollywood sub-title. They could not be persuaded that English people really talk like that. My Malvern patrons will know better.

G.B.S.

August, 1931.

Gordon-Craig and the Shaw-Terry Letters

(From an interview by G. W. Bishop, *The Observer*, London, November 8, 1931, on Craig's attack on Shaw in *Ellen Terry and Her Secret Self* as "a very large, malicious poke-nosed old woman with an idle and vindictive tongue spreading falsehoods up and down the street"; also in *The New York Times*, November 29, 1931)

Oh, bother Gordon Craig! The baby is squalling again, I suppose. It always squalls when it sees me; and nobody will whack it because it is Ellen Terry's baby. Well, let it squall.

Craig flew away from the nest the moment his wings were fully fledged; and he saw very little of his mother afterward. And he was perfectly right. He had to save his soul alive. Make no mistake about it: Ellen Terry, with all her charm and essential amiability, was an impetuous, overwhelming, absorbing personality. She could sweep a thousand people away in a big theatre; so you can imagine what she could do with a sensitive boy in a small house. It was not until he had put the seas between them that he himself developed an impetuous and charming personality; and the result was that Isadora Duncan ran away from him exactly as he had run away from his mother. And Isadora was no nonentity either, as I found when I met her. What makes this book of his so tragically moving—for if you disregard the rubbish about me, which is neither here nor there, it is a poignant human document—is his desperate denial of the big woman he ran away from and his assertion of the "little mother" he loved. He still resents the great Ellen Terry, the woman who would have swallowed him up if he had stayed within her magnetic field, so intensely that he is furious with me because I did not tear her letters up and stamp them and her into the earth so that the world would never have known her, and she could never have played Nelly the little mother off the stage. I quite understand that; and this book of his, which will perhaps seem rather a skimpy little one to those who do not understand it, is a very full one, and a very touching one, to me.

There is also the complication that I am the ally of his sister Edith Craig, the Edy of the correspondence. Now if you read the account of Edy's childhood which Ellen Terry wrote to me, and compare it with what Craig says in this book, you will see that Edy was unsympathetic to her mother in her early years because she was developing her powers of resistance to this domestic tornado that would have swamped her if she had not had the strong will to which Craig testifies, and much greater tenacity than either her mother or her brother. Edy finally got the upper hand, and so lost her fear of her mother and with it her hatred of her—the word is a hard one; but children do really hate their parents in their struggles for independence. She became the champion of the great Ellen Terry, and had no patience with Nelly. That is why the brother and sister are at loggerheads over the publication of the letters.

(Shaw was asked why Craig had shown an anti-Shaw complex long before the controversy over the correspondence.)

Well, perhaps there is no explanation needed. To many people I am a repellent person with an odious character. One of my professions is the profession of critic, a sort of literary gangster whose business it is to put my victims on the spot; and the more skilfully and accurately I do it the less they like it. Mr Craig is under no obligation to like me. His mother did not like me at first; quite the contrary. And then, consider Mr Craig's very odd profession: he has presented himself to the world, and to some extent conquered it, in the capacity of the thwarted genius. No doubt that began at home, when he was up against the all-conquering mother and her faithful lieutenant, the strong-willed sister. But he not only kept it up when he had thrown off the yoke, but actually made a profession of it. And he has not done so badly out of it, because the world does not know that all the geniuses are thwarted in this world of commonplace. . . . Look at the other men whose work in the theatre has been associated with mine: Paul Shelving, Norman Wilkinson, Albert Rutherston, Granville-Barker! Look at Edith Craig herself, who, under conditions that would thwart any genius if it were thwartable, has not only produced many interesting plays but dressed them as well. There was nothing to prevent Gordon Craig from doing what they did except that if he had he would no longer have been a thwarted genius. That is the worst of being a thwarted genius; the moment you do anything your whole stock-in-trade is gone; and so the thwarted genius instinctively recoils from a job.

But do not conclude that Mr Craig has been of no use. The people who do the jobs—who are dexterous enough to adapt themselves to all the circumstances, however desperate, and can yet produce a presentable result—people like myself, for instance—are the curse of the theatre because they accept its poverty and insecurity and subjection to commercial considerations instead of going on permanent strike against them, like Craig. To him they are artistic blacklegs. They undersell him at every turn. He demands a hundred thousand pounds—or is it a hundred million? I forget —with a free hand, absolute dominion, and a theatre to play with; and though he doesn't get it and never will get it, I am very well pleased that he should keep reminding people that such a thing as a model performance of a play today is quite impossible: even the most brilliant and satisfying of our productions is still a makeshift, acted by artists whose position is terribly precarious, managed and financed at risks which make failure ruinous, and saved from absurdity mainly by the imagination of the spectators.

(In a folder pocket attached to the back cover of *Ellen Terry and Her Secret Self* was a pamphlet in which Craig asserted that Shaw's comments in the preface to the correspondence were "a pack of deliberate lies, purposely invented to damage my mother, my father, myself, my family, Irving, and a few more." Asked if these statements were true, Shaw commented:)

Technically and literally, no; they are a string of flat whoppers. Here is his written consent to the publication of the letters: you cannot mistake the signature. You can quote it if you please. He not only consents to the publication but explicitly gives his word not to do what he has done in his book. But do not get virtuously indignant: his consent was extorted by circumstances, and his heart was not in his promise. I do not blame him, for I knew my man; and my object

was to make it impossible for him to attack his sister
and denounce the publication of the letters as an outrage without putting himself hopelessly in the wrong.
I guessed that he would be unable to resist doing it;
and I guessed right. But I shall not pretend to mount
the moral high horse at his expense; for he was not on
the spot, and does not know what really happened.
There was a change of attitude on my part which no
doubt misled him.

When Ellen Terry died, Miss Craig thought that a
volume of her letters might be compiled for publication; and she wrote to me as to other friends to ask if
I had any letters. I replied that I had some hundreds;
and I sent them to her so that she could pick out any
that were suitable for such a volume, just as Ellen
Terry, in her Memoirs, had included a suitable letter
of mine. You must understand that I had never read
the correspondence as a whole, and that I recollected
it at a distance of thirty years. But Miss Craig did
read it as a whole, and at once formed the opinion,
which has received such overwhelming confirmation
from the reviewers, that it brought her mother to life
in her real character and in all her strength with a
force and vividness which made it a duty to her
memory to publish the correspondence in full. At first
I was almost as stupid as Craig: I remembered only
the very intimate and affectionate character of the letters and declared that their immediate publication was
impossible. But as it was clear that some day or other
they would be published, and I had better leave a
document to explain them, I wrote an explanation for
posterity. This was entitled Preface to be attached to
the correspondence of Ellen Terry and Bernard Shaw
should it ever be published and was marked "Very
Private." I sent a proof of it to Mr Craig and another
to Edith Craig. Mr Craig declares, and will probably
declare to his dying day, that this document was a
pamphlet which I was circulating widely to confound,
destroy, insult, and ruin himself, his father, and his
entire family. It is now before the public as the preface

to the correspondence. Mr Craig and his family are none the worse for it; and I will give a penny to anyone who can discover in it the faintest disparagement of his father, Edward Godwin, whom I never met, and whose production of a Greek play at the old Circus in Argyle Street many years ago pleased me very much.

The effect on Miss Craig was that she made up her mind that the preface should be published at once as well as the letters. I was perplexed, and showed the proofs to a small court of honor consisting of two persons, one of them a famous soldier and the other a lady, the head of a religious house, much respected by both of us. Without the letters the preface suggested to them only a correspondence that should not be published. I accepted their verdict, but Miss Craig remained unshaken. Presently legal questions arose. Ellen Terry's executors had to realize her estate for the benefit of Miss Craig and Gordon Craig's children. My letters and Ellen Terry's copyrights were sold, and the assignee of the copyrights announced his intention of publishing Ellen Terry's letters by themselves if he could not induce me to consent to the publication of mine with them. Under this pressure I consented to the publication of a limited edition at a high price for the benefit of the Ellen Terry Memorial Institute which Edith Craig and Lady Maud Warrender were establishing at Smallhythe, in Kent, and which could be financed by no other means. It was the preparation of this edition which led to my reading the correspondence as a whole for the first time, and it converted me to Edith Craig's opinion.

When I make up my mind I do not make it up by halves, and I agreed that my hesitations had been absurd and that the limited edition should be followed by an ordinary unlimited trade edition at ordinary prices. But I made it a condition that Mr Craig should be consulted, and he, swearing he would ne'er consent, consented, as you have seen. I proposed that he should write a preface, and he entertained this until he learned that the proposal was suggested by me, whereupon he repudiated it with vehemence, declaring that it was a trap for him. He was treated by me throughout with inhumanly scrupulous correctness and by his sister with anxious consideration.

To sum it all up, I don't think the public will be misled by Mr Craig's grouch against me. After all, I wounded that sacred thing, a boy's idolatry of the first great actor he ever saw. And his psychopathic hatred of "the great Ellen Terry" will be forgiven for the sake of his romance about "little mother Nelly." But he has allowed his psychosis to carry him to the length of suggesting that his mother's last days were darkened by his sister's excessive surveillance, and then making the crazy statement that the stroke which killed her was caused by her eating something that disagreed with her when his sister was absent, implying that he was orphaned by this neglect. Here he seems to me to go beyond the bounds within which it is possible for even his greatest admirers to defend him: and at this point accordingly I throw up my brief for him and wish you good morning.

Arms and the Man on the Screen

(*Malvern Festival Book*, 1932)

Following up the experiment shewn last year at Malvern with the little film of How He Lied to Her Husband, I have this year repeated it on a larger scale with the screening of a full-length comedy. It may interest those who have seen the play on the stage to note how the physical and economic limitations of the theatre are expanded by the possibilities of the picture house. In the play the incident in the battle of Slivnitza, on which the story turns, is not seen: it has to be described in a lady's bedroom. The whole action of the play has to be confined to three scenes, two of them indoors. In the picture the battle is shewn, and the flight of the fugitive whom the heroine shelters. There is no pinning of the characters to one spot: they pass in and out of doors, upstairs and downstairs, into gardens and across mountain country, with a freedom and variety impossible in the room with three walls which, however scene-painters may disguise it, is always the same old stage.

As to the economic limitations, British International Pictures have, without thinking twice about it, spent as many pounds on this picture as any manager could afford to spend pence on the plainest and cheapest performance of the play.

Later on, these advantages of the picture house may enable it to supersede the theatre for all except very specialized work. It is in fact already doing so, though the accompanying spread of the taste for and knowledge of dramatic art has reacted favorably on the business done in the old theatres in the old way. But the films, in spite of all their splendors and enchantments, are still in their infancy. When dramatic poets (as they call us authors in Germany) realize the possibilities of the screen, and the performers master its technique, and the great producing corporations, still too much obsessed with the "movie" tradition, can be persuaded that a good play is not ready to be photographed until the actors have grown into it as completely as they do in the theatre after not only a month's rehearsal but a month's performance before the public, then every corner of the country in which a picture house can live will witness performances compared to which this one of Arms and the Man will seem a mere sketch, in which the talent of the actors has produced a few happy moments under difficulties not yet, but presently to be, triumphantly overcome.

G.B.S.

July 1932

Too True to be Good

(*Malvern Festival Book,* 1932)

Too True to be Good was written for Malvern; but
as the Malvern Festival comes only once a year, the
Theatre Guild of the United States captured the first
performance, with Poland a good second. The American critics (whom you must carefully distinguish
from the American public) on the whole disliked the
play. I am used to that; but this time they annoyed
me by taking the young gentleman-soldier-burglar-
chaplain in the play to be the mouthpiece of my own
opinions and the mirror of my own temperament, and
informing the world that I am finishing my life in a
condition of pitiable but theatrically very tiresome
disillusion and despair, having recanted all my professions, renounced all my convictions, abandoned all
my hopes, and demolished all my Utopias.

Many people are like that, both in America and
here: if you hint that there is not a paradise they call
you a pessimist, though they never stop grumbling
at the abominable way in which they are being treated
by their own Governments. They also never tire of repeating that I point out evils without suggesting
remedies, and am therefore not a practical man. Lest
our English critics should start all that over again when
they come down to Malvern—and many of them are
quite capable of it—let me hasten to assure them that
I have not recanted, renounced, abandoned, nor demolished anything whatever, and that extremely practical and precise remedies, including a complete political reconstitution, a credible and scientific religion, and
a satisfactory economic scheme, are discoverable by
anyone under thirty (the older ones are past praying
for) who will take the trouble to bring his or her education up to date by retiring into a House of Study and
Contemplation and reading my works carefully through

from beginning to end. I wrote them with a view to that; for though my trade is that of a playwright, my vocation is that of a prophet, with occasional lapses into what uncivil people call buffoonery. If my admirers dislike these lapses they should take care not to make me laugh, and to remember that there are others who think that I am endurable only when I indulge my unfortunate sense of humor.

In Poland, where criticism seems better equipped culturally, the success of the play so terrified the authorities, that they sacked the censor who had, in deference to my reputation, passed the play without reading it. Do not, however, waste sympathy on this enlightened official: he was reinstated three days later, presumably to avert a pro-Shavian revolution; and the play was allowed to proceed subject to the excision of all the disparagements of war in the last act. I invite the attention of the League of Nations, and of all Pacifist leagues and conferences, to this gesture by the Polish Government, and the light it throws on the real views of Poland as to the moral respectability—not to say glory—of war. Not that I would suggest for a moment that those views are a jot different from the views of the other imperialist States; but none of them have been quite so candid about it as the Polish Government in this instance.

The moral of my play, or rather the position illustrated by it, is simple enough. When wars were waged by professional armies, the reversal of morality which they involved was kept in a conscience-tight compartment: a civilian population might talk wickedly enough in its patriotic fervor; but it did not know what it was talking about: the actual slaughter and sack and rapine was only a story in the newspapers, not a real experience. But a war like that of 1914–18, in which the whole male population of military age was forced to serve, hosts of women volunteered for work under fire, and the new feature of aerial bombardment brought the bloody part of the business crash into the civilians' bedrooms, was quite another

matter. The shock to common morals was enormously
greater and more general. So was the strain on the
nerves. This time all the old romantic pretences of
"fearlessness" were dropped: nobody pretended to be
immune either from actual funk under the barrage or
from the wild reaction into security and hero-worship
when at home on leave. When terror had gone to its
limit, subsequent indulgence for everything, from the
pitch and tone of a night at The Byng Boys to the
manslaughter of a corespondent, obeyed the law that
action and reaction are equal. And so, for four years,
it was taken as a matter of course that young people,
when they were not under fire, must be allowed a
good time.

Now I do not at all object to young people having
a good time. I think they should have a good time
all the time, at peace as well as in war. I think that
their having a good time is one of the tests of civilization. But I very strenuously warn both young and old
against the monstrous folly of supposing that a good
time has any resemblance to those wartime reactions
after paroxysms of horror and terror, when the most
childish indulgence seemed heavenly and the most
reckless excesses excusable on the plea of "Let us eat
and drink (especially drink), for tomorrow we die."
Our difficulty now is that what the bright young things
after the war tried to do, and what their wretched
survivors are still trying to do, is to get the reaction
without the terror, to go on eating cocaine and drink-
ing cocktails as if they had only a few hours' expecta-
tion of life instead of forty years.

In my play the ex-war nurse and the ex-airman-ace
persuade a respectable young lady, too respectable to
have ever had a good time, to come with them and
enjoy the sort of good time they had in the nightmare
of 1914–18. My stage picture of the result of the experiment will, I hope, deter any respectable young lady
who witnesses it from relieving the tedium and worth-
lessness of idle gentility in that way.

The demonstration is rather funny at first; but I

know my business as a playwright too well to fall into the common mistake of believing that because it is pleasant to be kept laughing for an hour, it must be trebly pleasant to be kept laughing for three hours. When people have laughed for an hour, they want to be serio-comically entertained for the next hour; and when that is over they are so tired of not being wholly serious that they can bear nothing but a torrent of sermons.

My play is arranged accordingly.

G.B.S.

July 1932

An Aside

(From Lillah McCarthy, *Myself and Some Friends*, 1933)

I was very intimately concerned in the chapter of theatrical history which is also a chapter of this auto-biography of its leading actress. It did not seem an important chapter when we were making it; but now, twenty years after its close, it falls into perspective as a very notable one. I am often asked to write or speak of the development of the theatre, and to prophesy its future. I always reply that the theatre does not develop, and that it has, in the evolutionary sense, no future that will not repeat the past. From time to time dramatic art gets a germinal impulse. There follows in the theatre a spring which flourishes into a glorious summer. This becomes stale almost before its arrival is generally recognized; and the sequel is not a new golden age, but a barren winter that may last any time from fifteen years to a hundred and fifty. Then comes a new impulse; and the cycle begins again.

The impulse, like all creative impulses, is a mystery: that is, an unexplained phenomenon. Its outward and visible sign is a theatrical person of genius: a playwright or a player. The luckiest event is the coinci-

dence of memorable playwriting with memorable
acting. The present autobiography is the story of an
actress who was caught by one of these germinal
impulses; and, as it happened, I, as playwright, was
its vehicle (or victim) when it stirred up the depths
of our stagnant dramatic poetry and volatilized it into
tragi-comedy in the last decade of the nineteenth
century.

In 1889 the London stage had come into shattering
collision with the Norwegian giant, Ibsen. I say shattering advisedly because nobody could follow up Ibsen.
He knocked the fashionable drama of the day out of
countenance without effectively replacing it, because
his plays could never be forced on the London theatre
for more than a fortnight at a time except when some
player made a personal success in them. It was this
that distinguished his case from that of Wagner, who
not only delivered an equally smashing attack on the
old-fashioned Italian opera-houses but supplanted their
repertories by his own operas and music dramas so
completely that at last no one would pay a penny to
hear Lucrezia Borgia or Sémiramide whilst money
poured in for Lohengrin, Die Meistersinger, Tristan,
and even for The Ring. Wagner conquered and took
possession: Ibsen passed like a tornado and left nothing behind but ruin. When I say that he made even
Shakespear contemptible to inveterate Shakespeareans
like myself his effect on the standing of lesser playwrights may be imagined. They began to write unhappy plays, and, worse still, embittered plays. They
lost their ease of handling and their sense of humor.
They became a prey to doubts and compunctions
which they could not define: above all, they lost their
lightness of heart, without which nothing can succeed
in the theatre except illiterate sob-stuff and police sensation. And the ground lost in this way was not occupied by Ibsen, who soon seemed as extinct as the
least lucky of the playwrights he had destroyed.

And so the drama in London went staggering about

crazily for fifteen years. Everybody wanted a new drama of Ibsenian novelty and importance, but pleasant and with plenty of laughs at the right side of the mouth. No such drama was forthcoming at the West End theatres. The playwrights were all shell-shocked by the Norwegian broadside.

There was, however, one notable exception; and that was no less a person than myself. Ibsen had not shocked me in the least. Why was I immune? Because an earlier enchanter had taken me far outside the bounds of middle-class idealism within which Ibsen's bombshells were deadly. I am not by nature a good bourgeois any more than Shelley was; and I was a strong Shelleyan long before I ever heard of Ibsen from William Archer. And long after Shelley and yet still longer before Ibsen, came Karl Marx, whose indictment of bourgeois civilization, based wholly on English facts, utterly destroyed its high moral reputation and started throughout Europe a fire of passionate resolution to dethrone it and tear down its idols and laws and government, compared to which the commotion raised by Ibsen's Doll's House and Ghosts was a storm in a teacup. It is significant that though our press made a prodigious fuss about Ibsen as he sent the revolted daughters of the business and professional classes flying from the domestic hearth "to live their own lives" in all directions, the leaders of the proletarian movement which has overthrown Capitalism in Russia took no notice of Ibsen. They were not unaware of him; for at the first performance of A Doll's House in England, on a first floor in a Bloomsbury lodging house, Karl Marx's youngest daughter played Nora Helmer; and I impersonated Krogstad at her request with a very vague notion of what it was all about. But there is all the difference in the world between welcoming a dramatic poet as a useful auxiliary, which was the Marxist attitude towards Ibsen, and being wakened from a complacent satisfaction with Victorian respectability by a moral earthquake which threatened to bring every suburban villa crashing to the ground in a hurricane of Feminism and Anti-Clericalism and anti-Idealism.

I had the advantage of that difference. I had read Karl Marx fourteen years before Lenin did; and the shock of Ibsen's advent did not exist for me, nor indeed for anyone who was not living in the Victorian fools' paradise. All the institutions and superstitions and rascalities that Ibsen attacked had lost their hold on me. Consequently, whilst the fashionable Victorian playwrights who had never heard of Marx were reeling all over the place from the Ibsen shock, my self-possession and gaiety and grip of the situation were completely undisturbed; and when in response to various external suggestions and pressures I began writing plays, they were just as amusing and undistracted as if Ibsen had never been born. But they were also so strange to the theatre of that day, kept alive by a little group of fashionable actors who brought their artistic skill and attractiveness to the rescue of every successive rehash of the adulteries and duels which were the worn-out stock-in-trade of the Parisian stage and its London imitation, that when little private clubs of connoisseurs like the Independent Theatre and the Stage Society ventured on single performances of them, the Strand (as theatre-land was then called) could not accept them as plays at all, and repudiated them as pamphlets in dialogue form by a person ignorant of the theatre and hopelessly destitute of dramatic faculty.

Behind the scenes, too, I had my difficulties. In a generation which knew nothing of any sort of acting but drawing-room acting, and which considered a speech of more than twenty words impossibly long, I went back to the classical style and wrote long rhetorical speeches like operatic solos, regarding my plays as musical performances precisely as Shakespear did. As a producer I went back to the forgotten heroic stage business and the exciting or impressive declamation I had learnt from old-timers like Ristori,

Salvini, and Barry Sullivan. Yet so novel was my post-Marx post-Ibsen outlook on life that nobody suspected that my methods were as old as the stage itself. They would have seemed the merest routine to Kemble or Mrs Siddons; but to the Victorian leading ladies they seemed to be unleadinglady-like barnstorming. When Kate Rorke played Candida I seized the opportunity to pay her a long-deferred tribute to her beautiful performance of Helena in A Midsummer Night's Dream, which she had treated as a piece of music from beginning to end. To my amazement she changed color, and reproached me for making heartless fun of her only failure. When I convinced her that I was in earnest she told me how her musical rendering of that most musical part had brought on her such a torrent of critical abuse and misunderstanding that she had never ventured to attempt anything of the sort again!

No wonder I often found actors and actresses nervously taking the utmost care to avoid acting, the climax being reached by an actor engaged for the broadly comic part of Burgess in Candida, who, after rehearsing the first act in subdued tones like a funeral mute, solemnly put up his hand as I vengefully approached him, and said: "Mr. Shaw: I know what you are going to say. But you may depend on me. In the intellectual drama I never clown." And it was some time before I could persuade him that I was in earnest when I exhorted him to clown for all he was worth. I was continually struggling with the conscientious efforts of our players to underdo their parts lest they should be considered stagey. Much as if Titian had worked in black and grey lest he should be considered painty. It took a European war to cure them of wanting to be ladies and gentlemen first and actresses and actors after.

This difficulty was acute when I had to find a heroine for Man and Superman. Everybody said that she must be ultra-modern. I said that I wanted a young Mrs Siddons or Ristori, and that an ultra-

modern actress would be no use to me whatever in
the part. I was in despair of finding what I wanted
when one day there walked into my rooms in the
Adelphi a gorgeously good-looking young lady in a
green dress and huge picture hat in which any ordinary
woman would have looked ridiculous, and in which
she looked splendid, with the figure and gait of a
Diana. She said: "Ten years ago, when I was a little
girl trying to play Lady Macbeth, you told me to go
and spend ten years learning my business. I have learnt
it: now give me a part." I handed her the book of Man
and Superman without a moment's hesitation, and
said simply, "Here you are." And with that young lady
I achieved performances of my plays which will probably never be surpassed. For Lillah McCarthy was
saturated with declamatory poetry and rhetoric from
her cradle, and had learnt her business out of London
by doing work in which you were either heroic or
nothing. She was beautiful, plastic, statuesque, most
handsomely made, and seemed to have come straight
from the Italian or eighteenth century stage without a
trace of the stuffiness of the London cup-and-saucer
theatre.

It is an actress's profession to be extraordinary; but
Lillah was extraordinary even among actresses. The
first natural qualification of an actress who is not a
mere puppet, impotent without a producer, is imagination. Lillah had a great deal too much of it: she was
of imagination all compact. It was difficult to get her
feet down to the ground, and almost impossible to
keep them there. Her life was rich in wonderful experiences that had never happened, and in friendships
with wonderful people (including myself) who never
existed. All her geese were swans, flying about in an
enchanted world. When, as inevitably occurred from
time to time, real life and hard objectivity brought
her down with a stunning collision, she could be
tragically disappointed or murderously enraged; but
she could not be disillusioned: the picture changed;
but it remained a picture. On the stage she gave superb

performances with a force and sureness of stroke and a regal authority that made her front rank position unassailable; but if by chance her imagination started a fresh hare before she went on the stage she would forget all about the play and her part in it, and, whilst mechanically uttering its words and moving through its business, revel in the feelings of some quite different character. The effect of seeing an actress going through the part of, say, Lady Macbeth, under the impression that she is giving a touching representation of Little Nell is curious: at the Court Theatre we described it by the occasional dismal announcement that Lillah was blithering. In this way she was sometimes disqualified by an excess of qualification, like Shelley, who could not write a big poem without smothering it under a universe of winds and clouds, mountains and fountains, glories and promontories (with the accent on the Tories) until its theme was lost like a roseleaf in a splendid sunset. The one fault that authors and producers had to find with her was that she would not "stay put." And her friends complained, not without reason, of the startling discrepancies between her daily visions and transfigurations and the much less lovely facts of the case. You could not say that she had the faults of her qualities. Her faults *were* her qualities.

However, her technique fell in with mine as if they had been made for one another, as indeed they had. She created the first generation of Shavian heroines with dazzling success. Not merely playgoing London came to see her: indeed I doubt if playgoing London ever did to any great extent. Political London, artistic London, religious London, and even sporting London made the long series of performances in which she figured a centre of almost every vein of fashion except the hopeless old theatrical fashion. And she did this by playing my heroines exactly as she would have played Belvidera in Venice Preserved if anyone had thought of reviving that or any other of Mrs Siddons's great parts for her.

During the career of Mrs Siddons a play was regarded as an exhibition of the art of acting. Playwrights wrote declamatory parts for actors as composers did for singers or violinists, to display their technical virtuosity. This became an abuse: Wagner was quite justified in his complaint that singers thought only of how they sang, and never of what they were singing. Actors who had learnt how "to bring down the house" with a tirade were quite as pleased when the tirade was trash as when it was one of Shakespear's best. The cup-and-saucer drama, and the actor who, having no force to reserve, made a virtue of reserved force, were inevitable reactions against the resultant staginess, staginess being definable as much ado about nothing. The art of acting rhetorical and poetical drama, vulgarized and ridiculous, very soon became a lost art in the fashionable London theatres. Rhetoric and poetry vanished with it. But when I dragged rhetoric and poetry back its executive technique became again indispensable.

Lillah McCarthy describes in this book how she acquired and inherited from her father a love of verbal music in its loftiest ranges, and a physical necessity for declaiming it, with the inevitable accompanying craving for the beauty and dignity of noble architecture and statuary: a craving which could never be satisfied by dressmakers' and tailors' mannequins adorning "interiors" furnished by the best London establishments. Yet such actress-mannequins constituted the entire theatrical beauty stock in the cup-and-saucer drama. The continual efforts to give some sort of vital energy to these shop-window attractions by sex appeal, becoming less and less furtive until the interiors became bedrooms and the fashionable gowns had to be stripped off, mostly on no pretext whatever, in full view of the audience, seemed to Lillah poor stuff compared to a sonnet by Milton. When the new school arose she liked not only the matter of it (all the intelligent actresses did that) but its manner and method, in which she is today an adept,

and in the part of it which consists in the delivery of
English verse an unrivalled one. The horrible artificiality of that impudent sham the Victorian womanly
woman, a sham manufactured by men for men, and
duly provided by the same for the same with a
bulbously overclothed "modesty" more lascivious than
any frank sensuality, had become more and more irk-
some to the best of the actresses who had to lend
their bodies and souls to it—and by the best of the
actresses I mean those who had awakeningly truthful
minds as well as engaging personalities. I had so little
taste for the Victorian womanly woman that in my first
play I made my heroine throttle the parlor maid. The
scandal of that outrage shook the London theatre and
its Press to their foundations: an easy feat; for their
foundations were only an inch deep and very sandy
at that; and I was soon shaking more serious impos-
tures, including that of the whole rotten convention as
to women's place and worth in human society which
had made the Victorian sham possible. But for that I
needed the vigorous artificiality of the executive art of
the Elizabethan stage to expose and bring back to
nature the vapid artificiality of the Victorian play.

Lillah McCarthy's secret was that she combined
the executive art of the grand school with a natural
impulse to murder the Victorian womanly woman; and
this being just what I needed I blessed the day when
I found her; and, if I become Dictator (which may
happen to anybody nowadays), will most certainly en-
gage and command her, for an enormous salary, to
broadcast all the loveliest and splendidest pages of
English literature every day to them that have ears to
hear her.

Ayot St. Lawrence,
May 1933

Dramatic Antiquities at Malvern*

(*Malvern Festival Book*, 1933)

I sometimes wonder what the Festival pilgrims at Malvern, the real devotees who come and sit out the whole week's program faithfully, make of it all. Being themselves twentieth century products, they solemnly sit out a series of plays ranging from the seventeenth to the early nineteenth centuries. The seventeenth century plays are horrible, the eighteenth century ones silly and improper, the nineteenth century ones outrageously ridiculous. That does not diminish their attraction; people love horror if only it is horrible enough and they are not themselves the victims; and they are amused by silliness and impropriety gracefully and cleverly handled. They enjoy mockery well enough to tolerate the speeches of the heroines in Money and London Assurance. Besides, these plays are exhibitions of the art of acting; and people love the art of acting, and are bored by the elaborate suppressions of it which constitute so much of modern theatrical "production."

For the sake of all these luxuries, the Malvern audiences are ever quite ready to drop the question as to how far the old plays have any relations with real life. Many playgoers go to the theatre to escape from real life, and rather resent its intrusion into the fairyland in which wonderful beings "dress up" and pretend and enchant and make us forget our rates and our rent and our family and relatives and creditors, and our despair of the possibility of a revival of trade. There is no limit to the pretending that an audience

* The Malvern program of 1933, under the general title "Four Hundred Years of English Drama," included *The Conversion of Saint Paul*, *Gammer Gurton's Needle*, Heywood's *Fair Maid of the West*, Dryden's *All for Love*, *The Love Chase* by Knowles, and *The Dancing Girl* by Henry Arthur Jones; also the first performance of *A Sleeping Clergyman* by James Bridie.

will tolerate if the story is dramatically told, the dialogue witty, the spectacle picturesque, and the actors fascinating. A theatre of make-believe, utterly unconscionable, will never lack audiences when these conditions are fulfilled.

Yet the best plays are those made of the very stuff of contemporary life in its most deeply felt aspects. This was brought home to us in Malvern when Sir Barry Jackson went behind the seventeenth century and produced the medieval Hick the Scorner.* The effect was magical. Not only were the naïve rhythms of medieval stage poetry much more musical than the euphuistic blank verse of the Elizabethans and post-Elizabethans, but the world in which the persons of the drama spoke was our own modern war-wrecked world. The long speech with the refrain "Worse was it never" might have been written on the very day of the performance. It might have opened the World Economic Conference of last June, or any of the other futile Conferences in which our bewildered statesmen meet only to leave their confusion worse confounded.

After Hick the Scorner the Renascence plays, the Rococo plays, the early Victorian plays, though they were entertaining enough in their way, could not take us in. As pictures of life they were the most amazing trash, but very instructive trash, too. Their idealism is still doing as much mischief off the stage as it did before the terrible onslaught of Ibsen exposed its danger and falsehood on the stage. It may be that in the end they will become unbearable, and be driven out of the Malvern Festival by medieval drama and post-Ibsen modern drama. Meanwhile, however, we can, without moralizing about them, make the best of their conscienceless romance, their thundering rhetoric in tragedy and malicious or salacious wit in comedy, their exhibitions of unrestrained "all out" acting, and the delightful unreality which enables us to shed torrents of painless tears over the woes of their heroines (Mrs Siddons estimated her success by the number of

* Produced (as *Hickscorner*) in the 1931 Festival.

ladies who fainted in the audience), and work ourselves up to passions and furies which leave us quite
unexhausted because they are all nonsense.

G.B.S.

Playwrights and Amateurs

(*Drama* XII, December 1933. A verbatim report of
speech at the British Drama Conference at Edinburgh,
October 28, 1933.)

You have been induced to come here today by an
announcement that I was going to deliver an address
on "some aspects of the British drama." You have
been deluded. I have not the slightest intention of
doing anything of the sort. I never did such a thing
in my life. I am not here in the familiar person of
Bernard Shaw talking on his own. I am here as the
humble delegate of the Welwyn Garden City Theatre
Society, and it is my duty to move the following
resolution, which I shall read; and you will have to
listen very carefully, because it is very long and involved:

*"That this Conference urges the extreme importance
of disinterested nurseries of drama and of the art of
acting of small dramatic enterprises started spon-
taneously by local residents"*—this takes a lot of breath
—*"in villages and towns outside the commercial touring circuits and calls the attention of playwrights"*—
I am a playwright—*"to the wisdom of reserving to
themselves personally the duty of licensing performances of their works by such enthusiasts on terms
reasonably within their means though possibly not
worth collecting commercially by their professional
agents."*

Now this resolution has the advantage of explaining
itself. It is not necessary for me to add another word.
I am therefore here in the position of a Cabinet

Minister who has to make entirely superfluous speeches and to say as little as possible in the course of them.

You see, I write plays. And when I was a young man, which is now an unreasonably long time ago, the man who wrote plays got paid by the manager of the theatre—usually in the first instance a London theatre. Then his play went a certain tour through the provincial towns which had theatres, where he got paid by the managers of the touring companies. That was how he got his living. But he had one other string to his bow. In all the big provincial towns, and the suburbs of London especially, bodies of infatuated ladies and gentlemen, when they went to a theatre and when they saw, say, my friend Sir Gerald du Maurier and Miss Gladys Cooper enacting a play in a very finished manner, all the ladies thought they could do Miss Gladys Cooper's part, and all the gentlemen thought they could do Sir Gerald du Maurier's part. Accordingly, they used to get together, calling themselves amateurs because it was a very disreputable thing to act for money, and also by many excellent people was considered a very serious sin. They gave the best sort of performance they could; and if there were any profits—which there very seldom were—they were very careful to give them to a charity in order to expiate the sin.

I think I must make it clear to you that Fine Art throughout the world is only known to a few people as being a really good thing, as being an edifying thing, as being a necessary part of civilization. The ordinary man, the ordinary peasant, and very largely the ordinary townsman, is firmly persuaded that all fine art is vice, and that it is a thing to be indulged in secretly, shamefacedly.

I do not know if any of you are familiar with the collection of folk songs which was made by my late friend Cecil Sharp. I well remember when Cecil Sharp in the South of England—in Somerset—began collecting these songs. He was in the garden of the Reverend Mr Marson, also a friend of mine, when in

an enclosed fruit garden—they being outside the fruit
garden—they heard one of the gardeners singing a
song. Cecil Sharp was struck with the beauty of the
melody, and he scribbled down the song, and said to
Marson, "We must get to this man. He may know
another song." Well, they went into the fruit garden
and they found the gardener there. The moment he
saw them there was an end to his minstrelsy at once.
They went to him and said they had heard him singing his song and they wanted to know whether he
knew any other song. The man immediately threw
down his spade and declared before God that he was
an honest, decent, respectable man who had not done
such a wicked thing in his life, and that he deeply
resented the aspersion they had made on his character.
They talked to him soothingly for some time. They
did not succeed in convincing him that what he had
done was an innocent and even delightful thing; but
they did succeed in making him believe that they were
just as great blackguards as he was and therefore
might be taken into his confidence. And so the collection of songs began. The gardener introduced them
to other people in the countryside. Every man had
his song or two songs, and so the collection grew.
But what bears on what I am saying today is that they
all believed that fine art's a wicked and a naughty
thing.

You see in this the shady side of what you call the
"amateur." The amateur was a person who was trying
to give the best imitation of something that he had
seen in the theatre; but he had to keep himself
absolutely clear of any suspicion of doing anything so
disgraceful as making money, and he had to expiate
his sin by giving the money to charity. Every playwright who was a genuine artist and respected his
profession and his craft naturally loathed such amateurs. They were a standing insult to our art; but
nevertheless they were worth five guineas a time. In
those days the amateur became a byword for incompetence and vanity; so all the playwrights, myself in-

cluded, put down "Amateurs, five guineas." That was
in the old time. My difficulty today is that this practice,
which was quite proper at that time, now remains, in
entirely changed circumstances, as a superstition, and
a very mischievous one.

At that time, if you went round the villages and
through the countryside looking for anything like
dramatic art, all you could find was strange performances by mummers at Christmas time, not inspired
by a love of art but by a desire to collect money. A
few villagers would blacken their faces and put on old
hats with a number of paper ribbons streaming from
them; and they came in and recited some doggerel
about St George and the Doctor which made one
wonder what the verses originally meant. Bailie Adams
gave you a Scottish specimen yesterday; and I can
assure you that, although I think he put it forward
as poor stuff, it was absolutely magnificent poetry
compared with efforts of the mummers in the South.
And that was the only dramatic art you had among the
villages and the people.

All that is completely changed, though the five-
guineas amateur still pays his five guineas. Allow me
here to say with the greatest possible emphasis that
the British Drama League is not the British amateur
movement, as it has been called. I hope that the main
business of the British Drama League will be to get rid
of that sort of amateurism altogether. But all through
the country in the villages and towns you find people
who are genuinely enthusiastic for the drama, many
of them really desirous to do the highest and most
interesting type of play. This it is that brings them into
personal contact with me. And now comes the question. Very often these little devoted bands, before they
can give their performance—I do not say they actually
have to pawn their shirts, but it often comes to something very near that. Anyway, they manage to get up
a performance; and for an audience they may in a
village have a few rows of seats, and perhaps a few of
the gentry may be induced to come and pay half-a-

crown to sit in the front row—not very many. The rest
pay something like twopence. Sometimes performances
of my plays take place under those conditions. Well,
the receipts are, say, fifteen shillings. Now what is the
author to get? What can he expect under those circumstances? The authors who have never thought
about their position, those playwriting ladies and
gentlemen (we are not really ladies and gentlemen,
though we are politely called so)—what do they do,
many of them? They go to these unfortunate people
who have beggared themselves to give a dramatic
performance out of pure love of art and have managed
to get back fifteen shillings; and they say, "Five
guineas, please!" Well, are there any words of mine
that can sufficiently contemn such outrageous and unreasonable rapacity? In that happy land Switzerland,
plays can be performed by anybody on paying a
specified percentage—I think it is only 2 per cent.

I am very fond of money; and the older I get the
more fond I get of it; but if I were to charge five
guineas, what would be the result? Well, I should
not get it, because they could not afford to perform
my play. Am I to come with these ridiculous five-
guinea fees, which were previously a mere spoiling of
the Egyptians, to these people who are the very seed
from which the drama springs, from which all the
taste, the love of the drama, the power to act the
drama, the love of seeing it, all come? What do I do?
I don't let them off, because if I let them off with
nothing, that would be black-legging, that would be
unfair competition with my fellow-playwrights. I
charge them exactly what I charge the professionals—
that is, a percentage of the gross receipts. I cannot
see why, when these people have shown such devotion,
especially to myself, when they have chosen my play
as the sort of play they want to do, when they have
made these sacrifices to do it, when they have brought
the play to a place where no professional would ever
dream of bringing it—I cannot see why I should
charge them more than I should charge the very lowest

type of professional man who goes round with a disgraceful show, and, when he makes any profit, gets
drunk on it. I am not saying that this is the typical
professional. But that sort of professional will get his
license from the members of the League of British
Dramatists for five per cent or less. And then the
devotees of the drama are asked to pay five guineas!

I come back to that five guineas with loathing and
disgust. I ask whether there is any playwright— (I
have a B.B.C. microphone here and I hope a lot of
them are listening. I am supposed to be talking to you,
but I am talking at them.) I say that they do not deserve to have their plays performed at all unless they
are prepared to adapt them to the means of the very
poorest people. By all means let them go on with the
five guineas for the old lot of amateurs, who, I am
happy to say, are becoming extinct. But if I treat all
genuine drama lovers as I do, as professionals, if I
give them professional terms, they must not call themselves amateurs. My difficulty is that unless we of
the Drama League make it thoroughly understood that
we do not hold a special brief for amateurs—that we
do not want to encourage amateurs of the old type—
we will have all those little societies innocently calling
themselves "The So-and-So Amateur Players." Then if
they come to me, I say, "Amateurs, did you say? Five
guineas!" They must drop that term.

We had a meeting here this morning at which a
member of our League moved, with the best intentions, a resolution to the effect that in certain performances nobody should be paid; that the producer
should not be paid; and that nobody should make a
living out of dramatic art. I did not say anything on
that occasion, because I was speechless with rage. The
rule I want the British Drama League to make is that
everybody at all these performances should be paid.

What does constitute a professional performance?
If all the profits of the performance are kept in the concern for future performances, if the people call themselves the Portobello or What-You-May-Call-Them

Players, and if they keep a standing organization and keep on giving play after play, which is what they want to do, and if all the money that comes in is put to a reserve for future performances to build up a permanent arrangement, then unquestionably they are professional. What else is any professional supposed to do?

I have said that some professionals get drunk with the profits. Well, our people can do that also. If they prefer to go and have a jollification with the profits, nobody can question the complete professionalism of that. But when we try to make distinctions between people who are paid and people who are not paid, we find it impossible to distinguish between one class of performance and another. Take the most unquestionable professionals, people who are at the very top of their profession. Do you suppose that the old actor-managers—for instance, Sir Henry Irving, Sir Herbert Beerbohm Tree, or Sir George Alexander— do you suppose that *they* were always paid? There were many weeks in their lives in which, when they had paid everybody else, not only had they nothing left for themselves, but they were considerably out of pocket over the transaction. There are unquestionably professional companies in which the ghost does not walk, as the expression goes, and the principal performers have to come to the rescue of the manager and practically pay the deficit themselves.

Even supposing you say, as I am saying, everybody ought to be paid, well, it would be perfectly easy. Even the village players, if they could not scrape up money among themselves after paying my percentage, could at any rate borrow a shilling all round, and thus be in a position to say that everybody had been paid. I think that the only question is not whether these people should get professional terms, but whether they ought not to have less than professional terms. It sometimes happens that these people honestly write up to me in certain very difficult circumstances and say what they want to do, and my secretary writes

back to them and says she does not think I have taken
any notice of the letter and perhaps they had better
go ahead and say nothing about it. But I don't want
that altogether. I do like to get my ninepence or
one and sixpence. In the first place, it is rather a
pleasure to snub my fellow-playwrights who want their
five guineas, when I touch my hat to these poor people and request a renewal of their favors. There is
also this fact that I have to live in my modest way of
writing plays. It is a very difficult thing to do. Therefore I want to impress upon the minds of all the
players in the country, whether they are British
Drama League players or Repertory players or regular
professional players, that an author is a person who
has to eat and drink and clothe himself and lodge
himself, and that therefore they must not perform a
play without paying a little at any rate to the man
who wrote it. So, you see, I have my own little axe
to grind in the matter, as well as others.

You see now what I mean by this resolution. I want
the League of British Dramatists to get rid of this
nonsense about amateurism and professionalism altogether. All who are working for love of the drama
honestly to give the best dramatic performances to
the public they can, are entitled to professional terms.
You cannot draw a line and say, "On this side is
professional work, and on the other is amateur." The
only meaning that the words ever had is that on one
side there is bad work and that on the other there is
good work. That has ceased to be the case. I myself
have seen performances of some of my most elaborate
plays under the most difficult and ridiculous circumstances. I have seen them performed by people who
could not afford to dress their parts and were gro-
tesquely unsuitable to the characters they were playing, with no scenery whatever; and as to all the
business beloved by the old amateur of "make-up"
and lighting, there was nothing of that sort. There
were four boards and a passion, as the old saying goes;
and yet those novices got a quality into their per-

formance which you very seldom get in professional performances. It is partly because they are all doing it for the love of it, and partly because they have almost unlimited time for rehearsal. Their devotion produced the curious result that, in spite of all manner of difficulties, makeshifts, absurdities, and unsuitable casting, they got something that you do not always get in our metropolitan theatre.

Remember that Richard Wagner, the composer, said, quite truly, "Music is kept alive not in our great opera houses and in our concert rooms, but on the cottage piano of the amateur." I tell you—and this is my last word—that the drama in this country and in every country is not kept alive by the great theatres, although they do something for the highest departments of the art of acting, but by the love of the people for the drama and the attempts that they make themselves, when they are starved by the professional circuits, to give performances in the places the professional circuits do not reach. The object of the resolution which I now formally move is to make that as easy and as cheap for them as possible.

The Simple Truth of the Matter

(A reply to Joseph Wood Krutch's assertion in *The Nation* of March 6, 1935, that *The Simpleton of the Unexpected Isles*, with *The Apple Cart* and *Too True to be Good*, was pure vaudeville, devoid of meaning—"Shaw for Shaw's Sake." *Malvern Festival Book*, 1935)

Mr Krutch's article comes to me as a very welcome surprise from America. He found my play entertaining, and said so. Only those who have read the torrent of abuse with which the New York Press assailed and overwhelmed The Simpleton can appreciate Mr Krutch's courage in confessing that he enjoyed himself when sitting at it. The kindest thing his colleagues had to say was a description of me as "a dignified monkey shying coco-nuts at a bewildered public." It was really nice to call me dignified, though how a monkey shying coco-nuts can preserve the dignity of Jove hurling thunderbolts is beyond even my ingenuity as a stage-manager. Still, the softening adjective was kindly meant; and I was duly touched by it.

My heart goes out specially to Mr Krutch when he says, "I insist that Mr. Shaw's text is diverting; and the only way in which an intelligent spectator can prevent himself from enjoying it is by doing what intelligent spectators at Shaw plays have always been told to do: namely, try to discover its serious meaning." This is excellent. People come to a play as they come to all forms of art, to have their minds agreeably occupied in their hours of leisure. That is what they pay their money for; and my first duty as an honest theatrical tradesman is to give them their money's worth. As to their being "told to" look further and bother themselves with speculations about myself, I can only say that I object to it strenuously, and hereby curse to all eternity the officious duffers who do the telling. If I have ulterior designs, if in occupying the playgoer's mind agreeably I take advantage of his pre-occupation to extirpate his worn-out convictions and substitute fresh ones: in short, if I not only occupy his mind but change it, then the last thing I desire is that he should be conscious of the operation. The pickpocket does not want to be caught in the act. The burglar, however proud of his skill and daring, does not whistle for the police. I like my patients to leave the hospital without a suspicion that they have been operated on and are leaving it with a new set of glands.

But what takes place in a theatre is not always a simple matter of you please me and I'll pay you. If the playgoer is to keep up his (or her) power of enjoyment he must not stick in the same groove all his life. He must be prepared to come across from time to time a sort of play that quite upsets his notions of what a play should be. He may not like it at first; but if it takes a grip of the stage, he must go on enduring it until he does like it, or else give up going to the theatre and be derided by the young as a back number. When a play or a picture or a musical composition or a piece of sculpture is disagreeable at first sight, it is a mistake to run away from it, and revile its author for ever after. Of course, if there is nothing new in it, and its disagreeableness is due to mere folly and incompetence on the part of its maker, there is nothing more to be said. But if he is evidently a capable and skilled workman, and therefore must have made his work what it is on purpose and actually liked it, the chances are that you will like it too when you get used to it; for as he is a human being, built just as you are, his peculiar taste is a human taste and may therefore be acquired by any other human being at the same stage of civilized development. I can remember when Wagner's music was generally considered horribly discordant and quite destitute of melody. I can remember when Ibsen was denounced as an obscene and malignant lunatic. Plays of my own, popular enough now, were forbidden by the censorship for many years; and even today, when I am 79, the New York critics can see nothing in my latest play but the antics of a monkey. But they will get used to it in time; and when they shriek out their dislike of my next play, they will deplore it as an ignominious fall from the heights on which I produced that masterpiece, The Simpleton. All my plays are masterpieces except the last one. They always were. The donkey, no matter how fast he scampers, never overtakes the carrot.

There is, in fact, a force in nature which impels all born leaders in the arts continually to extend the scope of their works beyond the established and familiar form and content of such things. And, what is less often recognized, this same force impels audiences to come and endure this pioneering until they first discover that their old favorites have become stale and unbearable, and then that the new ones are not half bad when you get the hang of them.

As Malvern is, I hope, a much more cultivated centre of culture than New York, I have no hesitation in introducing The Simpleton to the British public at the Malvern Festival, though no doubt the London critics will make all their old mistakes about it as if they had not made them every time before. I can assure Mr Krutch that there has not been, as he suggests, any reckless new departure on my part: I have written The Simpleton exactly as I have written all my earlier plays, just as it came into my head. Naturally, it is more far-fetched than its forerunners, because I have already written plays on all the subjects that lay near to hand. I cannot go on repeating Back to Methuselah and Saint Joan, as musical comedy librettists go on repeating their old plots with nothing changed but the names and the tunes. I must go ever further and further afield except when I am coming nearer and nearer home; and it happens that in The Simpleton I am going further and further afield. And if you don't like it you must lump it—for a while—until you get used to the taste.

What I miss in Mr Krutch is a proper respect for the Apocalypse. As a child I was taught to fear the Day of Judgment, which was presented to my young imagination in so clear a fashion that once when I dreamt of it, I thought I had stepped into our garden in the middle of the night and seen above the gloom of the garden wall a great silver radiance in the sky, and in the middle of it a black equestrian statue like that of King William in College Green, Dublin, whom I immediately identified with God, come to judge the world. I did not call on the mountains to hide me; but I slipped back very quickly into the house and fastened the door noiselessly before the all-seeing eye lighted on me; for you cannot get it out of the head of a Christian child, or a Christian adult either, that God cannot be dodged and cheated like an earthly father.

That vision of judgment of mine was not more unlike any conceivable possible event than the great fresco by Michael Angelo in the Sistine Chapel in Rome, or that other one by Tintoretto in the ducal palace in Venice, or than the more compact painting by Albrecht Dürer. Such visions and pictures do not impose on the children in this age of science; and I should as soon think of dramatizing Jack and the Beanstalk as Michael Angelo's picture. But in rejecting all this imagery, we are apt to make the usual blunder of emptying the baby out with the bath. By all means dismiss the scenes painted by Tintoretto, Albrecht Dürer, and the rest as having no more reality than a Red Lion on a signboard. Cancel the authority of the Book of Revelation as the hallucinations of a drug addict which should never have been included in the canon. But do not think you have got rid of the idea of a judgment to which all human lives must finally come, and without which life has no meaning. On the contrary, the burning up of the old stage scenery and the exorcism of the old spectres only brings into clearer reality the need for justifying one's existence as well as merely enjoying or suffering it. The question "What good are you?" cannot be disposed of by the simple retort, "Mind your own business!" Even if it were not everybody's business in a civilized society, it is a question which people with properly trained social consciences cannot help asking themselves. In Russia, if the answer is not satisfactory, they occasionally go so far as to shoot you.

You may now declare that if this terrifying judgment is the theme of The Simpleton, you will take care to keep away from it. But you need not fear: you can depend on me to get plenty of fun out of the most dismal subjects and to improve your mind into the bargain. Even if you have to see beauty, chivalry, military heroism, and patriotic madness vanish like the phantasms of a long delirium, they will not pass away in a horror of September massacres, but in a very matter-of-fact and quite amusing manner. So take your courage in both hands, and face its first performance in England like a Briton.

One more word to Mr Krutch. I find it hard to forgive him for saying that I announced, in my last

Malvern play, Too True to be Good, that world
affairs are now irremediable, and that mankind is
damned beyond hope and redemption. I affirm, on
the contrary, that never before during my lifetime has
the lot of mankind seemed more hopeful, and the be-
ginnings of a new civilization more advanced. The
despair of the shell-shocked young gentleman-burglar-
clergyman who made such a pitiful attempt to be
happy by spending a lump of unearned money, is not
my despair, though I share his opinion of the utter
unsatisfactoriness of that popular receipt for a good
life. I made him a good preacher to warn the world
against mere fluency, and the result was that his
talking took Mr Krutch in. He must be more careful
next time.

This Year's Program*

(*Malvern Festival Book,* 1936)

On looking down the Festival program this year
I am apologetically conscious that there is too much
Shaw in it. The ideal program for Malvern would be
of new plays by new men. Here am I, by no means a
new man, offering one play 23 years old which every
playgoer in the universe must have seen a dozen
times, and another 12 years old and nearly as hackneyed as East Lynne. The only one with any pretence
of novelty is the three-year-old On the Rocks, unknown on the English stage outside London and
Birmingham, and still awaiting its first performance
in America this autumn. And it is wholly a political
play (the scene is in the Cabinet room in 10, Downing

* It included *Pygmalion, Saint Joan, On the Rocks, The Clan-
destine Marriage* by Garrick and Colman, S. I. Hsiung's *Lady
Precious Stream,* and first performances of *The Brontës of
Haworth Parsonage* by John Davison and of Helen Jerome's
Jane Eyre.

Street throughout); and though it has proved a striking example of how very funny a political play can
be without ceasing to be true to life, I wish I could
present something fresher and fitter for the Malvern
air. Unfortunately, the play on which I am at present
engaged, entitled Geneva, goes to the very depths of
politics. Besides, it is not finished.

What, then, is my excuse for reviving Pygmalion
and Saint Joan at this time of day? As far as I, the
author, am concerned, absolutely none at all. But the
art of the stage is not that of the author alone. The
actor is always the strongest attraction. People who
knew Shakespear's Hamlet by heart went to see
Garrick's Hamlet, Kemble's Hamlet, Macready's Hamlet, just as I during my long life have gone to see
Barry Sullivan's Hamlet, Irving's Hamlet, Salvini's
Hamlet, Forbes-Robertson's Hamlet, and, only the
other day, John Gielgud's Hamlet. From which you
may rightly affirm that I have a strong natural taste
for acting as distinct from writing, which is a different
affair. Shakespear could write Hamlet, but could not
act him (he had every opportunity) and had to content himself with a shot at the ghost, which is within
the capacity of any author with voice enough to read
his own lines. Stage history, which records the eminence of Burbage in the play, is silent as to the merits
of the author, who was also the spectre.

Now I, having this taste for the specific art of acting,
regard it as part of my business to provide effective
material for it. If you want to flatter me you must not
tell me that I have saved your soul by my philosophy.
Tell me that, like Shakespear, Molière, Scott, Dumas,
and Dickens, I have provided a gallery of characters
which are realer to you than your own relations and
which successive generations of actors and actresses
will keep alive for centuries as their *chevaux de
bataille*.

Take Pygmalion, for example. In 1913 its extraor-
dinary success in London was not the success of my
Eliza and my Higgins, but of Mrs Patrick Campbell's
Eliza and Beerbohm Tree's Higgins. What you see at

this year's Festival is Wendy Hiller's Eliza and Mr
Ernest Thesiger's Higgins, both entirely new and more
interesting than most new plays; for Thesiger is an
actor of great distinction whose range obviously ex-
ceeds that of the parts his cleverness as a comedian
often condemns him to play, whilst Miss Hiller's
sensational spring to the very top of the tree in
London in Love on the Dole makes her appearances
as St Joan and Eliza theatrical events of the first
magnitude. This is as it should be; for the Malvern
Festival would be nothing if it had not a tradition of
great acting as well as interesting dramatic literature.
Sir Cedric Hardwicke established this tradition from
the beginning; and Gwen Ffrangçon Davies, Edith
Evans, Phyllis Neilson-Terry, and Curigwen Lewis
have given performances which have made the Festivals
memorable quite independently of the authors who
were lucky enough to find such interpreters. With
that to fall back on, I need no excuse for myself. My
old plays and Garrick's old comedy will do as well
as the next best to shew what Malvern acting can do.

Besides, Sir Barry Jackson is ready, as usual, with a
new author who rouses my curiosity to eighty in the
shade. I have not read Jane Eyre since I was a boy
reading every book I could lay hands on (seventy
years ago, say); and I am keen to see what Curigwen
Lewis will make of her; or, shall I say, what she will
make of Curigwen Lewis? Not so bad a program, after
all.

Saint Joan Banned: Film Censorship
in the United States

Letter to The New York Times, September 14, 1936; also
   in London Mercury XXXIV, October 1936)

Some months ago statements appeared in the Press
to the effect that my play, Saint Joan, had been
adapted to the cinema by myself, and a syndicate
formed for the production of the film version with

Miss Elisabeth Bergner in the title part. These statements were duly authorized by me and by Miss Bergner's Press representatives. The facts were as stated;
and the way seemed clear before us. The play had
held the stage for eleven years throughout the civilized
world with such general approval, and especially with
such religious encouragement, that the possibility of
a conflict with the censorships which now control the
film world never occurred to me. Its revival in America by Miss Katherine Cornell has almost taken on
the character of a religious mission.

I am, of course, aware that there has been in the
United States a genuine revolt against pornography
and profanity in the picture theatres by good Catholics
who want to enjoy a beautiful art without being disgusted and insulted by exhibitions of silly blackguardism financed by film speculators foolish enough
to think that such trash pays. A body called the Hays
Organization has taken the matter in hand so vigorously that it now has Hollywood completely terrorized.
Without its sanction nothing can be done there in the
film business. The section of the screen industry which
is out for making money on the assumption that the
public is half-witted and depraved, has had a thorough scare, which was badly needed.

As I thought that the Hays Organization represented
unsectarian American decency, I never dreamt that
Saint Joan had anything to fear from it. Conceive my
amazement when I found that the censorship of the
Hays Organization includes that of a body called the
Catholic Action, professing, on what authority I know
not, to be a Roman Catholic doctrinal censorship.

It may be asked how a Catholic censorship can
possibly hurt me, as Saint Joan was hailed by all instructed Catholics as a very unexpected first instal-
ment of justice to the Church from Protestant quarters,
and in effect, a vindication of the good faith of the
famous trial at Rouen which had been held up to
public execration for centuries as an abominable conspiracy by a corrupt and treacherous bishop and a
villainous inquisitor to murder an innocent girl. The

reply is that I have certainly nothing to fear from
Catholics who understand the conditions imposed on
history by stage representation and are experts in
Catholic history and teaching; but as hardly one per
cent of Catholics can answer to this description, I
have everything to fear from any meddling by amateur
busybodies who do not know that the work of censorship requires any qualification beyond Catholic bap-
tism. And the Catholic Action turns out to be a body
of just such conceited amateurs.

Accordingly, I find myself presented with certain
specific requisitions from the Action to be complied
with on pain of having all Roman Catholics forbidden
to witness an exhibition of my Saint Joan film. What
will happen to them if they do, whether excommunica-
tion or a mild penance from the confessional, is not
specified. On my compliance and submission, and "if
the final film appears to be according to the truth of
the story, and does not contain anything against the
prestige of the Roman Catholic Church, the Catholic
Action (Azione Catholica) will declare that the shooting of such a picture has not met with any objections
from the Catholic authorities."

The censors of the Action object primarily that I am
"a mocking Irishman" (Ireland is now apparently *in
partibus infidelium*) and that my play is "a satire
against Church and State which are made to appear
stupid and inept." They follow this up with a heresy
which will make the Pope's hair lift the triple crown
from his head. In the play it is necessarily explained
that the Church must not take life. It could excommunicate Joan and hand her over to the secular arm,
but it could not under any circumstances kill her. The
Catholic Action is unaware of the existence of any
such scruple. It prescribes the following correction.
The Bishop must not say "the Church cannot take
life." He must say "The Church does not wish death."

At the Rouen trial Joan was spared the customary
torture, though she was threatened with it, and actually
shewn the rack, where the tormentors were waiting for
her. This incident, credited in my play to the mercy of

the Church, must, the Catholic Action demands, be omitted from the film, not because it is not true, but because it is "essentially damaging." The common use of torture by all tribunals, secular and clerical, in fifteenth century France, must not be revealed to the frequenters of picture palaces. No objection, however, is made to the revelation of the fact that Joan was deliberately burnt alive. The Action would have me teach that the Holy Office was far too humane to use the rack, but had no objection to the use of the stake by the secular arm.

But it is at the crux of the trial that the Action censor gets deepest out of his depth. There is no longer any obscurity on that crux: those who have not French enough to read Quicherat or Champion can read the excellent account by Mr Milton Waldman just published. When the Holy Office cleaned all the childish trifles out of the indictment, there was a perfectly clear issue left: the issue already raised by Wycliffe and Hus which subsequently developed into the issue between the Church and Luther. On this issue Joan convicted herself again and again in spite of the vain efforts of Cauchon and others of her judges to make her understand it. The question on which her fate turned was, Would she accept the Church as the inspired interpreter of the will of God instead of setting up her own private judgment against it and claiming that her conduct was a matter between God and herself? In this heresy she was adamant: no threat of torture, no argument, no affectionate appeal to her feelings could move her from it: George Fox himself could not have taken the Quaker position with more heroic obstinacy. The legal consequence was inevitable: there was nothing for it but to excommunicate her and deliver her over to the secular arm to be burnt; for no appeal to the Pope could have saved her: such an appeal must have had the same result as Cauchon's appeal to the University of Paris, which could not understand why he was hesitating.

To the last, Joan, strong in her spiritual experiences

and her voices, was sure she knew better than *"les gens de l'Église,"* of whom apparently she had much the same opinion as I now have of the Catholic Action's film censors. But when she did at last understand that she would certainly be burnt alive unless she recanted, she said with her rough common sense she would sign anything rather than be burnt. And sign she did: her immediate object, apart from the fire, being to escape from the indecent custody of Warwick's soldiers into the custody of the Church under conditions proper to her sex. But as Warwick would not let her go, her judges perforce broke their promise to her. Her voices reproached her for having betrayed them. She recanted her recantation, and thus became a relapsed heretic. As such she was beyond redemption. She had to face the stake and go through with it.

Perhaps as Joan could not make head or tail of the ecclesiastical law, the Action's censors may be excused for being equally at a loss. In desperation they have demanded the excision of all that part of the trial and of the incident of the recantation. This trenchant stroke would convert my account of a perfectly legal trial, in which the accused was, as far as the Church and the Holy Office were concerned, treated with special consideration and meticulous regard for the law, into a judicial murder like nothing except the trial of Faithful in The Pilgrim's Progress. It would restore the Belfast Protestant view of the Church which prevailed in literature until my play exploded it. That is what comes of conferring a power over the drama which would tax the qualifications of a Gregory or a Hildebrand on a body pretending to represent the Vatican without as much knowledge of Catholicism as any village gravedigger.

Besides, the Church was not finally beaten in the matter of Joan. The Church has a place for all types of character, including the ultra-Protestant. It admits that there are certain extraordinary persons to whom direct celestial revelations are vouchsafed. St Catherine

and St Michael, revealing themselves to Joan in the
fields at Domremy, and giving her divine instruction
as to her work and destiny, are no more outside the
belief of the Church than the Blessed Virgin in the
cave at Lourdes revealing herself to Bernadette Soubi-
rous. But just as persons of deep piety can attract
to themselves heavenly patrons and counsellors, so
equally can diabolically wicked persons, called witches
and sorcerers, attract to themselves hellish tempters,
personified in the fifteenth century as Satan, Belial,
and Behemoth, in heavenly disguises. It was inconceivable to the Rouen tribunal that Joan could be a
saint; and the alternative was to condemn her as a
witch. That procedure was strictly legal, strictly reasonable, strictly pious. In 1920, however, the Church
finally decided that Joan was a saint after all, and
canonized her.

This has settled the whole question for the Church.
Joan's voices came from heaven, not from hell. And
the Rouen judges were not corrupt, unjust, lawless,
nor any of the infamous things the Rehabilitation inquiry imputed: they simply mistook a very extraordinary saint for a witch. The Catholic Action must
be aware of the fact of the canonization; but it has not
yet readjusted its views to the 1920 situation. One of
the consequences is that Miss Elisabeth Bergner is
to be seen everywhere on the screen as Catherine of
Russia, Empress of Freethinkers and Free Lovers, but
may not make the world fall in love with a Catholic
saint as she did when she created the part of Joan in
Protestant Berlin when my play was new.

I cannot accept the pretension of the Catholic Action
to represent the Vatican. It has neither the knowledge
nor the manners to sustain such a part. It is as obnoxious to the United States Constitution as any of the
features of the New Deal forbidden by the Supreme
Court. It has no legal authority to enforce its vetoes.
Yet it has brought all the Hollywood financiers and
corporations to their knees by the threat that if they
dare to produce a film banned by it not one of the

twenty million Catholics in the United States will be allowed to cross the threshold of any picture house exhibiting it.

But what a paltry understatement of the Catholic position! The United States is not the whole realm of the Catholic Church, nor even as much as half that realm in America. What about South America and Quebec? What about the rest of the world? The Catholic population of the globe is estimated at 324 millions, of whom less than 50 millions are in the dominions of the United States and the British Empire. The Hollywood financiers believe that the Catholic Action can by a shake of its head keep twenty millions of Catholics out of the picture theatres. But if their belief is well founded it has but to hold up its finger to keep more than 324 millions of Catholics at home in the evenings.

I am not quite so credulous as the Hollywood financiers. I was impressed in my Irish Protestant infancy with the belief that every Catholic, including especially the Pope, must go to hell as a matter of divine routine. When I was seven years old, Pope Pius IX ruled that I, though a little Protestant, might go to heaven, in spite of my invincible ignorance regarding the Catholic religion, if I behaved myself properly. But I made no reciprocal concessions at the time; and no Catholic alive can bluff me into believing that, even had he the Vatican behind him, he could keep Papists (as I used to call them) even out of the saloons and speakeasies, much less out of the much more enjoyable theatres and picture palaces. I will make the Action a present of all the Catholics who never dream of going to a theatre under any circumstances; but I defy it to add a baker's dozen to that number by any interdict it can utter. And I promise it, in the case of Saint Joan, that wherever there is a cultivated Catholic priest who knows my play, he will do everything in his power to deepen the piety of his flock by making them go to see it, and urging them to make converts by inducing Protestants to do the same.

Did not one of the princes of the Church in America publicly decorate the first American impersonatress of St Joan? I hope this service of mine to the Church may be accepted as a small set-off against the abominable bigotry of my Irish Protestant childhood, which I renounced so vigorously when I grew up to some sort of discretion and decency that I emptied the baby out with the bath, and left myself for a while with no religion at all.

I make all this public because I believe very few inhabitants of the United States, Catholic or Protestant, lay or secular, have the least suspicion that an irresponsible Catholic society has assumed public control of their artistic recreations. I do not consider public control a bad thing in itself. I greatly prefer it to the irresponsible and sometimes vicious private control which is the real alternative. But I have again to point out that censorship is the wrong method. Whatever its moral and religious pretences may be, it always comes in practice to postulating the desirability of an official with the attributes of a god, and then offering the salary of a minor railway station-master plus a fee per play to some erring mortal to deputize for Omniscience. He who is fool enough or needy enough to accept such a post soon finds that except in the plainest cases judgment is impossible. He therefore makes an office list of words that must not be used and subjects that must not be mentioned (usually religion and sex); and though this brings his job within the capacity of an office boy, it also reduces it to absurdity. I find in the copy of my scenario that fell into the hands of the Catholic Action that the word paradise, and an allusion to a halo, are struck out because they are classed as religious. The word damned is cut out apparently because it is profane. The word God is cut out, St Denis is cut out, sentences containing the words religion, archbishop, deadly sin, holy, infernal, sacred office, and the like are cut out quite senselessly because they are on the list. Even the word babes is forbidden, presumably as immodest. These absurdities represent, not

the wisdom of the Catholic Church, but the desperation of a minor official's attempts to reduce that wisdom
to an office routine.

There is an epidemic of censorships at present raging
through the United States as a protest against a
very licentious anarchy which has hitherto prevailed.
Through a crowd of amateur regulations and lists of
words varying from State to State and even from city
to city the anarchists, the pugilists, the pornographers
can easily drive a coach and six, as it is useless to
check up on the letter if the spirit still eludes. But the
serious plays like Saint Joan get stopped because they
take the censorships completely out of their depth.
Presently the epidemic will abate, and the picture trade
pluck up enough courage and public spirit to insist
on the control of film morality being made a federal
matter, independent of prudes, of parochial busybodies, and doctrinaire enemies of the theatre as such.
As to the method of that control, there is only one
which has proved sensible and practicable. Have your
picture houses and theatres licensed from year to year
by the local municipal corporation, with power to the
corporation to discontinue the license on evidence that
the house is ill conducted or for other "judicial reasons." That will put an end to the irresponsibility of the
exhibitor without destroying the liberty that is vital
in those departments of social activity which are
roughly classed as highbrow. And as such departments
must be jealously guarded against the simplicity of the
lowbrowed (else must we stick in the mud for ever)
the initiative in prosecutions for sedition, blasphemy,
and obscenity should be taken out of the hands of the
common informer, and treated as a very delicate and
difficult function of the most responsible constitutional
department available.

For it must not be forgotten that the alternative to
amateur censorships is not complete anarchy but police
interference. The censorships are popular with managers and speculators because their licenses act as in-
surance policies against police prosecution, and keep

the agents of the criminal law quiet, without imposing any effective restrictions on the exploitation of vulgar pornography and criminal sensationalism. But as they do interfere very seriously with work of the class to which Saint Joan belongs I must continue to insist on the evil they do, on the good that they fail to do, and on the better ways of achieving their purpose that are readily available.

On the Festival Habit

(*Malvern Festival Book*, 1937)

Our municipalities are a trifle sheeplike and slow at the uptake, especially when the fine arts are in question; otherwise the example of Malvern would by this time have covered the English autumn with festivals. Even Malvern does not yet know what a good thing it has got hold of; for much as the Council has done to help the Festival of late years, the theatre, which the audience finds so pleasant and familiar, is, behind the scenes, inadequate both in dimension and equipment for the full exploitation of the Festival's possibilities. At Stratford, near by in these motoring days, the Memorial Theatre is so magnificent both before and behind the scenes that it brings in a steady and substantial income from the shillings of tourists who actually pay a shilling a head to look through it when there is no performance going on. That is what Malvern should aim at.

The Stratford Memorial Theatre is not a creation of municipal enterprise. The humiliating truth is that it is America's tribute to Shakespear rather than England's. But that it would have paid Stratford handsomely to build it is beyond question. If its citizens doubt this, let them suppose for the sake of argument that the Avon rose and swept the Memorial Theatre away, or that it was burnt down as the old one was.

Suppose that thereupon Sir Archibald Flower and the
Governors were to drop the whole affair, disbanding
the staff and company and leaving Stratford without
its theatre. How would the business men of Stratford
like it? A proposal to build a new theatre and organize
the Festivals municipally would be supported by rate-
payers who have never crossed the threshold of a
theatre and never intend to. The same would happen
in Malvern if Sir Barry Jackson were to throw up the
sponge and Captain Limbert to shake his head.

What applies to Stratford applies more strongly to
other places; for neither flood nor fire can take away
from Stratford the glory of being Shakespear's birthplace, and of the fact that, though he never did any
good until he left it, he came back to it when he had
made his fortune to build himself a mansion in the
middle of the town, and become Mr William Shakespear, Gent., instead of Will Shakespear, player, playwright, and ex-poacher. Stratford being famous for its
conflagrations, the mansion duly got itself burned down
after his death, but not before a clergyman tenant,
maddened by the forerunners of our autograph hunters,
cut down the Bard's mulberry tree. No matter: Stratford remains Shakespear's birthplace, and will always
be able to attract American tourists ready to pay a
silver dime to be shewn the more or less authentic
exact spot on which he breathed his first.

Buxton, which this year imitates Malvern by holding a festival, has no such indestructible asset. I doubt
whether it would appreciate an immortal poet; for in
Buxton every second person you meet is a centenarian
who looks about fifty. They cannot understand a town
which ranks as immortal a man who died at 62, an age
which in Buxton is infancy. Then there is the Valley
of the Dove, which is a very good equivalent for Ann
Hathaway's Cottage, to say nothing of the fact that
the view of Buxton from its own esplanade is most remarkably like the view of Jerusalem from the Mount
of Olives.

I am a booster of festivals because they are markets

for my plays. I have actually planted a municipal mulberry tree in Malvern, and thereby created a general impression that I was born there. In course of time visitors will be shewn for sixpence the room in which my first cries were heard. Thus will I become a source of wealth to Malvern in return for the extent to which it is at present a source of wealth to me. As the Festival habit grows from the seed sown in Malvern I hope to plant many mulberry trees, and end by having as many birthplaces as Homer.

My part of the program this year has an odd sort of topicality; for the new play is about a millionairess; and the recent death of Lady Houston has reminded us all that women with millions to throw about are facts of the Capitalist epoch in which we live, and are balanced by a much larger number of women whose standard wage is 2½d an hour. However, I was not thinking of Lady Houston, nor of any particular person, when I wrote the play. My acquaintance with Lady Houston was limited to a friendly correspondence in which she invited me to become a Saturday Reviewer. I had to inform her that I was a Saturday Reviewer before she was born, implying that she was under 40, which was perhaps stretching it a bit, Irish fashion. In her hands the famous old Saturday had become the vehicle of her prescription for the cure of a common cold. It would have killed a herd of rhinoceroses; and I hope her death was not caused by departing from precedent so far as to take her own medicine. Shakespear said, rather carelessly, that the purpose of playwriting is to hold the mirror up to nature. That is its purpose; but it is certainly not its method. If I in my play had held the mirror up to Lady Houston the result would have been rejected as an impossible fable.

The revival of The Apple Cart has also a topical air. In it a British king brings about the catastrophe by a threat to abdicate. And now a British king, very astonishingly, has abdicated. And note well, if you please, how natural and reasonable and probable the play is, and how improbable, fantastic, and outrageous the actual event was. There was not a single circumstance of it which I should have dared to invent. If you could raise Macaulay or Disraeli from the dead, and take him to the Malvern Theatre to see The Apple Cart just to ask him "Could this thing actually happen?" he would have replied "Oh, quite possibly. Queen Elizabeth threatened to abdicate; and Queen Victoria used to hint at it once a week or so." But if you had told him the story of the Duke of Windsor, he would have said, "If you put a tale like that into a play you will spend the rest of your days in a lunatic asylum."

So much for holding the mirror up to nature! Yet there was enough to tempt any playwright in the comedy of the utter helplessness of Earl Baldwin and the British Parliament while the affair was settled over their supposedly omnipotent heads by the Royal Family.

But the Malvern Festival program is not a political organ; so I must not pursue the subject, tempting as it is.

The Author's Apology for *Good King Charles*

(*Malvern Festival Book*, 1939)

In providing a historical play for this year's Festival[*] I have departed from the established practice sufficiently to require a word of explanation. The "histories" of Shakespear are chronicles dramatized; and my own chief historical plays, Caesar and Cleopatra and Saint Joan, are fully documented chronicle plays of this type. Familiarity with them would get a student safely through examination papers on their periods.

A much commoner theatrical product is the historical

[*] The 1939 Festival was unusual in that its program consisted of new plays—*In Good King Charles's Golden Days*, James Bridie's *What Say They?*, *The Professor from Peking* by S. I. Hsiung, Robert Vansittart's *Dead Heat*, Alexander Knox's *Old Master*, and *Big Ben* by Evadne Price and Rudy Miller.

romance, mostly fiction with historical names attached
to the stock characters of the stage. Many of these
plays have introduced their heroines as Nell Gwynn,
and Nell's principal lover as Charles II. As Nell was a
lively and lovable actress, it was easy to reproduce
her by casting a lively and lovable actress for the part;
but the stage Charles, though his costume and wig
were always unmistakeable, never had any other resemblance to the real Charles, or to anything else on
earth except what he was [not]: a stage walking gentleman with nothing particular to say for himself.

Now the facts of Charles's reign have been
chronicled so often by modern historians of all parties,
from the Whig Macaulay to the Jacobite Hilaire Bel-
loc, that there is no novelty left for the chronicler to
put on the stage. As to the romance, it is intolerably
stale: the spectacle of Charles sitting with his arm
round Nell Gwynn's waist or Moll Davis on his knees,
with the voluptuous termagant Castlemaine raging
in the background, has no interest for me, if it ever
had for any grown-up person.

But when we turn from the sordid facts of Charles's
reign, and from his Solomonic polygamy, to what might
have happened to him but did not, the situation becomes interesting and fresh. For instance, Charles
might have met that human prodigy Isaac Newton.
And Newton might have met that prodigy of another
sort, George Fox, the founder of the morally mighty
Society of Friends, vulgarly called the Quakers. Better
again, all three might have met. Now anyone who
considers a hundred and fiftieth edition of Sweet Nell
of Old Drury more attractive than Isaac Newton had
better avoid my plays: they are not meant for such.
And anyone who is more interested in Lady Castlemaine's hips than in Fox's foundation of the great Cult
of Friendship should keep away from theatres and
frequent worse places. Still, though the interest of my
play lies mainly in the clash of Charles, George, and
Isaac, there is some fun in the clash between all three
and Nelly, Castlemaine, and the Frenchwoman Louise

de Kéroualle, whom we called Madame Carwell. So I bring them all on the stage to relieve the intellectual tension.

But there is another clash which is of enormous importance in view of the hold that professional science has gained on popular credulity since the middle of the nineteenth century. I mean the eternal clash between the artist and the physicist. I have therefore invented a collision between Newton and a personage whom I should like to have called Hogarth; for it was Hogarth who said "the line of beauty is a curve," and Newton whose dogma it was that the universe is in principle rectilinear. But Hogarth could not by any magic be fitted into the year 1680, my chosen date; so I had to fall back on Godfrey Kneller. Kneller certainly had not Hogarth's brains; but I have had to endow him with them to provide Newton with an antagonist. In point of date Kneller just fitted in.

As to Charles, he adolesced as a princely cosmopolitan vagabond of curiously mixed blood, and ended as the first king in England whose kingship was purely symbolic, and who was clever enough to know that the work of the regicides could not be undone, and that he had to reign by his wits and not by any real power they had left him. Unfortunately the vulgarity of his reputation as a Solomonic polygamist has not only obscured his political ability, but eclipsed the fact that he was the best of husbands. Catherine of Braganza, his wife, has been made to appear a nobody, and Castlemaine, his concubine, almost a great historical figure. When you have seen my play you will not make that very second-rate mistake, and may therefore congratulate yourself on assisting at an act of historical justice. So if you are at Malvern this August be sure not to miss it.

But I must make an exception to this general invitation. If by any chance you are a great mathematician or astronomer you had perhaps better stay away. I have made Newton aware of something wrong with the perihelion of Mercury. Not since Shakespear made

Helen of Troy quote Aristotle has the stage perpetrated a more staggering anachronism. But I find the perihelion of Mercury so irresistible as a Stage Laugh (like Weston-Super-Mare) that I cannot bring myself to sacrifice it. I am actually prepared to defend it as a possibility. Newton was not only a lightning calculator with a monstrous memory: he was also a most ingenious and dexterous maker of apparatus. He made his own telescope; and when he wanted to look at Mercury without being dazzled by the sun he was quite clever enough to produce an artificial eclipse by putting an obturator into the telescope, though nobody else hit on that simple device until long after. My ignorance of these matters is stupendous; but I refuse to believe that Newton's system did not enable him to locate Mercury theoretically at its nearest point to the sun, and then to find out with his telescope that it was not there, but apparently somewhere else.

That is as far as I have gone. I grant you that if I had represented Newton as anticipating Einstein by explaining that Mercury is there all right and that its apparent dislocation is an optical illusion, this would have been a real anachronism. Happily I refrained.

For the flash of prevision in which Newton foresees Einstein's curvilinear universe I make no apology. Newton's first law of motion is pure dogma. So is Hogarth's first law of design. The modern astronomers have proved, so far, that Hogarth was right and Newton wrong. But as the march of science during my lifetime has played skittles with all the theories in turn, I dare not say how the case will stand by the time this play of mine reaches its thousandth performance—if it ever does. Meanwhile let me admit that Newton in my play is a stage astronomer: that is, an astronomer not for an age but for all time. Newton as a man was the queerest of the prodigies; and I have chapter and verse for all his contradictions.

Ayot St. Lawrence,
11th *July,* 1939.

(Revised and enlarged for Standard Edition, 1946.)

Granville-Barker: Some Particulars

(*Drama*, New Series No. 3, Winter 1946)

In the year 1904, when I was 48 years old, I was an
unacted playwright in London, though certain big box
office successes abroad, notably those of Agnes Sorma
as Candida in Germany and Richard Mansfield in New
York as the Devil's Disciple, had proved that my plays
were both actable, and possibly highly lucrative. But
the commercial theatres in London (and there were no
others) would have nothing to do with them, regarding
them as untheatrical and financially impossible. There
were no murders, no adulteries, no sexual intrigues
in them. The heroines were not like heroines: they
were like women. Although the rule of the stage was
that any speech longer than twenty words was too
long, and that politics and religion must never be
mentioned and their places taken by romance and
fictitious police and divorce cases, my characters had
to declaim long speeches on religion and politics in
the Shakespearean or "ham" technique.

Besides, I could not offer my plays to the established
managers because I was a noted professional critic,
and, as such, would have been understood as inviting
bribery.

I had, therefore, not only to publish my plays, but to
make plays readable. A leading friendly publisher
whom I approached had published the plays of a
fashionable playwright, and had shewn me the ledger
account of the transaction, recording absolutely no
sales except in the little batches indicating amateur
performances for which copies of the play had to be
bought for rehearsal.

I substituted readable descriptions for technical
stage directions, and shewed how to make the volumes
as attractive in appearance as novels. A young publisher, Grant Richards, rose to the occasion with pio-

neer pluck. His venture succeeded; and plays broke
into the publishing market as Literature. And I, though
unacted, made my mark as a playwright. My plays
formed a unique reserve stock available for any
management with sufficient flair to try the experiment
of a Shavian theatre.

Meanwhile, in looking about for an actor suitable
for the part of the poet in Candida at a Stage Society
performance, I had found my man in a very remarkable person named Harley Granville-Barker. He was
at that time 23 years of age, and had been on the
stage since he was 14. He had a strong strain of
Italian blood in him, and looked as if he had stepped
out of a picture by Benozzo Gozzoli. He had a wide
literary culture and a fastidiously delicate taste in
every branch of art. He could write in a difficult and
too precious but exquisitely fine style. He was self-
willed, restlessly industrious, sober, and quite sane.
He had Shakespear and Dickens at his finger ends.
Altogether the most distinguished and incomparably
the most cultivated person whom circumstances had
driven into the theatre at that time.

I saw him play in Hauptmann's Friedensfest and
immediately jumped at him for the poet in Candida.
His performance of this part—a very difficult one to
cast—was, humanly speaking, perfect.

Presently a gentleman with a fancy for playing
Shakespearean parts,* and money enough to gratify
it without much regard to public support, took the
Court Theatre in Sloane Square, made famous by the
acting of John Hare, Clayton, Cecil, Ellen Terry and
by the early comedy-farces of Pinero. He installed
therein as his business manager the late J. E.
Vedrenne, who, when his principal was not indulging
in Shakespearean matinées, kept the theatre going by
letting it by night to amateurs. Granville-Barker was
engaged for one of these revivals in the ordinary

---

* J. H. Leigh, a businessman friend of Martin Harvey, amateur
actor, reciter of Shakespeare, and husband of a would-be
actress.

course of his professional routine. I have said that he was a self-willed Italianate young man with qualifications far beyond those which the theatre could ordinarily attract. I need not describe the steps by which the Court Theatre presently became virtually his theatre, with Vedrenne in the manager's office. They began with matinées of Candida, the expenses of which were guaranteed by a few friends; but the guarantee was not needed: the matinées paid their way. More matinées of my plays followed with Barker as the leading actor; and before long Vedrenne and Barker were in a position to take the theatre over from the Shakespearean enthusiast as a full-blown management; and I ceased to write plays for anybody who asked me, and became playwright in ordinary to this new enterprise.

But it is not enough to have a fascinating actor for your heroes: you must also have an interesting actress for your heroine. She dropped from heaven on us in the person of Lillah McCarthy, who, having learnt her business in the course of a tour round the world as the beautiful Mercia in The Sign of the Cross after playing Lady Macbeth at the age of sixteen like an immature Mrs Siddons, burst in on me and demanded a Siddonian part. After one glance at her I handed her Man and Superman, and told her she was to create Ann Whitefield in it.

We were now complete. The Court experiment went through with flying colors. Barker, aiming at a National Repertory Theatre, with a change of program every night, was determined to test our enterprise to destruction as motor tyres are tested, to find out its utmost possibilities. I was equally reckless. Vedrenne, made prudent by a wife and family, was like a man trying to ride two runaway horses simultaneously. Barker worked furiously: he had not only to act, but to produce all the plays except mine, and to find and inspire all the artists whom he drew into the theatre to carry out his ideas. In the end he had to give up acting and devote himself entirely to producing, or, under all the pressure I could put on him, to writing plays. The Court was abandoned for larger and more central theatres, not always one at a time. The pace grew hotter and hotter; the prestige was immense; but the receipts barely kept us going and left no reserves with which to nurse new authors into new reputations.

At last we were in debt and had to put up the shutters. Having ruined Vedrenne in spite of his remonstrances, we could not ask him to pay the debts; and we were bound to clear him without a stain on his character. Barker paid all he possessed; I paid the rest; and so the firm went down with its colors flying, leaving us with a proved certainty that no National Theatre in London devoted to the art of the theatre at its best can bear the burden of London rents and London rates. Freed from them it might pay its way under a director content to work hard for a modest salary. For the evidence read the book Barker wrote in collaboration with William Archer.

The combination, Lillah-Barker-Shaw, still remained, and was reinforced by Shakespear. Barker reached the summit of his fame as a producer by restoring Shakespear to the London stage, where he lingered only in the infamous mutilations of his works by the actor-managers and refreshment bar renters.

But this was done at the cost of an extravagance which could not be sustained. Without Vedrenne to plead for economy Barker was reckless. Lord Howard de Walden came nobly to the rescue financially; and Barker gave him full value artistically, but made ducks and drakes of his heavily taxed spare money.

Quite early in this history, however, Lillah and Barker got married. I knew that this was all wrong; that there were no two people on earth less suited to one another; that in the long run their escapade could not stay put. But there was nothing to be done but make the best of it. Certainly, for the moment, it worked very well, and had every air of being a brilliant success. She was an admirable hostess; and her enjoyment of the open air and of travelling made her a most healthy companion for him. He, in spite of the vagabondage of his profession, was not in the least a Bohemian; and the dignity of marriage was quite right for him and good for him. The admirations and adorations the pair excited in the cultured sections of London society could be indulged and gratified in country houses where interesting and brilliant young married couples were welcome. And professionally they were necessary to one another, just as I was necessary to them. It actually made for the stability of the combination that they were never really in love with one another, though they had a very good time together. The appalling levity with which actors and actresses marry is a phenomenon much older than Hollywood; and I had no excuse for being surprised and every reason for finding the arrangement a convenient one. Still, I was instinctively dismayed.

My misgivings were finally justified by a domestic catastrophe. When we had tested the possibility of a highbrow repertory theatre in London to the insolvency and winding-up of the Vedrenne-Barker management, Barker, cleaned out financially, went to New York to consider an offer of the directorship of the new Millionaires Theatre there. Finding the building unsuitable, he turned down the offer, and was presently overtaken by the 1914–18 Armageddon and came back to present himself to me in the guise of a cadet gunner, and later on (he being obviously wasted as a gunner), as an intelligence officer in a Sam Brown belt. He looked the part to perfection.

In New York, however, the Italian volcano in him had erupted unexpectedly and amazingly. He fell madly in love—really madly in the Italian manner—and my first effective intimation was a demand that I should, before the end of the week, procure him a divorce, or a promise of one, from Lillah.

Not yet realizing that I was dealing with a lunatic, I naturally thought that Lillah was prepared for this, and that they had talked it out and agreed to it before

she left America. As I had never believed in the permanence of their marriage, and thought that a divorce
would restore the order of nature in their case and be
a very good thing for both of them, I approached
Lillah to arrange the divorce. I was at once violently
undeceived. Lillah was as proud as ten thousand
empresses. The unprepared proposal for a divorce
struck her simply as an insult: something that might
happen to common women but could never happen
to her. I had a difficult time of it; for I at once lost
the confidence of both parties: of Lillah because
instead of indignantly repudiating the proposed outrage and renouncing Barker as the infamous author
of an unheard-of act of *lèse majesté*, I was acting as
his go-between and treating the divorce as inevitable
and desirable: of Barker, because my failure to
obtain a decree nisi within twenty-four hours shewed
that I was Lillah's accomplice in the worst of crimes,
that of delaying his instant remarriage. There were
no broken hearts in the business; for this wonderful
pair, who had careered together so picturesquely, and
made such excellent and quite kindly use of the coincidence of their ages and gifts, had never really
cared a rap for one another in the way of what
Shakespear called the marriage of true minds; so that
now, in the storm raised by the insensate impatience
of the one and the outraged pride of the other, there
was no element of remorse or tenderness, and no point
of contact at which they could be brought to reason.
They had literally nothing to say to each other; but
they had a good deal to say to me, mostly to the effect
that I was betraying them both.

And now it may be asked what business all this was
of mine. Well, I had thrown them literally into one
another's arms as John Tanner and Ann Whitefield;
and I suppose it followed that I must extricate them.
I succeeded at last; but I could have done it easily
six months sooner if they had been able to escape for
a moment from their condition of passionate un-
reasonableness; and I came out of the conflict much

battered from both sides, Barker blaming me for the unnecessary delay; and Lillah for having extorted her consent by arguments that almost amounted to blackmail.

Happily the very unreality in their marriage that made the tempest over its dissolution so merciless also cleared the sky very suddenly and completely when it was over. The ending was quite happy. In a prophetic moment in the struggle I had told Lillah that I foresaw her, not as Barker's leading lady to all eternity, but as a handsome chatelaine with a title and a distinguished "honest to God" husband, welcoming a crowd of the best people on the terrace of a beautiful country house. She took this as being in the worst possible taste, her imagination being just then full of a tragic and slaughterous Götterdämmerung of some kind as the end of Lillah. But it is exactly what has happened to her. When these twain who worked with me in the glory of their youth settled down handsomely in the dignity of their maturity, I rejoiced in their happiness and leisure.

My part in the divorce had been complicated by the attitude of the lady who had enchanted Barker. This lady was not a private nobody. She was a personage of distinguished talent as a novelist and poetess. Unfortunately for me, she was an American, which meant that the latest great authors for her were Henry James and Meredith: the final politicians Jefferson and Washington. Socialism was to her simple sedition, and Shaw a most undesirable acquaintance for her beloved. Nothing I could do could conciliate her or maintain our alliance. After their retirement to Devon and then to Paris he became a highly respectable professor. Besides his Prefaces to Shakespeare, he wrote two more plays, and collaborated with his wife in translations from the Spanish. Virtually we never met again. Our old sympathy remained unaltered and unalterable; but he never dared to shew it; and I could not intrude where I was not welcome. He had well earned a prosperous and happy retirement after

his long service and leadership in the vanguard. I hope
his widow has come to see that the wild oats he sowed
with me have produced a better harvest than she
foresaw, and that his original contributions to our
dramatic literature are treasures to be preserved, not
compromising documents to be destroyed.

In what has been written lately, too much has been
said of him as a producer, too little as an actor, and
much too little as an author. Producing kills acting:
an actor's part dies if he is watching the others
critically. You cannot conduct an orchestra and play
the drums at the same concert. As long as I was
producing and Barker acting all was well: he acted
beautifully; and I took care to make the most of him.
But I kept pressing for the enlistment of other authors,
and urging Barker to write, which he did slowly,
repeatedly protesting that as it was not his profession,
and was mine, it was easy for me and very hard for
him. Galsworthy, Masefield, Laurence Housman, and
St John Hankin (for the moment forgotten or neglected, but a master of serious comedy) came into
our repertory, financed at first by revivals of my pot-
boiler, You Never Can Tell. Barker's production of
his own plays and Galsworthy's were exquisite: their
styles were perfectly sympathetic, whereas his style
and taste were as different from mine as Debussy's
from Verdi's. With Shakespear and with me he was
not always at his happiest best; but he was absolutely
faithful to the play and would not cut a line to please
himself; and the plays pulled him through with the
bits that suited him enchanting and the scenery and
dressing perfect.

He adopted my technique of production, but was
utterly inconsiderate in its practice. I warned him
again and again that the end of it would be a drastic
Factory Act regulating the hours of rehearsals as
strictly as the hours of weaving in a cotton mill. But
he would not leave off until the unfortunate company
had lost their last trains and buses and he had tired
himself beyond human powers of maintaining the

intense vigilance and freshness which first-rate production, or indeed any production, demands. I myself put a limit of such attention at three hours or less between breakfast and lunch, absolutely refused to spend more time than that in the theatre.

His only other fault was to suppress his actors when they pulled out all their stops and declaimed as Shakespear should be declaimed. They either underacted, or were afraid to act at all lest they should be accused of ranting or being "hams." I once asked a violinist of great experience as an orchestral leader, William Reed (Elgar's Billy Reed), whether he agreed with Wagner that the first duty of a conductor is to give the right time to the band. "No," said he. "The first duty of a conductor is to let the band play." I still want the Factory Act, and hold with Billy that the perfect producer lets his actors act, and is their helper at need and not their dictator. The hint is meant specially for producers who have begun as actors. They are the first instead of the last to forget it.

My Way with a Play

(*The Observer*, London, September 29, 1946; reprinted in *British Thought*, 1947)

Notwithstanding the easy terms of a friendly acquaintance with Allardyce Nicoll, I cannot contemplate his histories of the British drama without being somewhat overawed by the superhuman industry and devotion in which, as a great professor, he shames a mere practitioner like myself. The second volume of his History of Late Nineteenth Century Drama, 1850–1900, is a list of plays compared to which the telephone directory, compiled by an army of officials from ready-made information, is a trifle. It leaves me dumb with grateful wonder. I have not a word of criticism for its distinguished author: all I dare add as

an experienced practitioner is a note or two on the
limits and unavoidable misfits of any index which
presents the order of events in the commercial theatre
as the order of evolution in the art of the theatre.

For instance, a passage in Professor Nicoll's first
volume fairly made me jump. Because my vogue in the
fashionable London theatre came after that of Pinero,
Jones, Carton, Grundy, and Wilde, and supplanted it,
it is assumed that I developed in their school and
learned my art from them. As a matter of fact I was
furiously opposed to their method and principles, and
had my bag full of unacted plays before the limelight
shifted from them to me. They were all for "constructed" plays, the technique of construction being
that made fashionable by Scribe in Paris, and the
sanction claimed for it no less than that of Aristotle.
Plays manufactured on this plan, and called "well-
made plays," I compared derisively to cats'-cradles,
clockwork mice, mechanical rabbits, and the like. The
critics reported that my plays were not plays, whatever
other entertainment value they might possess.

Thus, instead of taking a step forward technically in
the order of the calendar, I threw off Paris and went
back to Shakespear, to the Bible, to Bunyan, Walter
Scott, Dickens, and Dumas *père*, Mozart, and Verdi,
in whom I had been soaked from my childhood.
Instead of planning my plays I let them grow as they
came, and hardly ever wrote a page foreknowing what
the next page would be. When I tried a plot I found
that it substituted the absorbing interest of putting it
together like a jigsaw puzzle (the dullest of all occupations for the lookers-on) for communicable dramatic interest, loading the story with deadwood and
spoiling it, as in the lamentable case of Goldsmith's
Good Natur'd Man, which without its plot would have
been a classic.

Shakespear's practice of recklessly borrowing his
stories from the books of contemporary novelists, and
filling them with his own characters, was not an example but a warning. The self-conscious poet hen-

pecked into murder by an ambitious wife, who is, in turn, termagant, drunkard, and somnambulist, was an absurdly incongruous imposition on the hard-fisted warrior of the Macbeth story. Walter Scott's Rob Roy is a thousand times more natural. Hamlet, brought up in militant barbarism, plunged in a blood feud, and finding himself incapable of the conventional revenge because he had evolved into a Christian without knowing it, is an amazing stride forward from the stage zany and village idiot of the old ghost story. Measure for Measure is a hopeless tangle of moral contradictions. No plot could restrain Shakespear's dramatic genius any more than the conventions of sonata form could restrain Mozart's; but the resultant incongruities are still there; and the attempts to imitate them by less gifted disciples are pretentious failures: the bane of the academic schools.

The art of all fiction, whether made for the stage, the screen, or the bookshelf, is the art of story-telling. My stock-in-trade is that of Scheherazade and Chaucer no less than of Aristophanes and Shakespear. I am quite aware that the jigsaw puzzle business, the working out of a plot, is necessary in detective stories, and helpful to playwrights who have talent enough to put their clockwork mice through amusing tricks, and hold their audiences effectively by jury-box suspenses. When I read a couple of acts of my first play to Henry Arthur Jones, all he said was, "Where's your murder?" But I needed no murder: I could get drama enough out of the economics of slum poverty. I scorned the police news and crude sexual adventures with which my competitors could not dispense. Clearly I had nothing to learn from Henry Arthur: he had something to learn from me, and did. But, as his vogue came before mine, Allardyce Nicoll, tied to the order of date, begins by placing my vogue as a development of Scribery. Later on, led away from chronology into criticism, he forgets this, and sets it right, leaving me nothing to complain of. I allow myself, nevertheless, to emphasize the fact that the difference between me

and the Scribe school was, and is, timeless, and that far
from turning the hands of the clock forward I whirled
them back to Scheherazade.

Like Gilbert Chesterton I was full of Dickens, and
had noted how vainly he bothers himself with plots.
He lets himself be persuaded that by inscrutable
complications his characters should turn out to be
somebody else, with secrets, hidden relationships, and
virgin heroines pursued matrimonially by repulsive
villains. But who cares for or can remember the plots
of Oliver Twist and Little Dorrit, or prefers the few
pages which unravel them to the straight stories of
David Copperfield and Great Expectations, though
even in that masterpiece the heroine turns out at the
end to be the convict's daughter and gives him a
movingly happy death? The happy ending of Pip and
Estella, imposed on Dickens by Lytton, is as false
as that of Benedick and Beatrice was declared to be
by Mrs Cowden Clarke.

Another timeless art inseparable from the history
of the theatre is the art of acting, which, as actors
have to live by their work, lands us at once in the
economics of the theatre. These, as our few up-to-date
historians have learnt from Karl Marx, are basic in
all histories. By leaving them out of account Professor
Nicoll has produced a hiatus in his history between
the retirement of Macready in 1851 and the advent
of Irving in 1871, during which Shakespear "spelt
ruin" in London, and speeches longer than a couple of
dozen words were considered excessive in modern
plays. The only steady income made by a famous
player in that period was in the British provinces by
a Shakespearean actor of what Walter Scott called
the Big Bow Wow school. His name is not even
mentioned in Professor Nicoll's index. He was Barry
Sullivan, the natural and sole successor to Burbage,
Betterton, Garrick, Kemble, Kean, and Macready in
the British dynasty of supreme masters of their art.
He was often described as an Irish actor; and his
statue is in Glasnevin, the Dublin Catholic cemetery;

but he was born in Birmingham of Irish parentage in 1821. He learned his business from his boyhood in the stock companies of Cork, Glasgow, and Manchester, where he played all sorts of parts, even including operatic ones.

After a brilliant success in London as Hamlet in 1852 he went to America for three years and to Australia for five, returning to England in his middle age a great tragedian, to be described in The Times as the leading legitimate actor of the British stage. He took a second-rate theatre, now a boxing arena. After spending too much on its renovation, and beginning with an obsolete program, he lost money in a month or two. This insult to his greatness he could neither afford nor forgive. He shook the dust of London from his feet, and decided to tour in the provinces, resolved that if he had to play there to ten people every one of them would come again and bring a hundred others with them. This actually happened. Soon he never left the provincial capitals without three hundred guineas in his pocket every week. He died opulently rich in 1891. And his chief author was Shakespear.

In the 1860's, when he was between forty and fifty, I, then a boy in my teens, saw him for the first time, as he had seen Macready in 1835. The play was Hamlet, which he played thousands of times throughout his long life. Such acting I had never seen or imagined before, nor was its impression weakened when, much later on, I saw the acting of Salvini and Ristori, the last of the great Italians, from whom I gathered what else I know of great acting.

Compare his career with that of Irving, who clung to London for thirty years, and was knighted and buried in Westminster Abbey as the unquestioned head of his profession. Beginning with a guarantee from a millionairess, he made much money for the owners of the Lyceum Theatre. For himself he made nothing by his continuous labor but his vogue and his living. At the end of the thirty years he left London with his pockets empty; returned to the provinces to repair his fortunes; and died there a much poorer man than Sullivan. The moral is obvious: London for reputation and quotable press notices; the provinces for money and artistic scope.

It was an old story. Macready had held out in London for six years only before taking to the road. Sullivan, beginning London actor-management at forty, when he was accustomed to continuous financial success, would not consent to make money for his landlords and employees whilst earning and losing it himself. He at once "cut his losses" and abandoned London.

This economic situation still persists. Sir Barry Jackson, who re-created and brought the theatre up to date from nothing to the Malvern Festivals, did so wholly in Birmingham. Having accomplished this he attacked London and had such success as is possible there. At its height he, too, shook the London dust off his feet and returned to Birmingham and Stratford-upon-Avon, where he got back to real artistic work again. Nugent Monck, who revived high drama and kept it alive in Norwich, ignored London. Rutland Boughton's Glastonbury Festivals, memorable events in operatic history, would have been impossible in London.

I could multiply instances; but these are enough to convince Allardyce Nicoll that a history of the drama which leaves the provinces and Barry Sullivan out of account, and describes my return to sixteenth-century practice (analogous to the pre-Raphaelite movement in painting) as a development of the practices of Scribe and of that adroit manufacturer of stage-Irish melodramas, Dion Boucicault, needs another chapter.

I did the old stuff in the old way, because, as it happened, I could do it superlatively well. I did not know this when I did it; but now I have outgrown it and can look back at it as the work of another person with whom I can no longer identify myself. It seems plain enough to me. Also from my boyish visits to the theatre (I began with a pantomime as a child) I had acquired that theatre sense which, when I am writing a play, keeps my imagination unconsciously within the conditions and limits of the stage, the performers, the audience, and even the salary list—all now extended enormously by the cinema.

This, too, has made an economic revolution needing perhaps another volume, for it has raised the profitable cost of production of a play from £2,000 to £2,000,000. Clearly there is plenty more for the Professor to do; but as I should be sorry to see him slain by his own prodigious industry, I refrain from further suggestion.

Sullivan, Shakespear, and Shaw

(*The Strand* CXIV, October 1947; also in *The Atlantic Monthly* CLXXXI, March 1948)

1

Barry Sullivan, son of an Irish Catholic Waterloo soldier, was born in Birmingham, in 1821, and died in 1891.

He was a great actor. He kept Shakespear and the tradition of great acting alive in these islands whilst in fashionable London Shakespear "spelt ruin" for theatre managers. For players, "cup and saucer" manners in the plays of Robertson and in adaptations from the French of Scribe's mechanically constructed "well made" pieces (I helped to kill them) had London all to themselves.

What was Sullivan like at the height of his power and glory? Why did his Hamlet, which he played every week (often twice) for forty years after his triumphant success in the part at the Haymarket in London in 1852, remain so imposing and satisfying, though he made no pretence of being a young student prince fresh from Wittenberg University? No doubt his splendid physical graces had something to do with it.

His stage walk was by itself worth going to the
theatre to see. When he killed the king by dashing up
the whole depth of the stage and running him through
again and again, he was a human thunderbolt. His
attitude as he threw off Horatio and Marcellus with
his "By heaven, gentlemen, I'll make a ghost of him
that lets me," his superb and towering contempt for
his guilty stepfather, and his gesture as he turned
away from Rosencrantz and Guildenstern with his
peculiar reading of "I know a hawk from a heron.
Pshaw!" were unforgettable.

But these ageless feats were not enough to carry his
Hamlet through over three thousand times. His secret,
which was no secret, was simply that he presented
himself as what Hamlet was: a being of a different
and higher order from Laertes and the rest. He had
majesty and power. As Richelieu, one of his greatest
parts, his dignity as he invoked the power of the
Church and drew the charmed circle of Rome round
the head of the heroine was literally supernatural. I
cannot believe any mortal actor ever surpassed it.

For boys like me he was irresistible. His Richard
was a monster of truculence. When he stabbed King
Henry with the words "For this, among the rest, was
I ordained" he swung his eyes one way and his sword
the other in a stage picture of villainy that from any
lesser actor would have made the audience laugh.
When he proclaimed that Richard was himself again,
he struck the attitude of a fencer on guard. His stage
fights with Macduff and Richmond were none the
less exciting because we knew quite well that what
we were witnessing was a prearranged battery of
what is known behind the scenes as "sixes." As the
Gamester, in which he had to die of poison in the last
act, his groans were frightful and heart-rending.
Every Crummles could, and did, attempt these "effects"; but nobody could get away with them like
Sullivan, nor any rival keep up the illusion of his
towering superiority.

He had classic taste and noble judgment for older

critics too. In Hamlet's scene with Ophelia he never sentimentalized it to drag in vulgar sex appeal as Irving did. As to treating the closet scene as an example of the Œdipus complex, such notions did not exist for him. His natural force was so great that he had not to stoke himself with drink as Kean, Robson, and even Dickens in America killed themselves prematurely by doing. Nor had he to husband his strength, as Salvini did, to give explosive contrasts to his outbursts. His ebullient energy, natural force, called for sedatives rather than for stimulants. Yet he lived to be seventy before his incessant activity killed him. And in his private life there was no scandal.

Beginning in his boyhood in Cork, he learned his business in the old stock companies in Cork, Edinburgh, Aberdeen, Glasgow, Liverpool, and Manchester (where he first headed the bill), and finally in London at £10 a week. He carried all before him there. The £10 a week ended as £80 a night.

For the rest of his victorious career he was a princely stroller, moving like Kean from city to city with his basket of costumes and swords, playing with local stock companies as he found them, in scenery with wings and flats, changes in full view of the audience on naked stages lighted by gas footlights and battens, to face which he had to paint his face with bismuth that damaged the skin almost as much as smallpox.

The substitution of gas for candles was to him an ultra-modern touch: all the rest of the stage equipment, its cellar with the three traps, one for graves, and two one-man traps for demons to pop up through, winches to raise and lower the skied cloths, and the pictorial act drop with its dangerously heavy roller that players had to be careful not to die under, and the final green curtain that showed the costumes so effectively when the wearers took their curtain calls, all the power of these contrivances being supplied by the muscles of the stage carpenters and scene-shifters, were as they had been for two hundred years past.

I once asked Bram Stoker, Irving's manager, why he did not introduce the then new hydraulic lifts and electric motors of the modern stages. He shrugged his shoulders and said he felt safer with eighty stage carpenters, who could not stop the performance (as happened at Drury Lane once) by short-circuiting the strange machinery. Sullivan was in the stone age of stage equipment compared to Irving, who at least had a modern switchboard.

2

There is no reason to doubt that Sullivan was among the greatest of the line of British Shakespearean star actors from Burbage and Betterton to Macready. That he was a provincial celebrity leaving no mark on London, and overlooked by theatrical historians or unknown to them, is not an artistic phenomenon but a purely economic one. He was expunged from Lewes's book on acting because when Lewes, a first-rate critic, was unwise enough to attempt a career as an actor in great parts, Sullivan, whom in his first edition he had described as "a very clever actor," contemptuously refused to act with him; and Lewes could not forgive the disparagement. That would not have mattered had Sullivan in the days of his greatness chosen London for his headquarters. Why he did not was because he could make a fortune in the provinces only to lose it in London. Irving headed his profession in London for more than twenty years, and finally had to return to the provinces penniless to live on his reputation and his knighthood. Since the palmy days of Kemble and Edmund Kean no big actor had held out so long as Irving in London management. Charles Kean returned to the provinces after nine years of it, and Macready after seven. Sullivan tried it for some months, and then shook the dust of London from his feet save for a few appearances, not as a manager, at the enormous salary of £80 a night.

Barry Sullivan was no scholar: he was a great actor and nothing else, and not ashamed of it. He could never have said, as Macready, his boyhood's idol, did: "I have seen a life gone in an unworthy, unrequiting pursuit. Great energy, great power of mind, ambition and activity that with direction might have done anything, now made into a player." Barry Sullivan was proud of his profession and of his eminence in it. He knew nothing of our educated gentlemen stars who are everything except great actors. He was a boy when he went on the stage. He did nothing for contemporary literature, his repertory including nothing more modern than Lytton's Richelieu.

A friend of mine who called on him began unfortunately with the words "I have written a drama." Sullivan at once interrupted him with "Sir: I do not play drama: I am a tragedian." To him drama meant melodrama, its technical sense on the stage. His famous Richard was Shakespear's Richard; but the text was the thing of shreds and patches put together by Cibber (which, by the way, is more effective on the stage than Shakespear's arrangement). Bar Shakespear, all the plays that Sullivan kept alive were obsolete. His professional mind was an eighteenth century mind, and his traditions those of Garrick.

I never saw great acting until I saw him; and from him and from Salvini and Adelaide Ristori I learned my stage technique and what great acting can do. Though a later generation saw Chaliapin and Coquelin, so little of it was remembered in London when I began to write plays that I was at once set down as ignorant of stage technique and my plays denounced as no plays, when I had in fact gone back to Shakespear and the sixteenth century (much as William Morris went back to the twelfth) and started from that date as a confirmed classic.

And now what does it all matter? Barry Sullivan has come and gone, like all the other great actors since it was said of an Elizabethan playgoer that

When he would have told how Richard died
And cried "A horse, a horse!" he Burbage cried.

The important truth is that the idols of adolescents, and to some extent of adults, are often founded on their admiration of great actors. It was certainly so in my own case. Whatever part Barry Sullivan played, a superman Hamlet or a villainous Richard or Macbeth, "he nothing common did, or mean": he was always great; and when I was a very impressionable boy he became my model of personal nobility.

As a playwright I have had countless letters from young women for whom St Joan has set up a standard which uplifted them beyond vulgarity and meanness. The schoolboy who, having seen my play, told his headmaster that he could pray to St Joan but not to Jesus Christ, justified the theatre as one of the most vital of public institutions. Without such uplift the playwright may be a pander or a buffoon, an actor only a mountebank or a common clown. It is this alone which can raise a theatre to the dignity and national value of a church.

Wherever "two or three are gathered together" to see great acting, both actor and playwright can claim equality with lords temporal and spiritual. Wise rulers establish or subsidize national theatres. When Napoleon had to transfigure himself from a successful military adventurer into an emperor he wisely went to a great actor for lessons. Cromwell, who closed the theatres as the gates of hell, opened them to the ultra-theatrical Opera.

The only British-speaking successor to Barry Sullivan within my experience who could do for Shakespear what he did was a woman, American Irish, born Ada Crehan, but through a happy error in printing which she adopted gladly, famous as Ada Rehan.

Rules for Directors

("Rules for Play Producers" in *The Strand* CXVII, July 1949; as "Rules for Directors" in *Theatre Arts* XXXIII, August 1949, with some deletions)

Play directing, like orchestral conducting, became a separate and lucrative profession less than a century ago. The old stage manager who arranged the movements of the players, and called every actor Old Boy and every actress Darling, is extinct. The director has supplanted him. Yet there is no established method of directing and no handbook from which a novice can learn the technical side of the job. There is not even a tradition, because directors do not see one another at work as players do, and can learn only by experience at the expense of everyone else employed in the production.

These pages are an attempt to supply a beginners' guide. They are not concerned with direction as a fine art; but they cover the mechanical and teachable conditions which are common to all productions, without knowledge of which the novice will waste hours of rehearsal time that should be devoted to acting. All playwrights should study these.

The most desirable director of a play is the author.

Unfortunately, as playwriting is a solitary occupation which gives no social training, some playwrights are so lacking in the infinite patience, intense vigilance, consideration for others, and imperturbable good manners which directing requires, that their presence at rehearsals is a hindrance instead of a help. None the less, they should know how to write for the stage as playwrights, and not as poets and novelists indulging their imaginations beyond the physical limits of "four boards and a passion."

The director, having considered the play, and decided to undertake the job of directing it, has no further concern with its literary merits or its doctrine (if any).

In selecting the cast no regard should be given to whether the actors understand the play or not (players are not walking encyclopedias); but their ages and personalities should be suitable, and their voices should not be alike. The four principals should be soprano, alto, tenor, and bass. Vocal contrast is of the greatest importance, and is indispensable for broadcasting.

The play should be read to the company, preferably by the author if he or she is a competent dramatic reader: if not, by the best available substitute. If none is available, no reading is better than a bad one.

To the first rehearsals the director must come with the stage business thoroughly studied, and every entry, movement, rising and sitting, disposal of hat and umbrella, etc., is settled ready for instant dictation; so that each player will be in the most effective position to deliver his lines and not have to address an intimate speech to a player at the other side of the stage, nor to follow such a player without a line or movement to transfer the attention of the audience accordingly. The exits must be carefully arranged so that the players leave the stage immediately on their last word, and not hold up the play until they have walked to the door. If the director arrives at the first rehearsal without this blueprint, and proceeds to waste the players' time improvising it at their expense, he will never gain their confidence; and they will be perfectly justified in going home after telling him not to call them again until they can devote all the rehearsals to their proper function of acting.

To appreciate the necessity for this laborious planning one has only to imagine a trial-at-law in a room without bench, bar, or jury box, or a service in a cathedral without altar, choir, or pews: in short, without an appointed place for anybody. This is what the stage is until the director has made a complete plan, called a prompt copy. Properly such a plan is the business of the author; for stage directions are as integral to a play as spoken dialogue. But the author may be dead. Or in view of the fact that writing dialogue (of Hamlet, for instance) is a pleasurable act of creation, whereas deciding whether the Ghost shall enter from the right or the left is pure drudgery, the author may leave the drudgery to the director. He mostly does.

It is not necessary to use a model stage for this job. All that is necessary is a chessboard with its chessmen, and a boy's box of assorted bricks. With these all scenes and furniture can be indicated and all movements made. Unless this is done some movements, especially exits, are likely to be forgotten by even the most experienced director.

The players should be instructed not to study their parts at this stage, and to rehearse, book in hand, without any exercise of memory.

When the movements are thoroughly rehearsed and mastered, the director should ask the players whether they are comfortable for them all, and if not, what is wrong.

All being satisfactorily arranged, books are discarded, and rehearsals called "perfect": that is, with the parts memorized. The director now leaves the stage and sits in the front of the house with an electric torch and a notebook; and from that moment he should watch the stage as a cat watches a mouse, but never utter a word nor interrupt a scene during its repetition no matter how completely the play goes to pieces, as it must at first when the players are trying to remember their parts and cues so desperately that they are incapable of acting. Nothing betrays the inexperienced director more than dismay at this collapse, with outbursts of reproach and attempts to get everything right at every rehearsal. The old hand knows that he must let the players memorize the words before they can act their parts.

At the end of each act, the director returns to the stage to explain or demonstrate such of his notes as may be judicious at the moment. But no fault should be mentioned or corrected unless and until its constant

repetition shews that the player will not correct it in
his or her own way as the play is gradually learnt.
When all the players are letter-perfect their memorizing will be so mechanical that if one of them makes a
slip by repeating an early cue later on, the rest will
pick it up again and repeat what they have just been
through, proving that the memorizing phase is over.
The director can now return to the stage and interrupt
as often as may be necessary.

The danger is that as the players can now utter their
words without thinking they will catch one another's
speed and tone, betraying to the audience that they
are only gabbling off a prearranged list of words, each
knowing what the other will say next and fielding their
cues like cricketers. The director must accordingly take
care that every speech contrasts as strongly as possible
in speed, tone, manner, and pitch with the one which
provokes it, as if coming unexpected as a shock, surprise, stimulant, offence, amusement, or what not. It is
for the author to make this possible; for in it lies the
difference between dramatic dialogue and epic narrative. A play by a great poet, in which every speech is
a literary masterpiece, may fail hopelessly on the stage
because the splendid speeches are merely strung together without provoking one another, whereas a
trumpery farce may win an uproarious success by its
retortive backchat.

The final phase of direction is that of "dress rehearsal" with costumes, scenery, and make-up all complete as for public performance, instead of everyday
dress and a bare stage with the doors marked with a
couple of chairs. It is now the director's turn to be
more upset by the change than the actors. Everything
seems to have become wrong and incredible. However, the director soon learns to be prepared for this,
even if he never quite gets over the first shock of it.
He is now back on the stage, going through the passages that need finishing, and generally doing what
he likes. A bad last rehearsal need not alarm him: in

fact he should connive at its failure lest the players should be too confident of success "on the night" and not do their utmost best.

The time needed for the direction of a full-length play on this method is roughly a week for the stage movements book in hand, with the director on the stage; a fortnight for the memorizing, with the director off the stage silent, watching, and taking notes; and a week for the dress, with the director on the stage again, directing and interrupting *ad lib.*

Rehearsals should be most strictly private. No journalist or lay visitor of any kind should be present. When for some reason it may be necessary to allow strangers to witness a rehearsal, no instruction nor correction should be addressed in their presence to a player; and the consent of every player should be obtained before the permission is granted. To emphasize the fact that what the visitors are witnessing is only a rehearsal, a prearranged instruction should be addressed to a stage carpenter, never to a player.

During the memorizing phase a muffled passage must never be repeated on the spot, even if the players desire it. The director's word must be "No; you will not be able to repeat it on the night; and you must not make a habit of a mistake. Go right on." A director who says "We must go over and over this again until we get it right" is not directing; he is schoolmastering, which is the worst thing he can do. Repetitions on the spot do not improve: they deteriorate every time.

Never find fault until you know the remedy; and never discuss a passage with a player; shew how the passage should be done as a suggestion, not an order; and exaggerate your demonstration sufficiently to prevent the player giving a mere imitation of it. A performance in which the players are all mimicking the director, instead of following his suggestions in their own different ways, is a bad performance. Above all, do not, instead of demonstrating a passage, say "This scene is essentially pathetic" (or comic as the case may be). If you do, the player will come to the next rehearsal bathed in tears from the first word to the last, or clowning for all he is worth all the time.

The notes taken by the director as he silently watches the players are a test of his competence. If, for example, he writes "Shew influence of Kierkegaard on Ibsen in this scene," or "The Œdipus complex must be very apparent here. Discuss with the Queen," the sooner he is packed out of the theatre and replaced the better. If they run "Ears too red," "Further up to make room for X," "Pleecemin," "Reel and Ideel," "Mariar Ann," "He, not Ee," "Contrast," "Change speed: Andante," "Shoe sole arches not blacked," "Unladylike: keep knees together," "More dialogue to give them time to get off," "This comes too suddenly," "?Cut this???" and the like, the director knows his job and his place.

When a play is by Shakespear such notes will crop up as "The green one red," "Tibbeeyrnottibeethat iz," "Become to Dunsinane," "Babbled," "Lo here I lenthee thishar pointed sword," meaning that the player should say "Making the green, one red," "To be? Or NOT to be? THAT is the question," "Though Birnam Wood BE come to Dunsinane," that Malone's silly "A babbled o' green fields" should be discarded for the original "His nose was as sharp as a pen on a table of green frieze," and that consecutive consonants must be articulated, as in "lend thee" and "sharp pointed." Othello must not change chaste stars into chaste tars.

In arranging hours players with only a few lines to speak should not be kept hanging about all day whilst the principals are rehearsing. Late night rehearsals are most objectionable. Neither players nor directors should work when they ought to be in bed. If such rehearsals are unavoidable the players who are kept too late for their last trains or buses should be paid their taxi fares home.

A play may need to be cut, added to, or otherwise altered, sometimes to improve it as a play, sometimes to overcome some mechanical difficulty on the stage, sometimes by a passage proving too much for an otherwise indispensable player. These are highly skilled jobs, and should be done by the author, if available, or if not, by a qualified playwright, not by a player, nor by the callboy. Copyright in all such changes passes to the author. A player who reveals the plot or words of an unperformed play to the Press can be sued for breach of confidence at common law or under the Copyright Act.

These rules are founded on experience. They are of no use to a director who regards players not as fellow-artists collaborating with him, but as employees on whom he can impose his own notions of acting and his own interpretation of the author's meaning. He must let the players learn the play, and not expect them to know it all as well as he does at the first rehearsal. He must distinguish between born actors who should be let alone to find their own way, and spook actors who have to be coached sentence by sentence and are help-less without such coaching. There are so many degrees between these extremes that the tact and judgment of directors in their very delicate relations with players are sometimes strained to the utmost; and there is no effective check on the despotism of the director ex-cept his own conscience, because only the most un-governable players dare risk being blacklisted by an authority so potent in the selection of casts as the director. This is why docile players are usually less often unemployed (which means running into debt) than better rebellious ones.

In stock companies, where the program changes from week to week or even from night to night, there can be no selection of the cast and no time to learn the play. Players have to "swallow" their speeches as best they can, and deliver them, not in the author's characterization, but in their specialties such as juve-nile lead, ingénue, walking gentleman, light comedian, low comedian, singing chambermaid (soubrette), heavy old man (*père noble*), old woman, utility, and so forth. Each plays every part in the same way: there

neither is nor can be any distinction between Polonius
and Lafeu, Adam and old Gobbo, Countess Rousillon
and Lady Macbeth, Juliet and Ophelia, Aguecheek
and Roderigo. Each male player has one combat
(sixes); and all have one stepdance for the Christmas
pantomime. Obviously the foregoing directing method
has a very limited application here; but the preparation beforehand of the director's prompt copy—if
there be a director—is doubly necessary to save time.

Repertory companies which, instead of "supporting" touring stars, rely on their own performances of
the best plays they can get, are genuine prentice
schools of acting, because the players are not "rats of
the theatre," in it only because as children of players
they are born to it, but because they come from the
educated laity, and have made their way into the
theatre against all prudent parental advice, for love of
it. Stock players are a hereditary caste. Though their
power of swallowing words in a few hours and im-
provizing (ponging) and gagging is amazing, they
finally become incapable of character study, and are
never really word-perfect. When age brings loss
of memory they have to be fed by the prompter word
for word, as Italian actors are as a matter of course.
They are obsessed with stage traditions and superstitions: to them all religious sages are Tartuffes or
Malvolios, all old husbands cuckolds, all women
either brides or Lady Wishforts, and all plays either
fictitious police news of murders committed by Heavies
(villains), or harlequinades, or an orotund but senseless variety of stage-work called shakespear.

Some good players can act sobriety perfectly, though
off the stage they are drunk and incapable. The same
is true of fever temperatures, sciatica, lameness, and
even partial paralysis. This curious fact, apparently
unknown to psychologists, must be taken into account
by directors lest they should sack an Edmund Kean
or Frederick Robson (who both drank themselves into
heroic fame and premature death) and retain a Gus-
tavus Brooke (a great actor when sober, reeling and

inarticulate when drunk, as he often was). In the logbooks of Drury Lane, when it was a patent theatre in the eighteenth century, are such entries as "No performance: Mr. Kemble drunk."

When a player repeatedly omits some physical feat or movement, the director must conclude that it is made impossible by some infirmity which the player would rather die than disclose. In such cases the business must be altered.

A director sometimes has an antiquarian job. He may be called on to direct a play by, say, Euripides or Aristophanes as it was produced in Athens 2356 years ago. Or one of the pious Mysteries as the Church produced them in the Middle Ages. Or an Elizabethan drama on an Elizabethan stage. Or a Restoration or early Victorian play on a stage with proscenium, wings, and flats.

He should know that the Athenian stage was an imposing tribune in the open air on which the actors, in mask, sock, and buskin, strutted in conventional hierarchic costumes, and that as scenery and curtains were undreamt of, and changes of place impossible, the action of the play had to pass in the same place on the same day. These conditions are called the Unities. On later stages and on the cinema screen they are negligible superstitions; but their observance still has great dramatic value. On the medieval stage unity of place was got rid of by a wide stage on which half a dozen different places were shown simultaneously. Heaven, the jaws of hell, the throne of the Blessed Virgin, the Garden of Gethsemane, the Mount of Olives, the Court of Pilate, the house of Caiaphas, were all in full view together, with the actors moving from one to the other as the story dictated. The Elizabethan stage, adaptable to innyards, had no scenery. The stage was surrounded on three sides by inn galleries, and had a balcony and an inner stage in the middle with curtains called traverses in which indoor scenes were played.

This inner stage, still in use at Oberammergau and elsewhere for Passion Plays, is important because it enables actors entering from the back at opposite sides to be seen by the audience before they can see one another, thus making possible such scenes as the first in Romeo and Juliet, in which the Montagues and Capulets talk out of sight of one another, and set the spectators wondering what will happen when they meet. The best example, however, is at Oberammergau, where the procession to Calvary starts upstage on the prompt side, and has to turn two corners before it passes out up the opposite avenue. At the first corner it is confronted with a comic character, Simon, going to market with his basket. He is seized by the soldiers, who compel him to help Jesus to carry the heavy cross. But as the fainting Christ in extreme exhaustion drags himself towards the second corner, the Virgin appears descending the avenue, and it is apparent that they must meet and turn the crude fun of the Simon encounter into the deepest tragedy.

It was for the sake of such effects that when the Elizabethan stage was succeeded by the Restoration stage, with painted scenery viewed through a proscenium acting as a picture frame, the scenes were pierced to provide avenues through which the actors could be seen before they could see one another. There were also doors in the proscenium through which the principal players could enter, with pages bearing the women's trains, not in historic costumes, but in the full court dress of the period. Old toy theatres preserve this type of stage. Every director should possess one; for effects are possible on it that are not possible in modern built-in sets. For instance, when there are three wide entrances between the wings on both sides of the stage a crowd can be cleared off it almost instantaneously. The very few who are old enough to have seen Queen Elizabeth and her court apparently sink into the earth and disappear when Ristori, as Marie Stewart, called her "the Bastard of England," will appreciate how a modern director is hampered by having to clear the stage through one door.

Modern direction includes film direction, in which there is no limit to scenic possibilities; and directors may spend millions of pounds profitably instead of a few thousands. The results so far include megalomaniac demoralization, disorganization, and waste of time and money. These evils will cure themselves. Meanwhile the art of the playwright and director remains basically the same. The playwright has to tell a good story, and the director to "get it across."

This is all that can be learnt by a director from anything but experience and natural vocation. Like all methods it depends for success on the taste and talent with which it is practised.

There is no sex disqualification for directing. Women directors are at no disadvantage in comparison with men. As in marriage and queenship, the grey mare is often the better horse.

The Play of Ideas

(*The New Statesman and Nation* XXXIX, May 6, 1950; reprinted in *Theatre Arts* XXXIV, August 1950. Shaw's answer to Terence Rattigan's article of the same title.)

I read Mr Rattigan's article on this subject, ... Let me say a word in his defence.

He is, of course, vulnerable as a reasoner; but he is not a reasoner, nor does he profess to be one. The difference between his practice and mine is that I reason out every sentence I write to the utmost of my capacity before I commit it to print, whereas he slams down everything that comes into his head without reasoning about it at all. This of course leads him into all sorts of Jack o' Lantern contradictions, dead ends, and even delusions; but as his head is a bright

one and the things that come into it, reasonable or
not, are all entertaining, and often penetrating and
true, his practice is pleasing, whilst my reasoned-out
syllogisms amuse my readers by seeming the first
things that would come into a fool's head and only my
fun, provoking hasty contradictions and reactions instead of stimulating thought and conviction.

Now there are ideas at the back of my plays; and
Mr Rattigan does not like my plays because they are
not exactly like his own, and no doubt bore him; so
he instantly declares that plays that have any ideas in
them are bad plays, and indeed not plays at all, but
platform speeches, pamphlets, and leading articles.
This is an old story! It used to take the form of
complaints that my plays are all talk. Now it is quite
true that my plays are all talk, just as Raphael's
pictures are all paint, Michael Angelo's statues all
marble, Beethoven's symphonies all noise. Mr Rattigan, not being a born fool, does not complain of this,
but, being an irrational genius, does let himself in for
the more absurd complaint that, though plays must
be all talk, the talk should have no ideas behind it,
though he knows as well as I do when, if ever, he
thinks for a moment, that without a stock of ideas,
mind cannot operate and plays cannot exist. The
quality of a play is the quality of its ideas.

What, then, is the function of the playwright? If
he only "holds a mirror up to nature" his vision of life
will be that of a policeman on point duty. Crowds
of people pass him; but why they pass him, who they
are, whither they are going and why, what they will
do when they pass on and what they have done before
they came into his field of vision, whether they are
married or single or engaged, which of them is a
criminal and which a philanthropist, he cannot tell,
though he knows that there are all sorts in every
thousand of them.

The policeman, however, is not always on point
duty. He has a home. He is a son, a brother, a husband,
a father, has cousins and aunts and in-laws, has been

an infant, a boy, an adolescent, has friends, male and
female. He has likes and dislikes, lovings and loath-
ings, lusts and appetites, jealousies, antipathies, pro-
pensities, tastes and talents, all the virtues, all the
vices, all the common needs and all the senses in
some degree. He keeps a dog or cat or parrot: perhaps all three. He has been to the seaside, and has
seen trees and flowers if he has not actually cultivated
them. Thus, though the passing crowd means nothing
to him, there is a cross-section of it, including himself,
under his daily observation that gives him as much
knowledge of human nature as his mind will hold.

Everybody, being thus provided with a sample
cross-section of the crowd and a faculty of observation,
reasoning, and introspection, has the data for at least
some biological hypotheses, however crude. But now
the mysterious activity I call the Life Force, and pious
people call Providence, steps in, with its trials and
successes and errors, its miracles and games and
caprices, its blessings and blunders and botherations.
It not only varies human capacity to such a degree that
what is child's play to a Napoleon, an Einstein, or
a Nuffield, is beyond the comprehension of common
men, but specializes them in the most fantastic manner,
notably for what children call pretending. And even
their pretending is specialized. One pretender will
have an irresistible propensity to figure as a King, a
High Priest, a Conquering Hero. Another must make
people laugh at him by pretending to be a liar, a
coward, a drunkard, kicked, fooled, and degraded in
every possible comic way. Now, as tragedians and
clowns alike must have fictitious stories and plots invented for them, another specialization produces a
class of professional liars who make no pretence that
their tales are true. Here is where your playwright
comes in.

But here also the differences in mental capacity
come in. One playwright is capable of nothing deeper
than short-lived fictitious police and divorce court
cases of murder and adultery. Another can rise to the

masterpieces of Æschylus, Euripides, and Aristophanes, to Hamlet, Faust, Peer Gynt, and—well, no matter: all these having to be not only entertaining, but intensely didactic (what Mr Rattigan calls plays with ideas), and long-lived enough to be hyperbolically called immortal. And there are many gradations between these extremes: tragedy and melodrama, high and low comedy, farce and filth.

Why this occurs I do not know. If I did, I should be the supreme god among all biologists, philosophers, and dramatists. I should have solved the riddle of the universe, as every criticaster complains I have never done. Of course not. Nobody knows. Only Simple Simons ask.

Theatre technique begins with the circus clown and ringmaster and the Greek tribune, which is a glorified development of the pitch from which the poet of the market place declaims his verses, and, like Dickens's Sloppy or a modern playwright reading his play to the players, reads all the parts "in different voices." On any fine Sunday in Ceylon the street poet may still be seen declaiming his works and taking round his hat: I have seen him do it.

But you need not go so far as Ceylon to see this primitive performance. Wherever there is a queue waiting for the doors of a theatre to open you may see some vagabond artist trying to entertain it in one way or another; and that vagabond may be an incipient Shakespear or Garrick. Nor need you go to the doors of a theatre to witness this parturition of pavement art. In Hyde Park I have seen an elderly man, dressed in black (his best, but old and seedy), step aside to the grass and address the empty air with the exordium "Ah, fahst EEbrews is very campfitn." Presently people stopped to listen to him; and he had a congregation. I myself have done the same on Clapham Common, and collected sixteen shillings in my hat at the end for the Socialist cause. I have stopped on the Thames Embankment; set my back to the river wall; and had a crowd listening to me in no time. A friend of mine who happened to pass described the scene to Henry James, who could not believe that such a thing was possible for a man of letters. He asked me at our next meeting was the tale true? I said it was. In his most impressive manner (he was always impressive) he said: "I could not do that. I *could* not." And from that day his affectionate regard for me was tinged with wonder and even veneration.

Now I, the roofless pavement orator, ended in the largest halls in the country with overcrowds that filled two streets. I harangued an audience of millionaires in the Metropolitan Opera House in New York. I was specially proud of a speech in the Usher Hall in Edinburgh, where 8,640 pennies were collected at the end.

Why do I tell this tale? Because it illustrates the development of the theatre from the pavement to the tribune and the cathedral, and the promotion of its outcasts to palaces, parliaments, and peerages. On the tribune there was no changeable picture scenery; but there were structures to represent houses, temple gates, or the like. When the tribune developed into a stage for the religious Mystery and Passion plays of the Middle Ages, these structures were multiplied until Pilate's pretorium, Herod's palace, the mouth of hell, the Blessed Virgin's throne in heaven, the Mount of Olives, the Hill of Calvary, and the court of Caiaphas were on the stage all through the play as now at Oberammergau, the players moving from one to the other as the action required.

Then came the Elizabethan stage (Shakespear's), with neither structures nor scenery but with a balcony above, an inner stage made with curtains called traverses, an apron stage projecting into the auditorium (relic of the innyard), and placards describing where the action was supposed to be taking place. The traverses distinguished indoor scenes from outdoor. The balcony distinguished castle ramparts from the plain below. But still there was no movable changeable scenery.

Suddenly Italian Opera came along and was tolerated and encouraged by Cromwell, who ranked the theatre as the gate of hell, but loved music. With it came changeable pictorial scenery, side wings, flats, and perspective. Still more sensational, women came on the stage as sopranos, mezzo-sopranos, and contraltos, replacing epicene boys, and founding the tradition that every actress is, or must pretend to be, sexually immoral. Opera taught me to shape my plays into recitatives, arias, duets, trios, ensemble finales, and bravura pieces to display the technical accomplishments of the executants, with the quaint result that all the critics, friendly and hostile, took my plays to be so new, so extraordinary, so revolutionary, that the Times critic declared they were not plays at all as plays had been defined for all time by Aristotle. The truth was that I was going back atavistically to Aristotle, to the tribune stage, to the circus, to the didactic Mysteries, to the word music of Shakespear, to the forms of my idol Mozart, and to the stage business of the great players whom I had actually seen acting, from Barry Sullivan, Salvini, and Ristori to Coquelin and Chaliapin. I was, and still am, the most old-fashioned playwright outside China and Japan. But I know my business both historically and by practice as playwright and producer; and I am writing all this to show that without knowing it historically and studying critically the survivals of it that are still in practice—for instance the Westminster School performances of the ancient Latin drama, where the women's parts are played by boys as Shakespear's women's parts were, and are so effective that Shakespear must have been as strongly against having them played by women as any Holy Willie—no playwright can be fully qualified, nor any theatre critic know what he is pontificating about.

And so I close, I hope, this series of essays started by Mr Rattigan, all of them entertaining in their way, but containing no convincing evidence that the writers have ever seen, written or produced a play.

Bibliography

The following list of additional uncollected pieces by Shaw on theatre and drama is selective and suggestive, not comprehensive. Shaw, throughout his prolonged career, wrote so voluminously and so frequently on so wide a range of subjects as to raise a doubt whether the most assiduous of bibliographers will ever compile a really definitive list. Among the items below are a very few that I have not been able to locate and examine; most of these will be recognized by the curtness of the entries.

1. Preface and Appendices to the Independent Theatre edition of *Widowers' Houses*, London, 1893.
2. "What Mr. Gladstone Ought to Do," a symposium, *Fortnightly Review* LIII (February 1893). Shaw's contribution, pp. 276–77, includes a brief comparison of Gladstone in action to Joseph Jefferson, Henry Irving, and the singer Maurel.
3. "The Religion of the Pianoforte," *Fortnightly Review* LV, February 1894.
4. "A Word More about Verdi," *Anglo-Saxon Review* VIII (March 1901), pp. 221–29. Reprinted in *London Music*, 1937.
5. *The Author's Apology from Mrs. Warren's Profession*, with an introduction by John Corbin, New York 1905. Reprinted from London 1902 edition.
6. Note on *Man and Superman* in *Stage Society News* No. 11 (March 30, 1905). Reprinted in Mander and Mitchenson, *Theatrical Companion to Shaw*, New York, 1955, p. 88.
7. Letter to V. Tchertkoff, in *Tolstoy on Shakespeare*, translated by V. Tchertkoff and I.F.M., New York, 1906, pp. 166–69.
8. "Ibsen," *The Clarion* (London), June 1, 1906, p. 5.
9. Broadside issued on opening night of first production of *Don Juan in Hell*, Court Theatre, June 4, 1907. Reprinted in Mander and Mitchenson, pp. 89–90.
10. Brief contribution to a symposium on "A National Theatre: Its Advantages and Disadvantages," *The Mask* II (July 1909), p. 84. Comment on Irving.
11. "The Reminiscences of a Quinquagenarian," with discussion, *Proceedings of the Musical Association, Thirty-seventh Session, 1910–1911*, London, 1911, pp. 17–27.
12. *"Fanny's First Play,"* letter to editor B. W. Findon, signed Flawner Bannel, *The Play Pictorial* XIX, #114 (1911), p. 50. Reprinted in Mander and Mitchenson, pp. 143–44.
13. "The Dramatic Censorship," *The Nation*, London, March 2, 1912, p. 886. Letter on censorship of Israel Zangwill's *The Next Religion*.
14. Flysheet issued on opening night for revival of *Captain Brassbound's Conversion*, Litttle Theatre, October 15, 1912. Reprinted in Mander and Mitchenson, pp. 75–76.
15. "To the Audience at the Kingsway Theatre," dated New Year's, 1913. Leaflet issued on opening night with program for

John Bull's Other Island, requesting restraint in laughter and applause. Reprinted in Mander and Mitchenson, p. 96.

16. "Bernard Shaw and the Heroic Actor," *Play Pictorial* X, #62 (October 1907), pp. 110–11; *ibid.,* XXI, #129 (June 1913), pp. 124–25. Reprinted in Mander and Mitchenson, pp. 63–64. Letter to B. W. Findon on Forbes-Robertson as Caesar.

17. Letter to Lady Gregory after production of *Blanco Posnet,* pp. 274–79, and "Bernard Shaw on the Irish Players," interview for New York *Evening Sun,* pp. 299–304, in Lady Gregory, *Our Irish Theatre,* New York, 1913.

18. Souvenir booklet accompanying program for *Androcles and the Lion,* St. James's, September 1, 1913. Reprinted in Mander and Mitchenson, pp. 151–52.

19. "The Art and Craft of Playwriting," reported lecture, *Oxford Chronicle,* March 6, 1914, p. 7.

20. Letter about *Pygmalion* and Mrs. Pat Campbell to George C. Tyler, October 12, 1914. Reprinted in Mander and Mitchenson, p. 160.

21. "Professional Association in Literature and the Fine Arts," *The New Statesman,* IX, April 28, 1917, Supplement, pp. 26–29. Includes a plea for an actors' union.

22. "Shaw's Portrait by Shaw, or How Frank Ought to Have Done It," in Frank Harris, *Contemporary Portraits, Second Series,* New York, 1919, pp. 312–45. Reprinted (revised) in *Sixteen Self Sketches,* 1949.

23. Program note for *Saint Joan,* New Theatre, London, March 26, 1924. Reprinted in Mander and Mitchenson, pp. 207–8.

24. "Bernard Shaw and the Bulgarian," *The Times* (London), October 9, 1924. Brief letter to *Berliner Tageblatt* concerning attack by Bulgarian minister on current production of *Arms and the Man.*

25. "Bernard Shaw on the Author," in William Margrie, *The Mighty Heart,* London, 1925, pp. 9–15. Prefatory letters concerning Margrie's drama *The Prince of Ireland.*

26. Translator's program note for *Jitta's Atonement,* Grand Theatre, Fulham, January 26, 1925. Reprinted, revised, in *Translations and Tomfooleries,* 1926.

27. Lawrence Stuckey, "Man and Superman," *Drama* (Chicago) XVII (March 1926), pp. 205–6. Report of Shaw's toast on Shakespeare's birthday at Stratford-upon-Avon.

28. "The Censorship of the Drama," letter, *Spectator* CXXXV (September 12, 1925), pp. 405–6.

29. Letter to author on meaning of *Candida* in James Huneker, *Iconoclasts. A Book of Dramatists,* New York, 1925, pp. 254–55.

30. Archibald Henderson, "George Bernard Shaw Self-Revealed," I. *Fortnightly* n.s. CXIX (April 1926), pp. 433–42; II. *ibid.* (May 1926), pp. 610–18.

31. Letters on playing and casting, Will A. Page, *Behind the Curtains of the Broadway Beauty Trust, including several letters by Bernard Shaw,* New York, 1927, pp. 214–25.

32. In Cyril Maude, *Lest I Forget,* New York, 1928, letter with much interesting side comment on Court productions, pp. 159–61; "The Interlude at the Playhouse," skit for Maude and Winifred Emery at opening of remodeled Haymarket, pp. 171–82.

33. Program note for revival of *Major Barbara,* Wyndham's, March 5, 1929. Reprinted in Mander and Mitchenson, pp. 105–6.

34. Reply to a questionnaire on a National Theatre, *Drama* VIII (January 1930), p. 54.

35. Program note for revival of *Misalliance,* Court Theatre, March 17, 1930. Reprinted in Mander and Mitchenson, pp. 135–36.

36. "G. B. S. and the 'Time Lag,'" *Manchester Guardian* (May 9, 1931), p. 13. Verbatim report of a speech at the luncheon in London of the Institute of Journalists.

37. Peggy Wood, *Actors—and People,* New York, 1930. "Bearding the Lamb" is an account of an interview with Shaw.

38. "Censorships Right and Wrong," letter, *Spectator* CLI (December 22, 1933), p. 934.

39. "A Letter to the Author about this play and all plays from Bernard Shaw," in Sir Henry Norman, *Will No Man Understand?,* London, 1934, pp. 11–15.

40. Notes on producing *The Millionairess,* letter and postal card to Matthew Forsyth, Bexhill, 1936. Reprinted in Mander and Mitchenson, pp. 248–49.

41. *"The Boy David," Time and Tide* XVIII (February 20, 1937), p. 231. Attack on Charles Cochran for closing Barrie's play written for Elisabeth Bergner.

42. "Bernard Shaw to John Farleigh: Letters concerning the illustrations to the 'Black Girl,'" *London Mercury* XXXV (March 1937), pp. 455–66. Contain much material showing Shaw's understanding of dramatic posture, gesture, and movement.

43. Broadcast prologue to *The Dark Lady,* April 22, 1938. Reprinted in *The Listener* (London) XIX (April 27, 1938), pp. 883, 914.

44. Program note to *Geneva, Malvern Festival Book, 1938.* Reprinted in Mander and Mitchenson, pp. 261–62.

45. Julian Park, ed. "Some Unpublished Letters of George Bernard Shaw," *University of Buffalo Studies* XVI (September 1939), pp. 115–30. To B. Iden Payne as director of Miss Horniman's Gaiety Theatre, Manchester; mainly on interpretation.

46. Spoken preface for American audiences to movie version of *Major Barbara, Variety,* May 21, 1941; also *The New York Times,* June 1, 1941, Magazine section, p. 7.

47. "Sixty Years in Business as an Author," *The Author, Playwright and Composer* (Society of Authors, London), Summer 1945, pp. 56–58; reprinted in *American Mercury* LXII (January 1946), pp. 32–36.

48. Letter on death of Granville-Barker, *Times Literary Supplement*, September 7, 1946, p. 427.

49. *Florence Farr, Bernard Shaw, W. B. Yeats. Letters*, ed. Clifford Bax, Dublin, 1941; New York, 1942.

50. "Art Workers and the State," *New Statesman and Nation* XXXIII (April 26, 1947), p. 291; also *Atlantic* CLXXX (November 1947), pp. 123–24.

51. "G.B.S. and Orchestral Basses," *Musical America* LXIX (February 1949), p. 303. Letter first appeared, under title "Basso Continuo," in *The Times* (London), October 25, 1948.

52. Program note to puppet play of Waldo Lanchester written by Shaw, "Shakes versus Shav" (Malvern, 1949). Reprinted in *Arts Council Bulletin* No. 113 (September 1949), pp. 5–9; *Buoyant Billions* (1951).

53. "Sumptuary Regulations at the Opera," letter to *The Times* (London), July 3, 1905. Quoted by Slominsky, *Etude* LXVII (November 1949), p. 5.

54. George A. Riding, "The Candida Secret," *Spectator* CLXXXV (November 17, 1950), p. 506. Contains Shaw's explanations of play's meaning to members of Rugby literary society in February 1920.

55. "A Letter from Bernard Shaw," *Drama* n.s #20 (Spring 1951), p. 22. To F. S. Boas on *The Change of Crowns*, by Edward Howard, ed. by Boas for the Royal Society of Literature.

56. Broadside, *"Blanco Posnet* Banned by the Censor," reprinted in "The *Blanco Posnet* Controversy," in *The Shaw Bulletin* #7 (January 1955), pp. 2–3.

57. Dame Laurentia McLachlan and George Bernard Shaw, "The Nun and the Dramatist," *Cornhill Magazine* #1008 (Summer 1956), pp. 415–58. Contains much about *Saint Joan*. Reprinted in *In A Great Tradition*, edited by the Benedictines of Stanbrook (1956).

58. Eleanor Robson Belmont, *The Fabric of Memory*, New York, 1957, pp. 33–51, 295. Letters from Shaw to the actress for whom he created Major Barbara.

Index